POSTMODERN UTOPIAS AND
FEMINIST FICTIONS

This study examines feminist speculative fiction from the late twentieth and early twenty-first centuries and finds within it a new vision for the future. Rejecting notions of postmodern utopia as exclusionary, Jennifer A. Wagner-Lawlor advances one defined in terms of hospitality, casting what she calls "imaginative sympathy" as the foundation of utopian desire. Tracing these themes through the works of a dozen fiction writers, including Margaret Atwood, Octavia Butler, Doris Lessing, Susan Sontag, and Jeanette Winterson, as well as those of well-known Muslim feminists such as Nawal El Saadawi, Shahrnush Parsipur, and Fatima Mernissi, Wagner-Lawlor balances literary analysis with innovative extensions of feminist philosophy to show how inclusionary utopian thinking can inform and promote political agency. Examining these contemporary fictions reveals the rewards of attending to a community that acknowledges difference, diversity, and the imaginative potential of every human being.

JENNIFER A. WAGNER-LAWLOR is Associate Professor in the Women's Studies and English departments at The Pennsylvania State University. She is the author of *A Moment's Monument: Revisionary Poetics in the Nineteenth-Century Sonnet* (1996), editor of *The Victorian Comic Spirit* (2000), and the coeditor of *The Scandal of Susan Sontag* (2009).

POSTMODERN UTOPIAS AND FEMINIST FICTIONS

JENNIFER A. WAGNER-LAWLOR

The Pennsylvania State University

CAMBRIDGE
UNIVERSITY PRESS

CAMBRIDGE
UNIVERSITY PRESS

32 Avenue of the Americas, New York, NY 10013-2473, USA

Cambridge University Press is part of the University of Cambridge.

It furthers the University's mission by disseminating knowledge in the pursuit of education, learning and research at the highest international levels of excellence.

www.cambridge.org
Information on this title: www.cambridge.org/9781107038356

© Jennifer A. Wagner-Lawlor 2013

First published 2013

Printed in the United States of America

A catalog record for this publication is available from the British Library.

Library of Congress Cataloging in Publication data
Wagner-Lawlor, Jennifer A.
Postmodern Utopias and Feminist Fictions / Jennifer A. Wagner-Lawlor,
The Pennsylvania State University.
pages cm
Includes bibliographical references and index.
ISBN 978-1-107-03835-6 (hardback)
1. Utopias in literature.   2. Feminism and literature.   3. Speculative fiction –
Women authors – History and criticism.   4. Postmodernism (Literature)   I. Title.
PN56.U8NW34   2013
809'.93372–dc23   2012051613

ISBN 978-1-107-03835-6 Hardback

For Len and Jonathan and to the memory of my mother,
Barbara Jane Wagner (1927–2012)

Contents

Preface

In an interview following the publication of *Paradise* (1998), Toni Morrison observed that "all paradises, all utopias," whether envisioned in literature, history, or holy books, "are designed by who is not there, by the people who are not allowed in."[1] *Paradise* is an extended meditation on exactly this observation, and "what on earth" a utopia would look like if that were not the case. In so identifying this aspect – she does not say "flaw" – of any representation of utopia, Morrison indicates the starting point of this study.

Postmodern Utopias and Feminist Fictions advances the following proposition in response to Morrison's dilemma: that postmodern utopia be conceived in terms of an absolute and therefore open-ended hospitality. The logic of exceptionalism that characterizes "all utopias" derives from an assumption that absolute hospitality is impossible. But the evidence of contemporary speculative fictions suggests the emergence of an alternate utopian logic, deriving not from *Logos*, but from *Eros*. Crucial philosophical implications emerge through and from this shift, and I come at this proposition from the philosophical angle first. But in contemporary fiction fully aware of its lineage in literary utopia and speculation, a radical shift from *Logos* to *Eros* has critical narratological and hermeneutic effects. These effects will mean tracing the entanglements of desire in the forms and figures, even the "function," of each text, as each author speculates on those that might accommodate, even welcome and celebrate, alterity.

It is no accident that an alternative conception of utopia should be derived from a feminist standpoint. The history of utopian and speculative narratives written by women is just one expression of feminist resistance – but it is exemplary. Feminist fictions confront not only the ways in which women's alterity has been and continues to be defined. They also confront ways in which specific communities – and even the very notion of community – do or do not integrate, or permit, others within their boundaries. A feminist standpoint must stake not only ontological but epistemological claims. Within the context of women's fiction-writing, this necessary intervention also means a narratological inventiveness.

Postmodern Utopias and Feminist Fictions begins therefore by introducing a figure who can advance those claims. Extending well-known feminist epistemological positions, I introduce the notion of a *speculative standpoint* and/as the figuring of a feminist traveler who stands there. A speculative standpoint signifies not only the "as is" (*speculum*), or the making visible of reality "more objectively," as a feminist standpoint proposes. Speculative standpoint also aspires to make visible the "as if," the projecting out or performance (*spectacle*) of possibility. These possibilities are different from what utopia theorists have called seeds of prediction; they are more like catalysts that capture the urgency of aspirations. One more sense of the word "speculative" adheres in this context: the sense of speculation as *risk*, which comes with the recognition of unpredictable, unseen, or unacknowledged possible futures. The agent of such risk is a speculator, and *Postmodern Utopias and Feminist Fictions* features the critical role of the speculative hero in disrupting what and how we "come to know" what we do.

Like her philosophical sister, the "scandalous witness" introduced by Donna Haraway, the speculative hero/ine's narrative is shaped from the standpoint of approaching *other* ways of knowing and other "ways of being nowhere."[2] The feminist speculator flees the nowhere that is everywhere, a universe of false objectivity created by a consciousness Haraway calls "the perfect knower," who is blind to the fantasy behind his own utopian constructions. The epistemology of that perfect knower is grounded in a particular form of rationality; his position is a privileged place. In contrast, the epistemology of the speculative knower is grounded in her acknowledged situatedness. But the imagination bears its own (inter)relational logic and extends its way of knowing to others. While "his" truths come from experiment, "hers" come from (situated *and* artistic) experience.

The role of art as the essential and ethical form of utopian work runs, therefore, through the entirety of *Postmodern Utopias and Feminist Fictions*. Readings of these texts reflect on the nature of each fiction's own form and genre, as well as on figures of those unforeseen conceptions and apprehensions of utopia itself. These figures introduce new subjectivities, new histories, new ways of being, new political economies. Other figures of alterity/alternatives are narratological. The achievement of speculation is often signaled by the apparition of a shifting "portal" (in Hopkinson's *Midnight Robber*, or Morrison's *Paradise*), or a staircase guiding "footsteps on the air" (in LeGuin's *The Telling*). These are quite evidently invitations to connect multiple ways of apprehension, of knowing, and of being. They connect alternative dimensions of reality, sometimes temporally parallel, sometimes not. Like Wordsworth's transitory spots of time, these moments may not always look benign. But for those who attend to such moments, these epiphanies urge the possibility that utopia is not achieved, and never achieved: the epiphany is that the utopian horizon is always shifting. The imagination always goes further. The "achievement" of a speculative standpoint, therefore, is to apprehend that epiphanic moment and hold it open long enough to describe what, where, how it is.

And of course, this is what art is best at. Susan Sontag argued that novels educate our feelings and our sensibilities, our attentiveness not only to ourselves but especially to others, "the larger world, and [break] out of the confines of narcissism and solipsism."[3] Asserting the priority of *imaginative sympathy* as the true north guiding her journey in art and literature, she argues that the work of art must be "an extension of my sympathies to other selves, other domains, other dreams, other words [*sic*; for "worlds"?], other territories."[4] Sontag describes an ethical turn that does not contain or immobilize. Art's ethical turn, on the contrary, always opens out, leads us away from ourselves, educates us in the ways of the world so that we return home "other" than we were. Without that turn, the future threatens to be "the same old story," a history based on what we already know, making room only for persons, ideas, and aspirations already familiar to us.

Thus, in addition to hospitality and art, a major theme in this study is, inevitably, history. Any instantiation of utopia draws from the archives of history as it tries to conceive a "not-yet" in a better time or place. But in keeping with a notion of utopia as erotic, these texts typically try to recover and interpret what Jeanette Winterson calls "archives of the heart." One set of archives will tell us "what happened"; but the archives of the heart give much more information about why it happened, what it was "like," and what the sufferings and celebrations of people around the same history have to do with what happens next. Imagination is critical to writing, and living, a history that does not retell the same story. Imagination too must be accommodated. "*There must be room for the imagination to exercise its powers,*" observes William Godwin, in an essay appropriately titled "Of Love and Friendship":

we must conceive and apprehend a thousand things which we do not actually witness; each party must feel that it stands in need of the other, and without the other cannot be complete; each party must be alike conscious of the power of receiving and conferring benefit; and *there must be the anticipation of a distant future,* that may every day enhance the good to be imparted and enjoyed, and cause the individuals thus united perpetually to become more sensible of the fortunate event which gave them to each other, and has thus entailed upon each a thousand advantages in which they could otherwise never have shared.[5]

There is a reason Godwin wrote political philosophy in the form of novels, and not just in treatises.

The concrete political implications of accommodating the imagination is explored most explicitly in the final section of the book (Chapters 4 and 5). Susan Sontag's *In America* portrays an immigrant's purposeful crafting of self and national identity aligned with the American myth of exceptionalism – betraying at once the strengths and weaknesses offered by this country's own aspirations. Sontag's novel of American utopianism leaves open the incompatibilities it exposes. Perhaps the irresolution is intentional, as it remains an open wound. But this irresolute stance is corrected in Toni Morrison's *Paradise*, which exposes the crafty bigotry adhering to any vision of America that demands partisan compliance (along racial and gender lines, in this case) to exceptionalist visions of community. *Paradise*'s offering of an erotic utopianism holds out a vision of hospitality supported by an economy of the human body, presenting the potential (though not yet, of course, the reality) of a truer version of America's democratic ideals and utopian promise.

This leads to the book's final turn toward a group of novels in which feminist utopian consciousness (or speculative standpoint), hospitality, and nationalism are considered from another "outsider perspective." In proposing a utopian hospitality confronting the "the strange that I am beginning to love,"[6] we face the question: Can a vision of humility and hospitality, even supposing it is achieved within one's borders, extend beyond a community or nation's borders? If we discover, as Octavia Butler's Lauren does, that our teachers are all around us, what lessons await from "others," not just inside our borders, but outside?

Indeed, it seems imperative to close this study on postmodern utopianism and/as feminist hospitality by reflecting back on ourselves. The final chapter therefore takes up the implied imperative: that we contest a contemporary Western rhetoric celebrating the "global community" while vigorously protecting its national interests and alliances, rather than seeking a standpoint toward others that is generous, humble, "accommodating" in a way that engages the other rather than merely tolerating her. There are also implications for thinking about global feminism and the kinds of affiliations it can or does propose. The Muslim feminist writers featured in Chapter 5 seem to offer visions of hospitality remarkably in line with previously sketched utopian visions in earlier chapters. But the distinct cultural genealogy of Eastern notions of hospitality *as an enactment of utopian consciousness* is a critical advance that is frankly more robust. A feminist vision of utopia-as-hospitality resonates powerfully and differently in these narratives, as analysis of the rhetorical and structural tropes and figures will show. While every text included in *Postmodern Utopias and Feminist Fictions* stages a representation of women's aspirational motives, what differs in these last narratives is an insistence on "spelling out" conflicting motives and strategies of domination, on either side. These women are more explicit about the requirement that these aspirations and visions be voiced, re-presenting them outside of fantasy. Thus once again, the power of art's mediation of feminist social and political dreams is held up: the work of art is a form of political agency, and all the more so in its dissemination or dispersal.

Like Morrison's *Paradise*, these novels imagine the evolution of a feminist vision of hospitality that takes in a stranger "as she is" (Parsipur). But the voicing of this imperative – that the imagination must "go further" (El Saadawi) – is more forcefully avowed. This may be because of the persistent cultural celebrity of a complex female legend, Scheherazade, who uses storytelling, and particularly the art of suspense, to hold time at bay and hold a mirror up to the "the strange within." Cultivating both feeling and ethical sensibility, Scheherezade reflects back to her royal auditor and tormentor the deeply distorted form of personal justice enacted by a serial "invitation" to marriage, to be consummated by each woman's death. Scheherazade's own invitation to *see yourself in your world as "other" than you "know" yourself to be* means recovering not only the humanity of the Sultan personally, but the very possibility of a generation of the future.

Margaret Atwood has lamented in post-9/11 interviews how easily we hand over our own political freedoms, and violate those of others, in the face of such inchoate enemies as "Islamic extremists"; how quickly we harden our vision of the world against the other; and how insistently and ruthlessly we protect ourselves within the walls, literal and metaphorical, that we imagine will ensure our safety. The contemporary risks of our global community – the purposeful violences of intolerance and ignorance on the one hand, and of environmental disregard on the other – appear in many of the novels treated here. While we find positive figures for a new generation of human being we are consistently warned against being "doomed by hope," as Atwood's Crake puts it, that there is always something *more and better*. If the story of acquisition and domination leads us to our own doom, the fault, Atwood grimly proposes, will be our own. The "privilege" of ignorance can easily betray us without the kind of anticipatory work that speculative art offers, and the ethical circumspection that imaginative sympathy demands.

"*What* are *our saving graces?*" Margaret Atwood once asked in an interview. In the study that follows, some of our best contemporary writers propose an answer.

Acknowledgments

There are many individuals who have contributed to this project with their emotional or intellectual support, and usually both. But I start with my friends Barbara Ching, Deb Tollefsen, and Gwenn Volkert, and their families. I can only hope they know how much they are appreciated.

This book would have been impossible without the support of friends and colleagues in the Department of Women's Studies at Penn State. Thank you to my department head, Carolyn Sachs, for creating such a congenial and stimulating environment in which to work. While I have learned from all my colleagues, I need to thank three in particular. Irina Aristarkhova, now at the University of Michigan, influenced my thinking in ways I could never have anticipated. Her work on hospitality and the matrix quite literally transformed my work, and her deep intelligence and compassionate spirit are sorely missed. Gabeba Baderoon also opened up theoretical avenues I am unlikely to have found on my own. To her I also owe wonderful times in Cape Town and Simonstown, South Africa, and an education in the ongoing richness of South African literature and art. Finally, Nancy Tuana's influence is obvious in my attention to feminist epistemology, but that fact says little about the extent of her professional support, and nothing about the extent of her steadfast friendship.

I would like to thank the College of the Liberal Arts at The Pennsylvania State University at University Park for the generous research support that helped me complete this book and find my way into new work and new commitments. I am fortunate to work with Dean Susan Welch and with Associate Deans Denise Solomon and Chris Long, all of whom fully support the research of their faculty.

Other colleagues at Penn State and elsewhere gave me words of encouragement and wisdom along the way. Thank you to Cheryl Glenn; to Susan Squier, who read a portion of the chapter on Margaret Atwood; and also to my recent research and writing collaborators, Karen Kiefer-Boyd and Eileen Trauth. Vincent Colapietro has read portions of my work on art, and pushed me to clarify certain lines of thought to clearer expression. Charles Berger, one of the best readers I know, commented on early drafts of the sections on Toni Morrison, as well as some of the work on Sontag. Special thanks to Brigitte Weltman-Aron, another longtime friend, whose ideas and critiques I always learn from.

I am grateful to Ray Ryan at Cambridge University Press for taking on this book with enthusiasm, and to Louis Gulino and others who have done a wonderful job seeing the project through on a thankfully brisk timetable. The Press's reviewers provided exceptionally thoughtful and constructive responses, for which I am deeply grateful. One of these was Phillip E. Wegner, who is quite simply an ideal reader for this book. I am indebted to him for reading the manuscript with such care, and responding with such generosity and thoroughness as well as with his characteristic grace. Thank you so much, Phil.

Stephanie Scott, a Ph.D. candidate at Penn State in English and Women's Studies, did a meticulous job proofreading the final manuscript. She saved me from a host of errors my eyes had skipped over a hundred times.

Karen and Joel Vanden and their children, Nick and Kelly, were the first new friends we made at Penn State, and I appreciate their continuing friendship. The same goes for Anna and Farhan Gandhi, and their children, especially Anand. Jane Hammerslough and Eve Glasberg are two childhood friends I have been lucky to reconnect with recently, just when old friends were needed.

Deep appreciation goes to the crew of dedicated environmental activists – too many to name – whom I have met in person or virtually through working with the Plastic Pollution Coalition (PPC). They remind me every day how even our smallest choices matter as they observe, measure, document, and publicize the way the earth is abused. Among them are two great women: Daniella Dimitrova Russo, executive director of the PPC; and Dianna Cohen, PPC co-founder, environmental activist, and visual artist. Both give me inspiration, ideas for projects, book recommendations, and silver linings. Dianna, special thanks to you for your encouragement, generosity, and time in helping with and contributing to my various projects. That includes giving me permission to reproduce your beautiful watercolor on the cover of this book. A perfect image of the "speculative woman."

Two other creative artists and utopianists in their own right, Lynn Book and J. Morgan Puett, encouraged me at just the right moment, as I approached the finish line. I met them for the first time in 2011, and the fact that their ideas resonated so deeply helped convince me I was on the right track.

To Kim Stanley Robinson, so well met in Australia in September 2010: for encouraging my various enthusiasms – musical, literary, and ecological, in about that order – and for sharing your own, thank you so much. But for you I'd never have known there was such a spectacular range of treehouse architecture. Or what hiking in the Sierras might look like, if I ever were to do it. Or that Galileo's dreams are, after all, ours.

My fellow utopianists from the Society of Utopian Studies are, after nearly thirty years, like a second family. All thanks and appreciation go to Jill Belli, Claire Curtis, Peter Fitting, Ralph Goodman, Brian Greenspan, Carrie Hintz, Naomi Jacobs, Corina Kessler, Tom Moylan, Ken Roemer, Peter Sands, Lyman Tower Sargent, Rebecca Totaro, Phil Wegner, and Toby Widdicombe for their many kindnesses, intellectual companionship, and gentle, generous spirits. Carrie Hintz included me in the CUNY Graduate Center's Fall 2010 seminar series on utopianism, and Ralph Goodman invited me to lecture at the University of Stellenbosch. I am grateful to them giving me opportunities to share this work.

Like all utopia scholars, I am indebted to Lyman Tower Sargent, who is endlessly generous in sharing anything and everything he knows with the rest of us. Sandra Stelts, the Rare Books Curator at the Penn State Libraries, has also been an ongoing supporter of all things utopian through her dedication to the Arthur O. Lewis Utopia Collection, which Lyman is diligently expanding on a monthly basis. I am grateful to Sandy for her hard work on the 2011 Society for Utopian Studies Annual Conference, which featured an exhibit from the University Libraries' extensive collection of texts related to all things utopian and speculative.

Love to my family, especially my mother, Barbara Wagner, who looked forward to seeing this in print but did not live quite long enough; my sister, Margaret; my brother, Jonathan, and his family; my brother, Daniel, and nephews Stephen, Dylan and Colinn; the family godmother, Marianne Heiden; and my stepdaughter, Casey Lawlor, and her partner Peter Tabor.

Finally, to "my boys," Len and Jonathan, to whom this book is dedicated. *Postmodern Utopias and Feminist Fictions* would never have been completed without the love, encouragement and, at times, extreme forbearance of my husband. Our son, "the singing boy" from infancy, brings humor, affection, sensitivity, joy, and music into my life every single day.

The generosity and spirit of everyone acknowledged here rejuvenate my own commitment to Margaret Atwood's challenge that we do more than "fare well," but that we "*fare forward.*"

Speculative standpoint and feminist intervention

THE NARRATIVE TASK OF UTOPIA

At the conclusion of her 1985 study, *Writing Beyond the Ending*, Rachel DuPlessis anticipates the narrative strategies that women writers might deploy as they move into the twenty-first century. Opening with a promise to survey the ground(ing) of narrative in romance, she maps the deceptively stable "'place' where ideology meets narrative and produces a meaning-laden figure." The meeting place is the "hard visible horizon" beyond which feminist narratives might aspire, rejecting the "conventional narrative resolution [including] all the endings of romance and death."[1] In the deployment of narrative strategies that resist "the pleasurable illusion of stasis," these texts reject every "happily ever after" conclusion, and insist instead on gaining access to the future(s) that might disrupt the illusion that "choice is over."[2] Such narratives offer "muted" utopian content, pushing toward an alternative to the conservative ideological imperatives that animate the form and content, the ways and mean(ing)s, of the traditional novel.

This book revisits the narrative strategies of feminist speculation, focusing primarily on novels that have appeared since the beginning of the new millennium DuPlessis anticipates. These are feminist fictions in which utopian content is occasionally muted, but more often amplified. Contemporary critics of feminist narrative since DuPlessis continue attending to the kinds of theoretical speculations, narratological inventions, and strategic interventions that stake out new grounds for exploring a feminist utopia as such, and feminist utopianism more broadly. Previous critics have defined feminist utopianism as "the sighting (in terms of the gaze) and siting (in terms of emplacement) of another possibility"[3] for female subjectivity and for feminist community. This study certainly follows in that tradition. *Postmodern Utopias and Feminist Fictions* extends a critical path cleared by DuPlessis, Nancy Miller, and other early feminist narratologists, particularly those interested in the specific developments of utopian and speculative fictions. Frances Bartkowski's *Feminist Utopias* (1989) was a model study – in fact the model I had in mind when I began this book; Sarah Lefanu's study appeared the same year. Following those were important books by Marleen Barr (1992 and 2000), Angelika Bammer (1991), Jenny Wolmark (1994), Jennifer Burwell (1997), and Lucie Armitt (2000). Barr, Bammer, and Armitt have been especially useful in their explorations of the relationship of feminist fabulation (Barr) to a masculinist postmodern literary canon offering "theoretical visions which define utopia as a Nowhere for women."[4]

Critical to my concerns is Bammer's critique of Fredric Jameson's notion of the unimaginability of utopia. Because, argues Jameson, utopian discourse is not so much a "mode of narrative [as] an object of meditation" he proposes that such discourse is therefore essentially plotless or characterless, its primary function to "jar the mind into some heightened but unconceptualizable consciousness of its own powers, function, aims and structural limits." Bammer contends, however, that not only *are* there plots and characters in the utopian discourse we call literature, but also both plot and character emerge "out of an impulse to narrativize."[5] This distinction between "utopian discourse" and utopian *literary* discourse, including speculative and utopian narratives, is critical. Utopian narratives may never represent the achievement of some ideal utopian neutrality as Louis Marin proposes.[6] But neutrality has never been a goal of feminist narratology, which seeks to mine narratives of difference, not sameness, for ways of deconstructing master narratives. One of those master narratives *is* the narrative of Utopia. Furthermore, should feminists countenance the notion that a utopian consciousness is impervious to conceptualization? Contemporary utopia theorists argue that utopia is both an object of self-reflexive meditation *and* a process.[7] In that case, feminism needs to conceptualize a utopian consciousness that can be enacted by the *practice* of critical thinking.

The central claim of this book is that feminist narratology, drawing from broader developments in feminist epistemology, does take on the task of discovering a figure of a feminist utopian consciousness. For this task, contemporary speculative fictions have proven themselves powerful formal tools for revis(ion)ing the shape of history and revaluing the role of imagination. Indeed this investigation participates in the ongoing recuperation of the imaginative faculty from postmodern skepticism. The imagination is defended not only as politically viable but as politically necessary, and the role of feminist epistemology is central to my defense.

Feminist epistemology is therefore more than just my starting point. It is the context for fleshing out as it were a figure of critical situatedness that I call *speculative standpoint*, whose "knowledge base" as it were is not only the empirical but also the imaginary.

Thus this book defends art of all kinds, and narrative in particular, for their "usefulness" – their practicality even – in imagining and implementing the practice of what I call "transitive imagining,"[8] a process of conceptualizing transition and transformation. Performance and storytelling in particular reveal themselves, in nearly every novel treated here, to be "practical technologies" of the imagination in action. In this regard, this book aligns closely with several recent studies, including Phillip E. Wegner's *Life between Two Deaths, 1989–2001* (2009) and John Su's provocative and rich *Imagination and the Contemporary Novel* (2011). Wegner's expansive analysis of American cultural texts from the "long Nineties" constitutes a sophisticated defense of the imagination deeply compatible with my own. His study appeals, as mine will, to "a shared commitment to a horizon of possibility that promises to transform everything."[9] It also requires a recuperation of the imagination as itself a powerful source of "information," which Wegner sees expressed characteristically as *allegory*, regarding the structures and occlusions of ideology. Su's excellent study focuses as well on the work that imagination does, while locating the vitality of new affiliative options in the urgencies of imaginative sympathy, or what our authors even call "love."

One of the overarching themes of this volume is, therefore, *work* – not the traditional utopian text's vision of efficient labor, but rather the speculative text's vision of "the work of art" itself as a (trans)active process making visible the outlines of desire.[10] This book launches a parallel inquiry into a specifically feminist reclamation of the imagination in speculative fiction. The feminist speculative fiction writers treated here characteristically defend the value of imagination and art – just one form of transitive imagining – in catalyzing feminist utopian movement. Ultimately, this valuation returns to epistemology, but to an epistemology of the *imagination* comparable to, and in dialogue with, traditional epistemological models. By extending feminist standpoint theory to include a *speculative* standpoint, this study reclaims speculative narrative as a robust challenge to claims that the imagination is politically useless. I argue that imagination is at the heart of art's "utility" in this world. Its "use-value" is not one of efficiency. The feminist speculative standpoint, partaking of information from rational inquiry as well as imaginative inquiry, is a figure of inventiveness that incites both narratological and historical disruptions. Its impulse is to narrativize difference, to propose risk, to anchor hope.

Each of the many authors touched on in this study no doubt concurs with Margaret Atwood's claim that "the full range of our human response to the world – that is, what it means to be human, on earth" is offered by art. The truth of art's fictionality will reside just here, in the artistic capacity to express "something that is true to itself.... That seems to be what 'hope' is about in relationship to art."[11] Art is the technology with which we measure the moral compass of individuals, societies, cultures, histories. In claiming, therefore, an ethical motive at the heart of these novels' attention to the imagination, this study proposes that both the speculative novel, as a form, and the imagination, as a faculty, cultivate sites of difference that hold at bay the modern drive to sameness. These works renew attention to the ways and means by which transitive imagining locates its own kinds of truths. This may be the only robust source of "hope" in the face of Fredric Jameson's challenge to the arts: that they offer some "coordinated" response, "philosophically and theoretically," to "the global frontier of capitalism" that has a stranglehold on our historical moment. Jameson proposes that we begin at just that "frontier" – the frontier that is also "the horizon of all literary and cultural study in our time." It is just here "where we ought to begin."[12]

WITH KNOWING IRONY

The postmodern suspicion, even hostility, toward the imagination as a form of false consciousness and "outdated humanist illusion" has been a formidable obstacle to a contemporary epistemology of the imagination. Richard Kearney's defense of the imagination as both historical and ethical is a starting point: "[t]he kind of imagination required to meet the challenge of post-modernism is, then, fundamentally historical. It is one capable of envisioning what things might be like after postmodernism. And also, of course, what things were like before it."[13] This is an apt description of the "narrative task" of utopian and speculative narratives, which are always meditations on the course of history, "archaeologies of the future," as Jameson memorably puts it, looking backward and looking forward to possible futures.

In promoting the relevance of imagination, however, we must account for the role of irony. Irony has been suspect for its potential to undermine the foundation of any political stance and the value of any frankly utopian projection. That suspicion has weakened the attractiveness of utopian speculation throughout modernity: What is the "use" of a theoretical no-place when the play of irony short-circuits or neutralizes a commitment to any position? A philosopher such as Kearney, who ultimately seeks a foundation stabilized in an ethical and religious worldview, denies a positive role to irony's destabilizing duplicities. But rejecting a role for irony is untenable in a study of postmodern literary texts,[14] and particularly of utopian and speculative texts. A recuperation of imagination requires that irony prove itself more than a political disability and a rhetorical liability. From an epistemic standpoint, irony makes critique possible, and most powerfully so when irony provokes critique *and* self-reflexivity. Any robust novel (and arguably any robust work of art whatever) discerns the workings of its own form, displaying a formal reflexivity that heightens the reader's awareness of the ways in which that text (or work of art) is tethered to its occasion and situated in literary history as well as in national and global histories.[15]

The centrality of irony to the evolution of the novel is a source not only of historical depth but also of hermeneutic depth, even where that depth is concealed. A conservative utopian vision that celebrates a naturalized, masculinist "culture of no culture"[16] may have motivated the novel genre's original rhetorical and political deployments. Indeed as Franco Moretti's brilliant study, *The Way of the World* (1987), has explained the bildungsroman – a form I turn to in Chapter 1 – exemplifies the in-forming of a conservative, and masculinist, utopian imperative supporting an advancing bourgeois class. Irony's role is critical to the form and function of the novel of education, designed to reinforce that advance: irony, Moretti observes, opens up an "'accessible' past," thanks to its "ability to stop time, to question what has already been decided, or to re-examine already finished events in a different light." Irony "will never suggest what would be done," he adds; "it can restrain action, but not encourage it.... [To] live is to choose, and decision cannot be eradicated from human existence or from history."[17] But the choice offered by Moretti's model is, as he acknowledges, limited by its own unacknowledged ideological greenwashing. Presenting itself as an exemplary "object of meditation," the classic bildungsroman presents a vision of an end-utopia. However conscious of "its own powers, function, aims and structural limits,"[18] the classic bildungsroman will – like any instance of utopian realization – disguise its designs on us by obscuring those limits as a closing off of invention and possibility. Moretti's identification of irony's conservative function makes sense, in that regard, and so does his claim that "therefore" the classic bildungsroman cannot accommodate "workers, women, and minorities."

But of course, postmodernism demands that we challenge those limits, insofar as one grants that irony *has* limits. Postmodern irony hardly aspires to stop time, but, at its most radical, to reimagine time. It thereby creates the conceptual time-space in/on which to imagine and to stage any number of possible futures. Linda Hutcheon's great study of "irony's edge" is helpful here. It is possible, she observes,

> to think of irony not as saying one thing and meaning another ... but, instead, as a process of communication that entails two or more meanings being played off, one against the other. The irony is in the difference; irony makes the difference. It plays between meanings, in a space that is always affectively charged, that always has a critical edge.[19]

The Janus-like character of irony will be an ongoing thematic in this study. Irony is Janus-like because it looks both backward, critiquing past actions and ideas, and forward toward a future, the shape of which is barely outlined. Double-edged and dialogic, critical and creative, irony is crucial in defining the ways in which feminist utopian thinking could develop future literary production.[20] Feminist utopia is not neutral, *pace* Marin, nor "unconceptualizable," *pace* Jameson. It is always already ironical.

In this book I claim that contemporary feminist utopian/dystopian as well as speculative narratives are always already, and necessarily, structured by irony's edge. The readings presented here reveal the critical role of irony's destabilizing and political charge. The charge splinters plot lines and shifts "out of joint" the structures of literary form. It multiplies figurations of dimensional shifts, which are temporal as well as spatial. The plot of many of these texts is an epistemological journey of a particular kind: a way of learning that teaches one how to look for such dimensional horizons, a way of knowing that allows one even to see the horizon, and possibly, to see beyond it. It may be that the horizon is the figuration of irony's edge, but in any case, it will not be the "hard horizon"[21] defining the separation of the past and the future.

It is hard – impossible? – to decide whether what happens at the horizon is revelation or creation. Irony may produce a moment of crisis in thinking and behavior. But the obverse is also possible and necessary. Irony is so Janus-faced that it both produces and is required by crisis. And the crisis may be more than "personal," but a crisis of the social space, of the community. This is why Nancy Miller has pointed out that textual stagings of crises of female subjectivity will "[call] for an ironic manipulation of the semiotics of performance" whereby feminist hope is negotiated "through [the production of] a new 'social subject.'"[22] More recently, philosophical work on "nomadic subjects" has continued the rejection, "within the feminist framework," of a passive nihilism or "cynical acceptance of the state of crisis as loose and fragmented. On the contrary, this crisis is taken by women as the opening up of new possibilities and potentialities. It leads women to rethink the link between identity, power, and the community."[23] It leads women to think of their situation.

One of the central arguments of this book is that the forms of contemporary feminist speculation require irony, but not of the endlessly enervating kind. As Linda Hutcheon has shown us, textual irony can offer an empowering, critical imperative, and in doing so gives the notion of utopia the political charge that drives utopian narrative. Utopia's critical edge requires irony's edge to sustain its challenge to, rather than its endorsement of, ideologies of all stripes. It also demands a vibrant evolution in the literary forms which re-present possible pasts, presents, and futures. Thus each chapter in this study tracks the ironic charge of its featured narratives in order to clarify irony's role in a specifically feminist epistemological project. From the beginning, of course, women had something to say about that. Recognizing the interests of the novel's insistence on realism as its primary mode, women writers intervened early on, exploring, for instance, gothic modes that disrupted realism's generic stranglehold. They told precocious tales of monstrous births – one of which stands, still, as a signal event in the history of speculative and science fictions. The nonsense they represented was figured, famously, as madness: the madwoman in the attic who raged her way into early feminist texts and literary criticism, and who lives on in modern and contemporary feminist literature. Monstrous women, however, must evolve as well, if they are to generate any "new woman," or any narrative, novel or otherwise, not similarly de-formed but rather *in*formed by a Janus-like duplicity.

"The chance of escaping the same"[24] has long shaped the motive driving modern feminist criticism of utopian, science, and speculative fiction; Jeanette Winterson's brilliant 2007 science fiction novel, *The Stone Gods*, represents only the most spectacular of recent feminist utopian speculations on that theme. This novel is driven by the urgency of having a "second chance," "begin[ning] again," and having "the chance to be human." The "capacity to affect the outcome" in a world that is "neither random nor determined" (181) can open up novel connections and correspondences via what Winterson calls "bridges of time." Connecting the familiar and unfamiliar recontextualizes both in ways that are not likely to be, as it were, commonsensical. These ways may even appear nonsensical to the "unimaginative" reader, as several of these texts acknowledge.

But this study insists on a specifically feminist motive for the possibility that revisioning is more than self-replication or parody. Narratologically, therefore, the sense of the ending in these texts is not oriented by the resolution of familiar, happy endings. Rather, they are reoriented entanglements of the real, the imaginary, the possible, and the potential, under such tension that the very frame of the text has to bend, or fold, or extend, or even suspend.

SPECULATING ON THE WORK OF STANDPOINT

The notion of imagination's "narrative task" is rich in implication, not least in its proposal of an active relationship between narrative self and other, although it presumes that each is actually listening to the other. Kearney will speak of fidelity to the other, or "commitment," but how do we account for this relationship? Similarly, Su problematizes what and how the imagination helps us *know*, as well as envision. Both Kearney and Su logically base their claims on a notion of sympathy that will always require the faculty of the imagination, as the nineteenth-century Romantics well knew. Su cites feminist epistemologists (he names Linda Alcoff, Donna Haraway, and Sandra Harding) as giving him his lead in theorizing an epistemology that recuperates imagination as knowledge, and "address[es] questions of knowledge with respect to subjects who are located in history rather than universalized."[25] This nod toward feminist contributions to his epistemology of imagination is left undeveloped, however.

For my analysis of a specifically feminist utopian consciousness, achieved in and through contemporary speculative fiction, this contribution needs to be outlined more fully. Feminist epistemology enables us to extend the traditional notion of knowledge (and the faculty we privilege as the "source" of knowledge), and also the notion of utopia. In this context, the work of Donna Haraway has been central, as she asserts that acknowledging one's standpoint "mean[s] specificity and consequential, if sometimes painful structures of accountability to each other and to the worldly hope for freedom and justice."[26] These "structures of accountability" are crucial to the emergent nature of a feminist utopian consciousness and a speculative standpoint within feminist speculative narratives. Each of these texts is a structuring of accountability. As such, the meta-narrative of feminist utopian and speculative literature will always "be about" disjunction and desire, and especially about the confusion of reality and fantasy.

This confusion, of course, we already know. The "perfect knower," as feminist epistemologists have called him, has covered over this confusion. The traditional "modest witness" is Haraway's term for the exemplary philosopher who uncritically regards his understanding of reality as absolutely objective and neutral. He is "modest" because he does not regard the claims he makes for reality as constructions, but "simply" a reporting of what is there, and true. In so asserting, this knower places himself in "the [transcendent] culture of no culture"[27] – a "god-trick," according to Haraway, which allows him to regard his description of the world as unified and natural. This is, however, nothing more than self-regard. In her essay "Postmodernism and Political Change," epistemologist Nancy Hartsock outlines the challenge to our inherited "faith in universal reason," which postmodernist philosophers – particularly Foucault, Derrida, Rorty, and Lyotard – have mounted. But she goes on to uncover the ways in which some of these theorists end up "recapitulat[ing] the effects of Enlightenment theories that deny the right of some to participate in defining the terms of interaction."[28] In other words, she argues, these theorists conserve the premises of what Lorraine Code calls the "monologic, self-interested enterprise"[29] undertaken by the disengaged nowhere-man, who does not recognize his own biases and exclusions.

Hartsock and Haraway thus challenge this accounting of "the world" as described by the so-called objective man of science, who conditions the very "nature" of our world. Haraway will spotlight this figure as "the witness whose account mirrors reality – [who] must be invisible, that is, an inhabitant of the potent 'unmarked category,' which is constructed by the extraordinary conventions of self-invisibility."[30] These conventions condition our culture with "all the authority, but none of the considerable problems, of transcendental truth. This self-invisibility is the specifically modern, European, masculine, scientific form of the virtue of modesty" – and it is "one of the founding virtues of what we call modernity."[31] It is also a false speculation on the nature of "virtue" – and on the particular utopian foundation on which that virtue is constructed.

The perfect knower, we have seen, is typically described as being "nowhere," and regards himself as being also "everywhere." In putting it this way, it is impossible not to think of the association with the original "Utopia," or No-Place. Originally troped as an island, utopia is located far from our own fallen lands, and its borders are characteristically and vigorously protected. Ever since that first sighting and siting, the feminist project has been to vex those borders, by way of reclaiming a land inhospitable to "others." Toni Morrison observes that utopia is as much about who is excluded from it as it is about who is included. This is the crux of the utopian dilemma for feminism: accommodation of the other, and the connections between epistemology, community, and utopia. Feminist standpoint theory proposes that the observer acknowledges her located-ness, and the situatedness of knowledge produced by "located practices at all levels."[32] Haraway's presentation of the weak, modest witness makes visible the false modesty of the invisible "we" who define the world from a standpoint grounded in a particular ideology that regards itself as self-evidently "virtuous" (a word etymologically coded as masculine, any-way),[33] but that can only be defended with violence.

The account that the "perfect knower" offers is not objective, nor transcendent, but riddled with subjective distortions. Two of these dis-tortions are critical to the feminist project taken up in this book. First, these distortions lead to what Haraway calls "a separation of the tech-nical and the political," and a disavowal of the "sociotechnical relations among humans and between humans and nonhumans that generate both objects and value."[34] A perfect knower does not see the seams and joints of his own constructions, or the political/ideological motives driv-ing his production of knowledge. This knowledge production is itself a form of elaborate fetishizing of the abstract as concrete, avoiding analy-sis of "a cascading series of self-invisible displacements, denied tropes, reified relationships."[35] That process of displacement leads to a second distortion. The "objective" and "elaborate" account leads to a devalu-ing of the body, even though the body indicates where we are situated. These types of divisions and diversions are of a piece with the deeply masculinist ideologies with which we are familiar: "female modesty was of the body; the new masculine virtue had to be of the mind."[36] This devaluation of the body and/as femaleness has been, to say the least, a radical source of political crisis for women.

Rosi Braidotti, like Donna Haraway regardless of their allegiances to different philosophical traditions, reminds us that "central to [a feminist] project ... is the need to detach the female feminist subject – that is to say real-life women as agents and empirical subjects – from the represen-tation of Woman as the fantasy of a male imagination. The struggle is therefore over imaging and naming; it is about whose representations will prevail."[37] That detachment is major surgery, as it were, that is painful to both subjects. In representing or "staging" that operation of detachment, we can see the kind of connective tissue, much of it scarred, that binds "real-life women" to fantasy images. We might see, given the female sub-ject's freedom from ideological binds, new conceptions of woman, man, and nature alike, and the kind of "imaging and naming" that will make sense of women's experience.[38]

Haraway offers a bridge from philosophical to literary perspectives on situated knowledges, and on what I am calling speculative standpoint. Following critic Katie King's proposal of the term "apparatus of literary production," Haraway pursues the notion of an "apparatus of bodily production" – of which her metaphors of "visualization technologies" are an example.[39] But literature itself is also such a visualization or figuration, as evidenced in Haraway's attention to Joanna Russ. "No wonder," she observes, "science fiction has been such a rich writing practice in recent feminist theory."[40] The subject emerges through the world into an "actual occasion" of its being-as-becoming, a birth into not only "an affective and political sensibility," but also "a kind of cognitive sensibility"[41] that I identify as speculative.

The ongoing crisis in the feminist movement leads me to this study on very recent contemporary feminist literature. If it is not obvious already, my own project is inspired by a notion of feminist standpoint that is closely informed by Donna Haraway's:

A [feminist] standpoint is not an empiricist appeal to or by 'the oppressed' but a cognitive, psychological, and political tool for more adequate knowledge judged by the nonessentialist, historically contingent, situated standards of strong objectivity. Such a standpoint is the always fraught but necessary fruit of the practice of oppositional and differential consciousness. A feminist standpoint is a practical technology rooted in yearning, not an abstract philosophical foundation.[42]

In this passage Haraway, following feminist critic, bell hooks, offers a word for ever-becoming forms of desire, and for the ever-moving process of utopia in which I am particularly interested: she calls it *yearning*. The urgency of yearning is located within the subject, the body and mind, in the present and future (and even, in the past): "Communication and articulation disconnected from yearning toward possible worlds does not make enough sense. And explicit purposes – politics, rationality, ethics, or technics in a reductive sense – do not say much about the furnace that is personal and collective yearning for just barely possible worlds."[43]

This book illuminates contemporary feminist authors' working through the apparatus of fictional production to speculate on and visualize other possible worlds. The comparative readings within each chapter are organized around emergent narratological tropes of ways of being nowhere that clarify how the (de)formations of literary form offer the feminist subject and reader the instruments of change. The chapters lay out an ongoing line of theoretical propositions that defend feminist speculative narratives as a critical, visionary, visualization technology. Whether a given text is utopian/dystopian fiction, science fiction, or speculative narrative with utopian visions embedded within, each foregrounds the cruxes: the variations of situated knowledges, the acknowledgment of accountability and responsibility, the uses and abuses of vision and invention, and the shiftiness of borders and horizons.

THINKING THROUGH SPECULATIVE STANDPOINT

Speculation (like utopia) has had a bad rap. To label something "speculative" is as often a dismissal as not. It connotes lack of full investigation; it can suggest bias: "That's just speculation." Nor is it, more seriously, speculation in the sense Marx criticized; that is, a mode of thinking unrelated to the world as it is, with all its dominations and injustices. Speculation, in the sense I am introducing it, opens pathways discredited or even invisible to the "common sense" enjoyed by the perfect knower. The "speculator" interrogates "what may count as the case about the world,"[44] as Haraway puts it. Only such an honest accounting, continues Haraway, can "bring the technical and political back into realignment so that questions about possible livable worlds lie visible at the heart of our best science." Science would include a concept of accountability that redirects a standpoint, always, toward the clarification of the relationship between the subject and the world. This relationship is not simply an experience of the world, but more specifically an experience of power in the world. As we know, especially following Foucault, the experience of knowledge is no different, embedded in conditions determined by power relations. We acquire knowledge of ourselves and others (human as well as nonhuman) and we understand the knowledge gained, not from the "view from nowhere" abstracted from concrete relations, but from a stronger position of disclosure regarding the relations of domination and suffering, injustice and violence. This is the gist of contemporary feminist standpoint theory: its political charge.

What is a speculative standpoint, then?

In introducing the term, I signal a concept of accountability that is even more provocative, sparked by the commitment to changing the here and now, but projecting beyond that here and that now. I propose a definition of speculation that emphasizes the potentiality for change and reconfiguration of "new and constructive ways to disclose aspects of the world."[45] Taking inspiration from Haraway again, we must conceive ourselves as – indeed, we must be – something more than modest witnesses; that is, we must do more than recount the way things are, and we must also reject the association of so-called wisdom with the past only. We must require ourselves to look around from the standpoint we occupy in the present to the horizon, which means that we look backward to the past and forward to the future. We can aspire to our ways of being nowhere – but this will not be speculation from the point of view of a nowhere representing false objectivity, a position that does not recognize the fantasy behind its own utopian constructions. We can aspire instead to the nowhere associated with the literary tradition of future-oriented fabulation. As we recuperate speculation, we recuperate utopia, and neither will look the same as it did.

The conventional division of time into three parts is immediately complicated. Instead of the traditional tripartite division of time, there is, as Winterson will say, simply "now" and "not-now." But this "simplification" gives us more. The not-now of both the past and the future inhabits the present. And therefore, our lives, our narratives, are best spent accounting for the "now" that exists within the "not-now" – and vice versa. Like Janus again, the feminist subject must look backward and forward – as well as "here and now" – to make visible the "painful structures" of past and present, as well as alternative structures that answer to "the worldly hope for freedom and justice."[46] Extending the epistemological project, in other words, to include what we can *imagine knowing* about the future, we create not just an accounting of (the "what"), but an accounting for (the "why"), and an accounting to – to the "who" (or the "what") of the past, present, and future. The knower/narrator is responsible not only to herself, but to those who will follow and indeed those who came before, whose worldly horizons might look very different based on epistemological shifts, and the critical and political potentialities that might emerge from an evolved epistemological position.

In my proposed extension of feminist standpoint theory, the not-so-modest feminist witness works at seeking alternative ways of being nowhere. Not just one way of being nowhere, because that is what Haraway and others show we have already, that is, a representation of reality formed and continually confirmed at the insistence of the masculinist perfect knower, who belongs to the "culture of no culture." This traditional way of being nowhere assumes and (self)affirms the rightness of that notional-utopia-made-real, which is the work (and the world) of a self-generating ideology. Instead, the feminist speculative witness pursues multiplicity through a critical epistemology that makes visible the tint of the lens through which a dominant culture sees the world, and sees herself. The speculative witness see(k)s ways that will always be plural, for her method will always be pluralizing, diverse, ironical, and inventive. She mirrors the view from nowhere; yet being multiple and multiplied by the not-now (which is not to say the nonexistent), her viewpoint will be more objective, "stronger."

Given the Marxist genealogy of contemporary standpoint theory and a correlative skepticism regarding utopian fantasies, the notion of a speculative standpoint might seem controversial. However, speculative standpoint means more than a critical witnessing of one's location in space and time, and of the various forces defining each individual's material existence and cultural awareness. It also means a "scandalous"[47] witnessing, flying in the face of the given facts and so-called truths. It is a witnessing that integrates where one stands now (and how one came to stand there) into a projection of where one could stand, which is something different from where one will stand. Both stands are "not-now." But the speculative standpoint is defined by the urgency of the aspirational ("not-yet"). It connects the real and the desired, and in the connection creates a dynamic field of longing or yearning that extends feeling and thinking outward into the future and the elsewhere. A speculative standpoint would offer a measure of one's place in "the world" by evaluating the presence of the past, in one direction, and the presence of the future, or what utopian theorists have called the "seeds of prediction." Speculative standpoint looks backward and forward, reflecting the "as is" (speculum); as well as the "as if," the projecting out, the performance (spectacle) of possibility. There is one more sense to the word, "speculation": the sense of risk that comes with a kind of anticipation of the future or of possibility; the agent of such risk is a "speculator." All these senses of the word resonate around the notion of a speculative standpoint.

If a speculative standpoint locates one both in this world and out of it, then what is to be proposed for "achievement"? What stands as "achievement" is altered by this potentially multi-dimensional locatedness. Speculative achievement would not reflect the concretization of desire in an approximate instantiation of an ideal or end. The achievement would stand always at a horizon, never achieved. The "real" achievement may not be concrete or even embodied, but projected, an imagined possibility or potentiality. This potentiality is akin to the "novum" described by Darko Suvin,[48] and certainly to the notion of the portal that has emerged recently. This achievement would be a dynamic, indeterminate, but "creative advance,"[49] something closely related to what recent utopian theorists have been describing as a *utopianism of process*. The indeterminacy of this creative advance is crucial; there is no finality as in a singular concrete achievement. Rather, each concrete moment becomes a launchpad for approaching the next, an endlessly inventive approach. Speculative standpoint would be dynamic, future-oriented, and mobile, always projecting a farther horizon, while never reaching it. Thus, the concrete achievement is always deferred; yet each provisional step catalyzes the ongoing yearning or urge to continue "travelling," if only imaginatively.

Achievement from a speculative standpoint would be, in a word, *invention*. And just as the notion of speculative standpoint brings numerous accretive resonances, so does the notion of achievement as invention. By definition, *invention* is both active and passive in its connotation: it is (1) the sense of something completed; (2) a creative power or ability, inventive skill; (3) the process of inventing or finding something. Invention is a form of work. And, of course, invention can also be a form of fabrication, something fictive, even a lie. Nancy Hartsock anticipates this conclusion in seeing standpoint theory as making available new epistemological options "open possibilities that may or may not be realized," yet they "can claim to represent a truer, or more adequate, account of reality,"[50] exposing systemic power relations in any event. But to achieve that visibility, we need to be attentive to the fictiveness of reality and to the reality of fictive visions. Haraway's "passionate detachment" eschews "innocent 'identity' politics and epistemologies,"[51] but from that standpoint, she embraces the guilty risk-taking (or speculating) of those who create other subjectivities, other epistemologies, other politics, through the polymorphous figurations of art and the imagination. The feminist speculative fiction writer has worked consistently alongside the philosopher as a student of ontological and epistemological models, but she is licensed to go further; an intellectual world-traveler with a passport to, and through, the portals of possibility that the figurations of fiction can conjure.

WOMEN SCANDALIZING UTOPIA

Whereas this book treats utopian and speculative fictions published since 2000 (with a few important exceptions), the transgressive woman, as previously noted, has been on the scene from the beginning of women's utopian and speculative literature. Think of Margaret Cavendish's self-anointment as "Margaret the First," ruling her own alternative

"Blazing World"; the founding women of Millennium Hall, each of them with an "indecent" and even criminal history; Connie Ramos in Marge Piercy's *Woman on the Edge of Time*, regarded as "human garbage," criminal and insane, "Monster"-ous; the scandalous "four J's" in *The Female Man*; the various grotesque females inhabiting novels by Angela Carter, and by Jeanette Winterson, up to and including the figure of her adoptive mother, Mrs. Winterson. Each madwoman breaks through conventional boundaries of space and time, and all manner of decorum. She is comparable to Haraway's "Coyote or Trickster" figure of the "witty agent"[52] who, like the traditional figure of comedy or "topsy-turvy" reveals ideological contradictions and absurdities as a form of play. She may be judged contaminated, even criminal, because she is a transgressor – but she is ultimately valuable precisely for her disruptiveness. She is critical, self-critical, and inventive. And the texts she inhabits? Scandal sheets.

This will have formal implications important to this study. Haraway's turn to the rhetorical history of science writing points us toward an important linking of epistemology and historicity of narrative forms. The emerging method of scientific objectivity, she notes, is paralleled by the invention of a new genre: "the written report," in which "the rhetoric of the modest witness, the 'naked' way of writing, unadorned, factual, compelling, was crafted."[53] The development in the rhetoric of science writing has extremely important parallels in literary history as well. By the eighteenth century, the measure of the value of fictional prose is taken by its adherence to the realism and "truth" of description. At just the period Haraway refers to, the novel emerges out of narrative romance as literary prose's premier genre, its truthfulness to reality assumed by its common self-description as history. As literary historians have amply shown,[54] however, the novel's own hybrid origins in both romance and report have always complicated its truth claims, and spurred authorial play on the truth of fiction, the fictionality of truth, and the transparency of the novel's representations of "the world." Thus, what Haraway says of science writing is strikingly true of novel writing as well: "The self-contained quality of all this [scientific work, based on the masculinist 'projection' of nature] is stunning. It is the self-contained power of the culture of no culture itself, where all the world is in the sacred image of the Same. This narrative structure is at the heart of the potent modern story of European autochthony."[55]

The narrative structure of the same is precisely the source of feminist unease with traditional narrative conventions, as feminist narratologists have long observed. The "heart" of the contemporary fiction treated in this study will not be that potent story of self-generated knowledge, but rather invention, generating new ways of thinking and knowing, and images of ourselves and a world in which women are intelligible and "make sense." These narratives of difference, eschewing sameness, reimagine the world in forms that can for now be "only" visionary, speculative. They reimagine, too, the figure of "the future of humanity" that some feminists and queer theorists have regarded as the most suspect and retrograde: the birth of a baby. A new "generation" of the same? Or of difference?

The critical opposition of feminist narrative of otherness or difference to the masculinist narrative of the same is of course what prompts Haraway's promotion of Joanna Russ's 1975 speculative fiction, *The Female Man*, as a "founding text" for feminist fabulation. To say as Haraway does that "[t]he form was its content" is hardly controversial; the novel's fractured structure is celebrated for making visible the invisibility of woman in the world, and for challenging the coherence and "common sense" of the world that woman inhabits. More interesting is her connection of Russ's enterprise with her own:

This book [*The Female Man*] made gender a patent scandal of the imagination, the intellect, nature, language, and history – all those hoary categories in the romances of modernity....The linguistic and genetic miscegenation of both Russ's Female Man and my FemaleMan© is a tool for provoking a little technical and political intercourse, or criminal conversation, or reproductive commerce, about what counts as nature, for whom, and at what cost.[56]

The question, as Haraway suggests, is always what is "at stake," and "at what cost" a feminist revision of reality is mounted. Russ's text does more than make visible the invisibility of woman in the world, and challenges the coherence of the world that woman inhabits. The positive scandal of Russ's great novel lies in its blustering insistence that both men and women *see* the nature of ideological unknowing, and admit to the self-interestedness in dwelling among the community of "partial knowers" who are too afraid or too stubborn to learn. This scandalizing also accounts for the irony and humor of Russ's book. The comic techniques of her writing point toward feminism's ability to "narrativiz[e] social change" through the "process of comically transforming outcomes as an act of *imaginative revision*."[57] The structural multiplicities of *The Female Man* generate a comic mode that achieves a transgressive (feminist) utopianism driven by something other than the desire to possess: "the profit does not consist in the possession of truth, but rather in the opening of further alternatives and possibilities."[58] Russ's novel also makes visible the cost of that disruption: the hostility that sharpens the critical consciousness and the restlessness of a character like Jael; the literal dislocation of the four J's from their original historical context. Jael is not exemplary of speculative standpoint; her war against men sends her backwards in time. Janet, the anthropologist from the future, is a more congenial possibility, although her refusal to take up arms stands as an anticlimactic end to her story. Certainly not Jeannine. Perhaps not surprisingly, the exemplary one will be Joanna, the figure of the author, whose splintered identity is drawn together at the end of the novel.

The author's achievement, in terms of standpoint theory, is her final gesture of letting her book loose into the world to do its playful work.[59] Its narrative task is to enact that release into the world, and into the minds of its readers. Arguing the exemplary nature of Russ's novel, Haraway admires its inventiveness in figuring a new and multiplicitous view from nowhere. The figuration of ongoing utopian process in this novel resides neither in the keeper of past knowledge, the librarian Jeannine; nor in the representative of a future knowledge, Janet; nor in the keeper of the rage, Jael; nor even in the artist, Joanna. It resides in the work of art itself, at the moment when Joanna affectionately sends the (momentary) achievement of her own yearning "on its way" with a final envoy, a gesture of hope in finding or forming a new community of readers hospitable to alternative vision/versions of the world.

WELCOMING "THE STRANGE": THE ROMANCE OF COMMUNITY

The notion of "cognitive estrangement" has, of course, been central to analyses of narrative utopia and science fiction for years, most famously articulated in the work of Darko Suvin, Fredric Jameson, and Tom Moylan, in particular.[60] But in feminist speculation, "the strangeness" we would avoid – the madwoman we would rather leave in the attic, for instance – will out. Moroccan sociologist Fatima Mernissi will locate the central figuration of feminist identity in the legendary character of Scheherazade, who uses storytelling as an instrument to explore "the strangeness inside" of her king's serial violence against women. This model of critical thinking is repeated in Jeanette Winterson's *The Stone Gods* (2007), where we also explore what the narrator calls "the strange that I am"[61] in a sexist, technological culture.

The contemporary turn toward an ethics of reading also, clearly, informs this study. The "ethical turn" does not mean simply a commitment to a listening other, to whom one acknowledges "who I am and where I stand."[62] There is not just one story to tell about oneself, or about another. Feminist speculative standpoint can break the deadlock (and historical dead-end) of self-generating knowledge, or the illusion thereof. Its operations also break the deadbolts locking the virtuous in, and all the rest out. Speculative standpoint gestures toward a vision of utopia defined not in terms of inclusivity and exclusivity, but in terms of a radical hospitality that admits of – in fact celebrates – imagination's political and ethical possibilities.

Peter Melville's study of Romantic hospitality (2007)[63] therefore joins John Su's work in tracing to the long nineteenth century a persistent attention to and engagement with the figure of "the stranger." As Melville observes, Romantic writers characteristically admit "having designs on the figure of the stranger, and in doing so, they also welcome the destabilizing singularity of that figure. They embrace the stranger's ultimate resistance to accommodation, its singular refusal to be incorporated by a text that would otherwise wish to assimilate difference into a discourse of similarity." He adds, these texts "situate themselves in an 'ethical' space that renders each scene of reading the foreign an experience of responsibility" *for and to* another.[64] A similar pattern of resistance to accommodation is evident in many texts included in this study. But where Romantic texts rarely get past that resistance, these contemporary texts describe a performance of hospitality in which the stranger is accepted "as she is."

The plotting of these texts focuses not only on the alterity of the "elsewhere" to which we are transported, but the alterity(-ies) of the world in which we already live, the "strangeness within," which is much harder to see. The ability to perceive the virtue in alterity is *itself* a virtue. These texts investigate the "truth-content" of feminist fictions that "tell" (that is, that both account for and narrate) a new vision of identity and community based upon this newly defined virtue.

In bringing forward a feminist articulation of strangeness, my goal is to revise dominant characterizations of narrative utopia that do not take into account a deeply occluded germ of feminist utopian thought and narrative. A speculative standpoint defining itself against the so-called neutral standpoint sharpens the visibility of feminist anticipations of a subject liberated from a deep-seated masculinist ideology of individualism. Phil Wegner speaks of the "shadow images" that narrative utopias project, images appearing "on the extreme peripheries of our conceptual retina, [images] of a situation whose truth-content necessarily resides somewhere else."[65] They are narratives of "return," but not conventional ones that suture the wound of nostalgia. Sick of shadows, the speculative figure rarely returns to her original home. Home is in the future.

The novel readings in this book highlight the ways in which "truth-content" lies in the perception of "the strange that I am," not only within the subject itself, but in the context of social interaction habituated to ignoring its own strangeness. As these novels turn their attention to female subjectivity and community, they project shadow images of communities that welcome strangeness rather than shun it. The trace left behind in each novel is the proposal of a communality based in what Winterson calls a "beginning to love," the potentiality of which is figured at times as a search for a way to a home that the feminist subject has never inhabited – and thus is figured at other times as a portal of possibility. *Postmodern Utopias and Feminist Fictions* emphasizes that this way of knowing oneself as "the strange" – and thus as open to self-consciousness and to imaginative sympathy – leads to a consideration of a theme not often directly treated in analyses of narrative utopias: the theme of hospitality.

Herein lies the background pattern in the carpet. Whereas this book begins with a focus on individual subjectivity in the context of a particular model/ing of and by feminist epistemology, the problem of community moves forward with each chapter. Not one protagonist within these texts is ever actually "at home" in the conventional sense. She may not be literally homeless (although she often is), but she does not belong and is not welcome in the place where she is. Like many a narrative hero, her journeys are plotted out in stages as she alights, temporarily, in search of a landing place, in the hope of arriving at a home, somewhere. Whether a particular narrative can be described as either utopian or dystopian depends on the subject's ability not only to learn the ways of the world in which she lives, but also to imagine the possibilities of the home that she desires. Postmodern narrative utopias are unlikely to offer a floor plan for any such home, or a comprehensive map to such a homeland. Such narratives therefore often gesture toward a new dimension – spatial, temporal, or both – of locational feminism.[66] Where she is "at home somewhere."

For the feminist speculator, desire does not reside in the "nowhere" of pure mind; as Tobin Siebers has proposed of postmodern utopianism generally, her desire "is about desiring to be elsewhere. . . . Utopian desire is the desire to desire differently, which includes the desire to abandon such desire."[67] One could wish that such yearning as Haraway and Siebers write about could be satisfied; but part of the drive for accountability discussed earlier makes such a wish implausible, if not nostalgic. As we enter the worlds of the novelists who populate this study, she is either "on the road" or at a temporary home regarded more as a way station than as a permanent dwelling. This pattern of movement is best described by one of the traveling women of Shahrnush Parsipur's *Women Without Men*, which I will discuss in Chapter 5. The character Munis has just been invited into one of the many "safe havens" we see in this literature, and she observes the following:

Unfortunately, this is not a good time for a woman to travel alone. She has to be invisible to travel, or just stay at home. I can't stay home any longer, but because I am a woman, I must stay home somewhere. I can make a little progress, then get stuck in house, then go a little further, and get stuck in another house. At this rate I might be able to go around the world at a snail's pace. That's why I accept your invitation with pleasure.[68]

Whether literally mobile or only imaginatively so, her travels in and to such spaces are figurations of a libratory process – not necessarily (in fact, rarely) achieved. Nevertheless, her approach to the world is not one of suspicion, but of openness and hospitality; she engages the body as well as the mind. Her priorities are more "sensible," inventive, curious; they emphasize the importance of others, of sympathy, and of communal inclusiveness. Imaginative sympathy will be the critical faculty in play as I argue for a feminist version/vision of a hospitable utopia.

Similarly, these texts aspire to constructing a relationship of author and reader that is characterized by safety and welcome, not by mastery and control. Siebers reminds us that *reading* gathers together narrative's *aesthetic and ethical* tasks. The aesthetic work resides "in [narrative's] attempts to represent the repetition of experience and the nausea of ethics in a specific figure, word, or plot. *But the nausea of ethics cannot be so located. All we can do is retell or reread the story one more time.*"[69] The ethical work lies in narrative's offer of its vocation. This offer is troped in Russ's gesture of an "envoy" in search of a friendly audience; in Rajaa Alsanea's appeal to readers, Arab and non-Arab, to meet up in whatever safe havens they can find: houses, online chat rooms, "in the phone lines that spring to life after midnight."[70] Narrative makes possible those havens for ethical imaginings: in the stories, "songs and poems, too numerous to count," where the reader can take on the role of authoring her own otherworld. These creative novelistic approaches to new horizons endorse the Qur'anic verse with which Alsanea opens her own novel: *Verily, Allah does not change a people's condition until they change what is in themselves.*

The speculative knower inhabiting the fictive worlds I explore in this book understands herself to be the impure, contaminated subject who thinks and feels, who reasons and imagines: recall here Haraway's description of feminist standpoint as not simply "an empiricist appeal to or by 'the oppressed'" but a "practical technology rooted in yearning."[71] She travels in pursuit of a reality that she can intuit, desire, envision, and maybe partially realize. Her ways of being nowhere will be not only a manner or method of being, but the multiple pathways from the nowhere of insignificance (say, for instance, Offred's abjection in *The Handmaid's Tale*) to the "nowhere" of positive signification. Unlike traditional utopian texts, in which travel generally takes place within the utopian space – for example, the "tour-guide" plot that characterizes so many of such texts – feminist speculative texts map the coming in or upon (Lat. *in-venire*) the possibilities for utopia. The speculative observer may, like Munis, perceive herself as a kind of exile, and only by traveling and understanding that unstable position does she "[grow] a narrative of her own."[72] The achievement of the speculative traveler will be the invention of the journey itself, and her assurance that while that journey will be incomplete, she is that much closer to the (moving) horizon. The trip is risky, however; she must avoid "shipwreck," a nautical and narratological trope repeatedly employed in the novels, as these authors reach back to the novel's generic origins in order to conceive (of) alternate beginnings and endings, and generate new figures and figurations of history.

CHAPTER I

Learning the way of the world, and beyond
Utopian imperatives and the female bildungsroman

Even to be a stranger is to enter a world constituted from within as strange. The strangeness itself is the mode in which it is experienced.
– Dorothy E. Smith[1]

If a feminist utopian consciousness is always already ironical, the task of feminist speculative narrative is primarily epistemic: to find new ways of *knowing* that reveal new ways, paths, and bridges to nowhere. I begin then with the literary form most consciously about epistemology. The novels considered in this chapter are already classics, particularly Angela Carter's *Heroes and Villains* (1969) and Octavia Butler's *Parable of the Sower* and *Parable of the Talents* (1993, 1995). Nalo Hopkinson's *Midnight Robber* (2000), the final text treated here, should – and I expect will – become a classic.[2] All four speculative novels are also novels of development or bildungsroman narratives. The bildungsroman, of course, flourished as a symbolic form celebrating a bourgeois culture into which a young male successfully integrates. As I have noted in the Preface, the exclusion of women from this "classic tradition" of the form is explained by Franco Moretti's 1987 analysis; however, the formal and ideological conservatism of the bildungsroman was aggressively challenged early on. Charlotte Brontë's *Jane Eyre* bridles against formal limitation in the same way its heroine does. Jane's traumatic imprisonment in the obviously womblike red room is a conceptual moment: the anger at exclusion from the house, from the familiar, is embedded here – and is the narrative impulse driving Jane to find her way in the world despite the "ways of the world." The novel's domestic conclusion is an anticlimax and, as many have recognized, a ruse. What stirs us is the cruelly inhospitable treatment of this young girl, the difficult taming of her independent nature in and by a society indifferent to her desires and talents. What haunts our memories is Jane's disturbing self-recognition in the grotesque figure of Bertha, whose illicit accommodation in the attic pushes this early female bildungsroman toward the gothic mode. Irony, the gothic, the grotesque: these are modes, regardless of the forms they inflect, that women writers have found more fitting than the comic mode for capturing female experience. Brontë is only one of the earliest to wrestle with the muscular ideology molding a literary form that supports the construction of an "idea" of culture and invests an emergent figure of the "ideal citizen." But the weight of the bildungsroman's symbolic content, including its exclusion of the woman, is still being cast off.

The novels treated in this chapter are in fact not typically thought of, first off, as female bildungsroman narratives because their focus is on more spectacular (and catastrophic) visions of future society. Nevertheless, they are clearly postclassical – indeed, postmodern – bildungsroman texts, and consciously so.[3] Set in historical moments that are not merely postcapitalist and postmodern, but indeed postapocalyptic, the ideal and ideological teleologies of a classical bildungsroman text are intentionally destabilized, and this will naturally have profound implications for the symbolic form of these specific texts. Their specifically *speculative* mode, encumbered by the anachronistic imperatives of the bildungsroman, stimulates a return to "the problem" of history's centrality. This problem is hardly a matter of paradise lost and regained; restoration in these visionary (as opposed to realistic) representations of individual education and social development is neither expected nor desired. Between the comedy guiding the original trajectory of the bildungsroman plot and the apocalypse recalibrating that trajectory, the possibility of a hospitable resting place is uncertain. The end of these texts is not to confirm "the way of the world," conforming to "*a priori* lessons to be learned,"[4] but to pursue ways to other worlds without being tricked into false hope.

Therefore, the texts must return to "the problem" of education: what we learn, how, and why. Under the dangerous social and nearly post-historical conditions that are the settings of these texts, "*a priori* lessons" only misguide. Blind conformity to traditional knowledge systems proves foolish, if not deadly: it is impossible to see ahead. The "specific pedagogical ideal"[5] of the classic bildungsroman cannot reflect the reality of the apocalyptic speculation – but like *Jane Eyre,* these contemporary narratives explore exactly how anachronistic the metaphor of history informing the bildungsroman is. The reality of such speculation will require a mobile, modest witness, as Haraway teaches us, a self-reflexive epistemic standpoint that resists assumed categories of knowledge, and that understands history to be not "simply" linear, closed, or unidirectional, but complex, with multiple lines of possible futures, presents, and pasts entangled with one another. The extent to which each heroine locates a new epistemic and pedagogical ideal determines how successfully she can mature to be a citizen of an aspirational new world. Some novelists have told us that the goal of their art is to make us see: the goal of *these* novels is to make us see beyond. They must be, therefore, what Susan Sontag calls "out-landish" narratives and seek to educate for a radical mobility.

THE WAY OF THE WORLD "NO MORE": THE LIMITS OF FEMALE BILDUNGSROMAN

Among recent critics of the classical literary bildungsroman, there is no question that Franco Moretti has offered the most comprehensive and coherent reading of the symbolic form of the genre called the "classical bildungsroman." Yet Moretti's groundbreaking 1987 study, *The Way of the World*, acknowledges that his literary-historical account does not account for more recent versions: "[t]he bildungsroman," he adds, "seemed to have *its own private ideology*"[6] – and indeed, it self-reflexively thematizes privacy as the foundation for sociality. Susan Sontag brilliantly describes an ideological imperative of this kind as a characteristic feature of the novel genre's "*mandate of its own normality*."[7] The normality defined by the ideal form of the bildungsroman, according to Moretti, belongs to another time (mid-eighteenth to mid-nineteenth century), another place (Europe – mainly Germany, France, and England), and "necessarily" to the male gender. He allows for readings of postclassical bildungsroman texts up until 1914, and permits consideration of *Jane Eyre* and *Middlemarch* as legitimate postclassical examples. But the pressures of women and war alike bring the classical period (the term itself suggesting the highest point of its development) to a halt. Moretti observes, following Lukács presumably, that "formal patterns are what literature uses in order to master historical reality, and to reshape its materials in the chosen ideological key"; "if form is disregarded, not only do we lose the complexity (and therefore the interest) of the whole process – we miss its strictly political significance too." This suggestion of transcendent form is what supports his view, then, that the genre will be an inhospitable workspace for "women, workers, African-Americans"[8] – and he is right, strictly speaking. But Georg Lukács's theory of the novel includes a description of what happens when the original conditions "under which [a genre] came to be given form" are so changed as to render "the basis of artistic creation ... homeless."[9] Under such circumstances, artistic form becomes a more complex "entangling" of one genre with another – in our contemporary parlance, formal hybridity. Entanglements, homelessness, hybridity: these will also be useful words for describing the feminist aims of the authors in this chapter and beyond.

Even before Moretti's magisterial study came out in 1987, studies of female bildungsroman narratives began to appear and continue to do so.[10] Todd Kontje warned early on against trying define a "female form" of the bildungsroman in too simplistic a manner; we are as likely to "grow impatient" with such parallel definitions as with "the aesthetic and ideological conservatism of earlier definitions of the male Bildungsroman.... In fact, searching for positive female role models in the Bildungsroman threatens to play into the hands of those who would continue to marginalize women's fiction as 'trivial' literature."[11] However, Susan Gubar helpfully remarks that women's writing generally, and women's novels of education in particular, develop a utopian imperative that alters obsolete literary forms.[12] Postmodern and women novelists obviously challenge the nineteenth-century novel's commitment to linear plotting and realist mimesis in pursuit of their own goals of deconstruction and reconstruction, and of a narrative form adaptable to those new commitments. If plot variations among the bildungsroman novels generate differences "in the ways in which plot generates meaning"[13] – about history, about time, about identity – what meanings can we ascribe to recent narratives of education that clearly *affiliate with* the original form, even if they neither parody it, nor replicate it, but "entangle" it?

I begin with Angela Carter's *Heroes and Villains* (1969), which is clearly and self-consciously a bildungsroman, although critics focus almost exclusively on its catastrophic vision of the future. The novel's nearly post-historical setting quickly brings into focus the crisis of her heroine's community. The traditional, ideal teleology of Marianne's father maps out for her a utopian narrative of individual improvement and social progress, of paradise lost and regained in the protected calm of the private and the civilized.[14] The utopian aesthetic of comfort and security that enriches our civilized lives loses all credit when, by the end of chapter one, no one is left who cares about that utopian fantasy; it becomes a bankrupt vision, its traces kicked into nonexistence. Other than entropy – which stands at the end as a real possibility – the only alternative is emergence, although "into what?" and "why" are central, unresolved questions. But those are the questions directing Marianne's education during the crux time in which she exists, as she self-consciously strains toward new ways of learning about and conceiving of the individual and/in history.

Heroes and Villains' conscious rehandling of the classical bildungsroman is signaled instantly by the name of Carter's protagonist: "Marianne" alludes to the female love-interest of Goethe's paradigmatic *Wilhelm Meister's Lehrjahr* – although, of course, Carter reverses the relationships in order to draw the portrait of the young woman rather than the young man. Set in a post-apocalyptic period, there is evidently no national government left, no fixed borders, and a weakening grip on any notion of culture and humaneness. The "comfort of civilization" is limited to a small community in which heroine Marianne is born, and she is in many ways the typical bildungsroman hero/ine at the novel's opening: she is restless, seeking "the meaning of life," "intense,"[15] and will soon reject her home for the wilderness beyond the tower and walls that mark the town's geographical boundaries.

Integration into this society is clearly her father's goal for her, and as a professor of history, he provides the resources for discovering a "sense of belonging"[16] to a wider community of human beings: "He [Marianne's father] taught his daughter reading, writing, and history. She read his library of old books" (*Heroes and Villains*, 8). Her classroom is within a "white tower" – call it an "ivory tower" – of steel and concrete, left from the nuclear war that has reduced the world as we know it to a shadow of its former self. So long as she remains safely within the tower and enclave walls of the Professoriate she, too, can participate freely in this dedicated preservation of humanity's rich history, the whole of its knowledge, its "civilized" ideals. As one of the Professoriate class – "the only ones left who could resurrect the gone world in a gentler shape, and try to keep the destruction out, this time" (8) – she would enjoy the "certain privileges" of that class, such as the "deep shelters" that had allowed them to survive a nuclear holocaust. In this opening scene, however, Marianne sits in the study of the tower reading and looking out, from this god-like vantage point, "across the fields to the swamps and brambles and tried to imagine a forest of men" (7). Her extravagant curiosity and lack of belonging are evident in the first paragraph of the novel:

Marianne had sharp, cold eyes and she was spiteful but her father loved her. He was a Professor of History; he owned a clock which he wound every morning and kept in the family dining-room upon a sideboard full of heirlooms of stainless steel such as dishes and cutlery. Marianne thought of the clock as her father's pet, something like her own pet rabbit, but the rabbit soon died and was handed over to the Professor of Biology to be eviscerated while the clock continued to tick inscrutably on. She therefore concluded the clock must be immortal but this did not impress her. Marianne sat at table, eating; she watched dispassionately as the hands of the clock went round but she never felt that time was passing for time was frozen around her in this secluded place where a pastoral quiet possessed everything and the busy clock carved the hours into sculptures of ice. (1)

Time itself imprisons Marianne, its mechanical cyclical actions mocking her gaze outward toward the unknown, those "forests of men," from atop her tower, like so many a fairy-tale princess.

The professor's white tower is a clear opening trope of what Rosi Braidotti, following Haraway, describes as the perspective of "masculine standpoint," the "'cannibalI/ eye' of unlimited disembodied vision that is the fantasy of phallogocentrism."[17] Marianne's ordered existence feels empty and cold to her, its principle of continuity coming only from the inexorable, mechanistic spring of the clock, artificial and passionless. The Professors' Society of the Tower in fact parallels descriptions of ideal, aristocratic societies in the earlier examples of the bildungsroman. In these aristocratic cultures, notes Moretti, there are no apparent conflicts within their walls, and the aristocracy is portrayed as self-sufficient. As Moretti puts it, "its authority merg[es] with everyday activities and relationships, exercising itself in ways that are natural and unnoticeable." This endorsement of the aristocracy, he adds importantly, is the "hidden logic of the everyday life of the classical bildungsroman" and the point to which the hero must return at last.[18] So here, a community "self-supporting at the simplest level" (2), pastoral, but civilized, a throw-back to a sort of Platonic Republic: "primarily a community of farmers with the intellectual luxury of a few Professors who corresponded by the trading convoys with others of their kind in other places. And the Soldiers were there to protect them all" (8).

Marianne's rugged truthfulness betrays her community's false self-sufficiency from the outset. The novel's second paragraph warns how fragile a community the Professoriate is, not least because its inhabitants close their eyes to the dangers outside: "Beyond the farmland was nothing but marshes, an indifferent acreage of tumbled stone and some distant intimations of the surrounding forest which, in certain stormy lights of late August, seemed to encroach on and menace the community though, most of the time, the villagers conspired to ignore it" (1). Marianne does not. Intent even as a child in setting herself apart, she was left out of the children's games "but she did not care"; she also "marked all her possessions with her name, even her toothbrush, and never lost anything" (3). Marianne's precocious discernments reveal a community more closely resembling the inhabitants of Plato's Cave, not of Plato's Republic. Jean-Jacques Rousseau and Lewis Mumford, two authors featured in her father's library, contribute to the Professor's magnum opus on "the archaeology of social theory" (8), but beyond their theories of social contract, urban development, "technics and civilization," is the real question: "Is there still a living choice between Necropolis and Utopia?"[19]

Marianne consumes her father's books and dictionaries as offered, but they say little to an adolescent living in a present that looks only to the past: the texts "had ceased to describe facts and now stood only for ideas or memories" (7). Sneaking outside the town walls she discovers, among lacerating and flesh-eating plants and "bottomless vents in the ground," the ruins of a city reduced now to a "dangerous network of caves." The subterranean bowels of these ruins not only hide "obese and hugely fanged rats," but also the remains of a surviving population so skeletal and disorganized that Marianne had initially concluded they were ghosts. They *are* ghosts, the narrator explains, "only in the sense that they had forfeited their social personalities" (8) as their bodies starved. This "picture of misery" portrays the so-called Barbarians, whom Marianne had regarded as a force of brute nature, as "explosions of violence produced by the earth itself" (14) to shake the security of their tower society. Marianne's boredom is such that she actually *hopes* for a direct experience of them: "at least a visit from the Barbarians would make some kind of change" (2). Watching dispassionately from a tower room where she had been locked up for "curiously indulging her spitefulness in several ways" (3), she had found such attacks "very interesting" – although the most recent one had killed not only most of the livestock, but also her brother.

Marianne's willingness to survey objectively her surroundings as if she were disconnected from them – her acceptance of a speculative standpoint in other words – gives her the kind of attentiveness that allows her effectively to defamiliarize the familiar and to open her mind to critique. She refuses the easy categorizations of her father and the Professoriate, whose reading of the world, she suspects, is at best irrelevant. She observes with curiosity, but not judgment, that women from her own village are apparently assisting the attackers in their plundering. Marianne's refusal to play Soldiers and Barbarians, a common childhood game in which "'The Soldiers are heroes but the Barbarians are villains'" (2) is attributed to her stubborn contrariness. But it is also a seed of prediction. As a young teen, Marianne thoughtfully informs her father that "it was impossible for her to consider marriage with any of the young men in the community.... 'I don't see the point. I could maybe marry a stranger, someone from outside, but nobody here. Everybody here is so terribly boring, Father'" (11). Her wise parent, with a maturity that ennobles his "retreat from life,"[20] advises her that "chaos is the opposite pole of boredom" but moments later, Marianne yawns at his lecturing: "She loved him but he bored her"

(11). Neither wise nor mature, she opts for chaos. And she chose wisely: Marianne's father is killed shortly thereafter not by a chaos-bearing Barbarian but by her own childhood nurse, who like others in the community had suddenly gone mad; the kind of event that "[n]ow and then" broke the community "from its trance" (9). After that, there is no reason for her to stay, "nothing but custom to keep her in the village and nothing she wanted to take away with her. Not a single one of all those things she had once possessively marked with her name now seemed to belong to her" (18).

So much for the comfort of civilization that stabilizes the conventional bildungsroman. Yet Marianne prepares for her own initiation, underscoring her unwillingness to be absorbed into her community. In crafting her appearance as a "demented boy" (15) by chopping her hair off, she not only turns away from the prospect of monotony (and marriage) but becomes a parody of the male initiate of the bildungsroman form.[21] She also burns her father's books, and finally "drown[s]" her father's clock: "It vanished under the yielding earth, still emitting a faint tick" (15).[22] The Professors and Priests may struggle to retain the woof and warp of memory that keeps the weave of this social fabric together, but that veil is rent for good when another Barbarian attack pulls the community closer to collapse. Escaping in the company of Jewel, a Barbarian leader, Marianne braves a new world: "it seemed the real breath of a wholly new and vegetable world, a world as unknown and mysterious to Marianne as the depths of the sea; or the body of the young man who slept … in her lap" (22). Later, she notes the passing of the season, *"outside time and known space"* (52; emphasis added), and this ambiguous dimension welcomes her journey into "pure potentiality."[23] The slate, she thinks, is clean and she walks in with eyes wide open.

As in the paradigmatic bildungsroman, the meaning of the heroine's quest promises to emerge through her "ordeal"; like so many such heroes, the period of trial consists of "becoming aware of such a state of affairs."[24] Marianne is courageously open to every incident, thinking, interpreting and waiting for the meaning to come to her, although she is also naively eager to judge: "you," she condescendingly informs the young Barbarian leader, Jewel, "are a perfect illustration of the breakdown of social interaction and the death of social systems." She calls him the "noble savage in her father's researches" (24) and nominates him the "ragged king of nowhere" (53), in a bow to this novel's utopian forbears. This assumed "brute," however, reveals his intelligence quickly enough, informing his family that Marianne is "the daughter of a Professor of History … She knows which way time runs" (31). Even more pointedly, when Marianne loftily informs Jewel that "[t]hinking was [my father's] function," he responds, "he had the time to think about things, did he? ... Or was he a preserved brain at the best of times?" (57).

Heroes and Villains' comic Mrs. Green, another nurse figure to replace the one who went mad, blithely observes upon her arrival that "'Tomorrow you'll have to sleep with Jewel, won't you. That's *the way of the world*'" (59, emphasis added) – and suddenly Marianne faces a social logic that is mysterious to her. Trying to orient herself in the intellectual landscape of Plato, Rousseau, and the Western culture learned from her father, Marianne discovers rather quickly what she already intuited and is therefore ready to accept: that "the way of the world" into which she was born is itself an anachronism. Her father's work on Rousseau does not prepare her for this new community, where "[s]he felt herself removed to a different planet," isolated "as though she were in quarantine" (41). Indeed, to the Barbarians she *is* a kind of disease; she notices at the sight of her that the newly met Barbarians guard themselves by making "the sign" against the evil eye – a gesture that she recognizes, much later in the novel, as the long-forgotten sign of the cross. Given their obvious super-stitions, she muses that "If time was frozen among the Professors, here she lost the very idea of time, for the Barbarians did not segment their exis-tence" (41). As if to drive that point home, she notices among the cloth-ing of a little girl named Jen "a dead wrist watch on her arm, purely for decoration; it was a little corpse of time" (44). She muses further on this girl, who reminds her of "an Ancient Briton": "Marianne contemplated the archaic child and wondered if her clothing were proof of the speed with which the Barbarians were sinking backwards or evidence of their adaption (*sic*) to new conditions" (43).

Such speculations on history and culture hardly ease her "integration" into this wild society to which she was willingly, naively, even roman-tically, drawn. For just here, Marianne, the self-proclaimed "virgin of the swamp" (50), is matter-of-factly raped by Jewel upon her first and only effort to return home. It is no accident that the primary topic of their post-coital banter is time, interpretation, and anachronism. Coldly observing her ravisher, with his amulets and tattoos, Marianne concludes, "You are a complete anachronism" (57). Asked to define the last word, she responds, "A thing that once had a place and a function but now has neither any more." Anachronism, she adds, is a "pun in time" (56). That is when Jewel launches the barb concerning her father's "preserved brain." The point is clear: not only is her father an anachronism, but so is her own attachment to the past, and to her father's rational categories, which were represented once by all those words, ideas, and so-called facts (7). Although she regards herself "the only rational woman left in the whole world," Jewel reminds her again and again that her kind of reason serves no useful function anymore. Thus, in that Barbarian logic that Marianne does not understand and cannot challenge, Jewel announces that "I've got to marry you, haven't I? That's why I've got to take you back" (56).

In the classic bildungsroman, marriage is a metaphor for the social contract. Typically performed in a ceremony filled with symbolism that connects the individuals to society at large, marriage according to Moretti fits the lives of the two into a "symbolic construction" that "always 'connects' the 'individual moments' of a text with all the others: they are thus 'preserved' in their singularity, while simultaneously made 'meaningful' – they 'point beyond themselves.'"[25] The conflict between individualization and socialization thus dissolves in the coalescence and coincidence of "desire" in all its forms, social, economic, sexual and moral. The same could be said to be true in the coupling of Marianne and Jewel – although we must read the symbolic construction of this marriage rather differently. We know by now that the Barbarian society of Jewel is a grotesque version of the utopian social contract envisioned by Rousseau. This marriage ceremony too is characterized by symbols emptied of their original significances and redefined – although the scene is more specifically nuanced than Sarah Lefanu suggests in describing it as a "grotesque parody of a fairy-tale wedding."[26] The couple's commitment is not secured through a reciprocal exchange of vows and the "consummation" of those vows, but through the violence of a forced intercourse by which Jewel claims Marianne.

The marriage in this novel does not function, generically, as a metaphor for the social contract; rather, this marriage signifies the rending of that contract, symbolized by the tearing or "giving way" of Marianne's hymen, graphically described in the narrative. The ironic reversal of elements in the marriage plot is complicated by further references to one of the most famous bildungsroman texts, *Great Expectations*. One of *Heroes and Villains'* jokes is that Mrs. Green supplies a decaying wedding dress that she removes from a wooden box. In that box are a few other possessions from the old days, "a few dresses, several aprons, her hairpins and a book which was no less precious to her because she had forgotten how to read it. This book was a copy of *Great Expectations*" (37). The naming of the Dickens novel just here places the grotesque wedding ceremony behind the looking glass. For "this crumbling anachronism" of a dress that Mrs. Green pulls from the box along with the book is a replica of Miss Havesham's wedding dress, the very tissues of it disintegrating as it is pulled from the box. In case we miss the joke, the dress is burned after the wedding, although *without* its wearer inside it this time. Marianne demands its destruction, and Mrs. Green, who herself alternates between sentiment and callous indifference, does the honors.

Other intertextual puns adhere to this moment in the text: the elaborate tattoo depicting the Fall of Man traced permanently into Jewel's back, for instance. "'It's hideous,'" says Marianne of the tattoo, "'It's unnatural'. But," the narrator tells us, "she was lying again; the tattoo seemed to her a perilous and irresistible landscape, a terra incognita on the back of the moon" (86). The tattoo's symbolism holds open for her until the bitter end the hope that she and Jewel hold in their union the potential for a future in this fallen Eden, despite the "devils" at every turn. Here is a world she can explore – perilous but irresistible. And so she does for the remainder of the novel, "[c]ourting her own extinction" (87). At night, however, she and Jewel give life, as it were, to a hybrid creature, "this erotic beast" (88), the "dual being they made." Once again, what is emphasized is the "universe" of desire these two individuals create, allowing her to "[deny] him [Jewel] an existence outside." Indeed, to deny the existence of anything outside: "Then their bed became a cold, black, silent world and its sole inhabitants were denied all other senses but those of touch, taste and smell" (88).

In the afterglow of these episodes, separating "out to themselves, again, they woke to the mutual distrust of the morning" (89), and the contraction of their world to only "two dimensions, flat and effectless.... [A]ll these activities were no more than sporadic tableaux vivants or random poses with no thread of continuity to hold them together" (89) in "this disintegrated state." The singularity of their lovemaking has an effect opposite to what Moretti describes: far from finding meaning "beyond" themselves, Marianne's transcendent experience in the bedroom has meaning only there and then. In a comment reminiscent of Charlie Marlow's, the narrator describes Marianne's feeling that "It's a small world.... It's as small a world as the Romans found and much smaller than Uther's, getting smaller all the time. Contracting, tightening, diminishing, shrinking" (95–96).

This brutal marriage does permanently change Marianne and leaves her, at least until the end, *not* "entirely without hope" (59). The narrative offers out something after all: love. As they endure their wedding night, an unlikely thing happens: "the strangeness of the events of the day combined almost to subdue her." She begins unplaiting Jewel's long hair, slowly, "an action altogether *out of time*" (78; emphasis added). While Jewel mocks her educated idiom – "Lead me by the hand to the gates of paradise" he jibes (to which she responds, "Why are you putting me through this ordeal by imagery?" [81]) – she accepts the ironized come-on. They "make love" for the first time, "clutch[ing] one another's hands with almost the same kind of terrified relief" (81) and in this way, the narrative concludes, "they effected a truce" (82). That is as good as it gets in this marriage: hardly a commitment, but a temporary truce at best. The outcome of that truce I shall turn to in a moment. But here, Marianne knows even this truce is a precious thing, because it reveals something "real." It is her first authentic experience. Their lovemaking "bore no relation to anything she had heard, read or experienced ... she was filled with astonishment that the room contained the world or the world had become only the room; but she put her arms around him and caressed him." The gates of paradise indeed. "And," this paragraph concludes, "if anything else but this existed, then she was sure it was not real" (83).

The hope for love seems fragile at best, and delusory at worst. For this reason, we are suspicious when Marianne finds herself, in the days following, surprisingly and for the first time "comfortable." This feeling of comfort reminds her of her father and his ilk, "gathered together over their after-dinner, home-brewed blackberry brandy when they would discuss apocalypses, utopias and so on. Marianne suppressed a yawn but, all the same, she felt at home" (93). She has found "familiarity," even a little comfortable boredom. But as her new cohort of nomads move out toward the sea, which she has never seen, these connections continue to confuse her: "And Marianne knew in her heart that none of this was real; that it was a kind of enchantment. She was in no-man's-land" (103). Furthermore, "she could find no logic to account for her presence nor for that of the people around her nor any familiar, sequential logic at all in this shifting world; for that consciousness of reason in which her own had ripened was now withering away and she might soon be prepared to accept, since it was coherent, whatever malign structure of the world" (106).

The symbolic form of the classical bildungsroman, with its goals of comfort, compromise, autonomy and independence, was clearly apparent to Carter, who overturns those goals time and time again in setting the novel at a moment of civilizational collapse. Whereas the Professors "at least make the pretence of nourishing such a thing [as hope]" (123), Jewel, Marianne's own "unorthodox" tutor, rejects any proposal of hope in the future. Marianne concurs, signaling that her "researches into the *moeurs* of savage tribes [are] completed" (132). She observes that a return to the Professors is a meaningless conclusion to her education: "'The Barbarians are Yahoos but the Professors are Laputans,' she said" (123); both peoples, in other words, are parodies of themselves and neither of them worthy of much admiration. Why seek existential moorings or Morettian objective foundations among either party? She refuses to play "Heroes and Villains" here among the Barbarians, just as she did at "home"; now, the game cannot be played at all, for "I don't know which is which any more, nor who is who, and what can I trust if not appearances? Because nobody can teach me ... because my father is dead" (125). Neither the Barbarians' nor the Professors' societies can offer any positive symbolic legitimacy.

Up to the bitter end, Marianne is pulled between anachronistic hope and abject despair. She continues on with Jewel, at once disgusted with and attracted to her "husband," and is "abashed" at what she suspects is merely nostalgic sentimentality. Thus, as the couple reaches the last real horizon – the sea – the narrator invests this final major scene with allusive ghostliness. Like the first couple, they stand before "all the wonders of the seashore, to which Marianne could scarcely put a single name, though everything had once been scrupulously named" (136). Adam's reign is over. Yet Marianne and Jewel's arrival in this primeval scenario is shadowed, too, by the knowledge that they have also reached the end of the world, an analeptic arrival of a new Adam and Eve. The beach recalls other post-apocalyptic scenarios on beaches – not only Neville Shute's but also, and uncannily, H. G. Wells':

Losing their names, these things underwent a process of uncreation and reverted to chaos, existing only to themselves in an unstructured world where they were not formally acknowledged ... Jewel and Marianne walked along the beach of this wide, unfrequented bay not as if they were discovering it, or exploring it, but *like visitors who have arrived too late*, without an introduction, are unsure of their welcome but, nevertheless, determined to brave it out. (136–137, emphasis added)

Reaching such an indifferent horizon, the traces of their footsteps "already filling with water,"[27] Marianne still considers beginning a new world with Jewel, even as she skeptically predicts failure: "[A]t best, they might begin a new subspecies of man who would live in absolute privacy in secret caves ... This fearless and rational breed would eschew such mysteries as the one now forcing her to walk behind the figure on the shore, dark as the negative of a photograph, and preventing her from returning home alone" (137).

The influence of "home," with its associations of hospitality, comfort, familiarity, and family, is not what resolves this plot; the very idea of home ("as if somewhere there was still the idea"[52]) is mocked by the inhospitable state of nature that Mrs. Green calls "this hell on earth." Indeed, a cruel reminder of her former affiliations faces her at just this moment, as Marianne gazes on "a time-eaten city up to its ears in the sea" (137), a negative image of the place from which she came. In a last confusion of sentimentalism, Marianne interprets the sight of twin towers, a white tower (her own?) and a lighthouse, as landmarks telling her to "abhor shipwreck [and] go in fear of unreason. Use your wits ... She fell in love with the integrity of the lighthouse." The narrator is quick to remind us that Marianne is nostalgically recalling the culture of "the defunct clock" (139), and momentarily she sees the reality of the ruins' "rotten concrete."

The only possible ending is what Moretti calls the "implausible" kind: crisis, a divorce, or death. With Marianne suspecting that the "grand design" in this world has little to do with human sociality, much less love, she and Jewel examine one another "with marvelling suspicion, like heavily disguised members of a conspiracy who have never learned the signals which would reveal themselves to one another" (148). When he leaves for the last time, she suddenly feels a stranger even to herself: "she was surprised to find herself dislocated from and unfamiliar with her own body" (148). Moretti reminds us that "[t]he [classical bildungsroman] story ends as soon as an intentional design has been realized."[28] The same is true in this novel, except the intention here is to evacuate static utopian ideals. Its conclusion hardly satisfies the conventional sense of an ending. "No more" – the words used to inform Marianne of Jewel's death – is to be given, taken, exchanged, or demanded. Thus, with that death, the narrative almost immediately shuts down, but not before Marianne experiences the truly *unheimlich*, catching a reflection "in a misty, cracked mirror on the wall: there stood Marianne, *unrecognizable to herself*, leaning over the cauldron" (149; emphasis added). Visions of her entire life history, like a ghostly triumph of life, parade before her in the curling steam, including the figure of the murderous Nurse, "her ... forgotten face grinn[ing] triumphantly for, in some sense, her prophecy had been fulfilled" (149): "If you're not a good little girl, the Barbarians will eat you" (2). Last in the parade is her father, "who merged imperceptibly with the image of the blind lighthouse and then disappeared in the slowly rising bubbles" (149), just as his timepiece sank into mud. Marianne tries a new ending, claiming the inheritance of Jewel's authority and legitimacy: "'I'll be the tiger lady and rule them with a rod of iron'" (150). The

civilized comforts of her White Tower home are devolved into the infan-
tile terrors of the fairy tale.[29]

Whereas the classic bildungsroman endorses the "triumph of meaning
over time,"[30] this novel faces the triumph of time over meaning. Carter's
novel reflects urgently on the purgatorial conditions of life that make
narrative possible, and what kind of imagination will preserve the task
of narrative. Carter's strategic choice of the bildungsroman exposes with
profound irony the falseness of Marianne's own misguided naiveté and
hope long before she admits it to herself. The dismal lesson: the odds were
against her from the outset. In a post-historical setting, where it is doubtful "which way the time runs," another principle of hope must be discovered. The most one can say of Marianne's quest for self-discovery is
that she does not despair in her suspicion that she goes forward into this
"realm of bare life,"[31] shrugging at the fact she is pregnant. This sense of
an ending overturns the promise of that conventional mark of futurity.

"ANOTHER PLACE. ANOTHER WAY": THE RECONSTRUCTION OF THE FEMALE BILDUNGSROMAN

Octavia Butler's *Parable of the Sower* (1993) and *Parable of the Talents*
(1998), as well as Nalo Hopkinson's *Midnight Robber* (2000), offer far
more robust, if indeterminate, trajectories for narratological and historical possibility. In doing so, the texts propose new conceptions of community and affiliation, other ways of living, and new ways of learning
and of knowing. As in *Heroes and Villains,* wisdom proves to be more
than knowledge of the past, but requires attention to realities of the present, and a commitment to, if nothing so optimistic as a "dream of," the
future. The preoccupation with education therefore remains, as do the
formal structures of the bildungsroman. Education is not simply forma-
tive, but self-critical and ultimately transformative, such that the heroines in these novels can lead out (*educere*) toward "another place" and
"another way," as Butler's Lauren Olamina will put it (76). These novels
have happy endings, however fragile, and their "sense of an ending" is a
kind of sixth sense, far removed from the "common sense" endorsed by
traditional ways of the world.

The near-future vision of the United States projected in Butler's famous
Parable of the Sower is unsettling because it feels so familiar – a social
tinderbox that finally ignites and is fueled by racism, economic collapse,
depleted resources, and head-in-the-sand politics. As *Parable* opens, the
walled community of Robledo, California manages to stay relatively

secure, its residents drawing together to protect the integrity of their way of life, such as it is. Only the young Lauren recognizes how ill-conceived is this quarantine approach, how short-sighted their goals, how delusional their fantasies of America's present, not to mention its future. All the more galling for her, therefore, is to see her father and stepmother, themselves teachers, blind to those fantasies and to their responsibility to make the other members of community see that change is inevitable, with or without walls. There are no ivory towers in this community, but plenty of walls separating it from the wild spaces outside. In an ironical allusion to utopia's characteristic trope, Robledo is described as "an island surrounded by sharks" (50); later, Lauren describes her home as "our island community, fragile, and yet a fortress" (135). But for her as for Marianne, the boundaries are increasingly blurred: one night, Lauren sees the very wall itself as "a crouching animal ... more threatening than protective" (5). Thus, for Lauren as for Marianne, "home in the neighborhood" is already an anachronism maintained by sentimental memories of a so-called civilized nation.

The uniqueness of her commitment to "something else" is registered in her possession of a private space: "my room is still mine. It's the one place in the world where I can go and not be followed by anyone I don't invite in. I'm the only person I know who has a bedroom to herself" (51). Like Marianne again she wants to mark something, and the introspection and self-possession encouraged by this privacy is critical. However, the space she seeks is not simply the other side of the city wall but undiscovered, or at least unconsidered, spaces that promise a break from history and a new, self-generating and regenerating state of nature: "There are islands thousands of miles from anywhere – the Hawaiian Islands, for example, and Easter Island – where plants seeded themselves and grew long before any humans arrived" (78). Lauren extends this utopian geography to outer space, "[w]ell out of the shadow of their parent world" (83). A future that simply reproduces what is here, defects and all, is a narrative Lauren rejects. She pursues a motive for the journey she understands she must and will take, "some place other than down the toilet" (21). That is her task and her commitment.

For this reason, Lauren consciously concerns herself with the function, the form, and the content of her own education. Her stepmother Cory teaches the local elementary school-age children, and has taught her. Her father, the community preacher, also teaches at a local college outside Robledo. These Christian teachings, disseminating a dour passivity and acceptance of suffering, are the first ones Lauren contests: "My

favorite book of the Bible is Job. I think it says more about my father's
God in particular and gods in general than anything else I've ever read"
(16). Learning to endure may be wise if one fears damnation from an
angry God. But to Lauren's mind, America is already, like Carter's purgatorial landscape, "a hell ... on Earth" (21). Lauren is "not some kind
of potential Job" (25), ready to settle down into some "version of slavery"
(37) or another, assuming she survives at all. Hence the irrelevancy, to her
mind, of any standard curriculum her stepmother Cory would follow, on
the one hand, and any homilies on acceptance and submission her father
offers, on the other. Neither prepares these Americans with the appropriate knowledge for physical survival or for a spiritual strength that does
not reside in blind faith.

Even worse, the stubborn habits of her friends and family poison the
ground for any seeds of change, despite the obvious fact that sexism,
racism, economic inequality, and fear, including fear of change, are unrav-
eling the social fabric – and allowing the reintroduction of such social evils
as debt-slavery to corporations that promise jobs, housing, and security in
high-walled, prison-like compounds. Lauren recognizes that American ideals are degraded precisely by our habit of arguing only in terms of dichoto-
mies – male/female, black/white, old/young, violent/nonviolent, rich/poor,
high class/low class – in fact, any configuration of *them vs. us.* This stance
is itself a kind of enslavement within an ideological prison house out of
which America cannot easily escape. As Lauren puts it:

> All struggles
> Are essentially power struggles,
> And most are not more intellectual
> than two rams
> knocking their heads together. (94)

Hence Lauren's decision that "Given any chance at all, teaching is what
I would choose to do" (124) in order to articulate what *is* relevant to learn.
Her course is not the usual fare. The instruction of her friend Joanne with
books "on survival in the wilderness" is not welcomed as the common
sense that it is, but as nonsense. "Do you think our world is coming to
an end?" her father asks, "and with no warning at all," Lauren records,
"I almost started crying. I had all I could do to hold it back. What
I thought was, 'No, I think *your* world is coming to an end, and maybe
you with it'" (62) (emphasis in the original). Her future is not the story of
suffering and promised reward in the next world. If this world is dying,
the next has to be created – and Lauren's goal crystallizes. To educate

herself and others is not only to survive, but to do so precisely by learning to see through, over, under, and beyond physical, mental, and ideological walls. Only then can the way to a next world be discerned, and that "way" is Earthseed – as predicted by her vision of an island where "plants seed themselves" (77).

Lauren's difficulty in characterizing what Earthseed is – religion? philosophy? way of life? – resolves itself when she understands that it is an *embodied* curricula (not curriculum, as it is inherently plural) educating for the endlessly contingent events of entangled histories. Acknowledging the ways in which past, present, and future influence one another, the curricula are constantly self-reflexive and self-critical, producing knowledge that accommodates uncertainty and contingency as its context, and resists so-called impregnable ideals or universals. Her notion of God is too impersonal – *indifferent* (25) is the word she uses – to take sides or even countenance the categories of victim and victimizer, eschewing the politics of opposition. Her deity "is Change," a "Power," and an "Intelligence" that does not demand obedience in any conventional religious sense, yet does demand "ongoing, individual adaptability" (29). Therein rests the key: Earthseed promotes a critical intelligence[32] that is itself adaptable, ironical about what it knows and thus, is self-critical as well as critical. Lauren's notion of Intelligence commits itself to exposing the willed ignorance that has brought herself, her family, and her country to unprecedented levels of anarchy and rampant cruelty.

Earthseed's tenets also mean that no single person possesses the truth, or the "right knowledge." There can be neither one teacher nor only one way because Earthseed is by definition always a becoming. Taking over Cory's position as elementary school teacher in Robledo, Lauren levels the typical hierarchy of a teacher-student relationship, partnering older kids with kindergartners, to "let everyone get a taste of teaching or learning from someone different" (95). Later, on the road with her growing cohort of followers, she reminds them that each is equally "qualified" to teach and learn: "'Everyone who's surviving out here knows things that I need to know,'" I said. "'I'll watch them, I'll listen to them, I'll learn from them. If I don't, I'll be killed. And like I said, I intend to survive'" (173).

Trust is a primary theme in this novel – and Lauren "embrace[s] diversity" and the intelligence of others in order both to learn from them, and to gain their trust in learning from her: "We must find the rest of what we need within ourselves, / in one another / in our Destiny" (200). She banks on the greater wisdom of the *group* rather than of an individual, and in doing so promotes an epistemological "modesty":

> Earthseed
> Cast on new ground
> Must first perceive
> That it knows nothing. (179)

Young as Lauren is, she reconceives the purpose of education as adaptability, not indoctrination or even integration – not when the so-called ideal is an image of corrupt community from the top down. Finding a way of learning that is also a way of living, Lauren educates her few followers for speculation, not expectation. With such leveling in place and in play, Butler envisions an inherently unstable but hopeful utopian alternative in which the situated knowledges of all members of society are valued, and through which ossified structures of contemporary culture may evolve, if erratically, in a network of affiliated communities that can explore other models of civility and civilization.

It is no accident, finally, that Lauren's ordeal is informed by the fact that she is a "sharer," or hyperempath (11). She suspects that society would be more coherent and more ethically nuanced if everyone were a sharer. This suspicion pressures the shape of her plans, and the form of her narrative. Rather than pursuing a path designed "to build the Ego, and make it the indisputable centre of its own structure,"[33] she trains for a quickened sense of perception, an attention to things beyond herself, that maintains the modesty of her standpoint. Lauren records how routinely people do *not* pay attention, either to her or other children (8, 9, 33) or to the clear signs of social dysfunction and imminent disaster (38, 55, 90, 117, 131). Her curricula, therefore, do more than urge people to "get ready" (55). They teach students – whether children or adults – how to see what *is*, not just what they expect or hope to see: "Someday," she notes, "when people are able to pay more attention to what I say than to how old I am, I'll use these verses to pry them loose from the rotting past, and maybe push them into saving themselves and building a future that makes sense" (79). Just as Earthseed is "[t]he life that perceives itself / Changing" (126) – life that in other words pays attention to itself and "keeps [its] eyes open" (178) – so a proper relation to the Earthseed "god" is not standard worship but a more basic activity: "We perceive and *attend* God" (17; emphasis added). This is not submission but admission by "the ones who will make our first schools possible" (*Parable of the Talents*, 389), and prevent the suicidal consequences of "lack of attention to the wider world" (*Talents*, 81).

Attentiveness gives Lauren and her followers a perceptual portal to that "more objective" account of experience and history. And only this more objective view, shared by others, makes possible something more than a faint hope of social maturity. This potentiality is troped as an ascent from ignorance to intelligence, and from immature dependency to independence, *through* cooperation. The ascent is given not to a single savior figure, but offered to everyone in the community. But each member must have the maturity to *choose*, rather than expect, or hope, to *be* chosen. The initial "launch" of Lauren's *The First Book of the Living* on the Internet, a step toward disseminating her teachings to worldwide audience, picks up the metaphor of growth and ascent:

> Earthseed is adulthood.
> It's trying our wings,
> Leaving our mother,
> Becoming men and women.
> ...
> We are men and women now.
> We are Earthseed. (*Talents*, 394)

This maturity is only possible through the historical "rebirth" that Earthseed represents: "it's like watching a birth" (*Talents*, 391), remarks one of her publishers.

In the second of the series, *The Parable of the Talents*, Lauren Olamina's daughter Larkin confirms Earthseed's widespread success, rooted in the cultivation of a new educational system. Constructing her own story from her mother's journals, Larkin acknowledges her mother's important recognition that in a disintegrating American economy, even if you have no property or financial wealth, there is always "something to exchange" of value: information. This trading in knowledge has a literal side in Lauren's early efforts: each member taken into her newly created Earthseed community is required to learn at the very least reading and writing (those being desirable and dwindling "commodities" in Butler's twenty-first century America) as well as a practical trade. The directive to be educated and then to educate is one of the first "duties of Earthseed ... to learn and then to teach" (*Talents,* 74). Furthermore, any knowledge acquired is shared: "Anyone who had a trade was always in the process of teaching it to someone else" (24); "You help us teach others. You help others the way we've helped you and your sisters" (77). By the end of the *Parable of the Talents*, Earthseed is wealthy and widespread, but the power of money and reputation is focused on education, on financing science and technology research, and on "[helping] the communities to launch themselves toward the stars and to live on the distant worlds they found circling those stars" (*Talents*, 379).

Lauren Olamina's vision avoids the impoverishment of Marianne's "narrowing" of "actuality (daily life, reality)," as Bakhtin puts it. Instead, the utopian imperative driving her bildungsroman narrative accomplishes the goal that Bakhtin ascribes to that form: that reality be "at the same time filled with an equally real future that is growing out of it." Earthseed comprises in itself the Bakhtinian chronotope that informs his and Butler's notion of the bildungsroman genre. Time and space "merge here [in the novel form] into an inseparable unity, both in the plot itself and in its individual images."[34] And so it is in the *Parable* narratives: Earthseed, as both a process and an idea, catalyzes the becoming of a new time and of a vision of a "real future." The series' plot is the time-space of plotting and seeding the community that will be called Acorn. The individual images of the chronotype include seeds of native plants that Lauren gathers; and also *space travel*, an anticipatory vision of historical shift in *The Parable of the Sower* that is realized, although not without irony, in *The Parable of the Talents*.

"'I KNOW WHAT I'VE DONE'": ATTENDING TO THE FUTURE

This sounds like a confession. And that's how Larkin regards that statement by her mother, as she opens the ambivalent sequel to *The Parable of the Sower*. As Butler maps a second bildungsroman narrative, *The Parable of the Talents*, we learn at once how well her mother has succeeded in creating a new social ideal, and how skeptically that ideal can be taken. Ruth Levitas teaches us that "the shift to late modernity produced a shift in utopian thought such that it is no longer possible to say anything about the nature of utopia itself, but only the communicative processes by which it may be negotiated. Thus the only kind of utopia which is possible is the processual and communicative."[35] This aptly describes the presumed accomplishment of Lauren Olamina and Earthseed – but Levitas warns that "[in] practice, such claims tend to sneak assumptions about the actual character of utopia in by the back door" – can any such process be politically neutral? In retelling Olamina's story through her own eyes, Larkin charges her mother with exactly this form of (unwitting?) self-interestedness.

Larkin/AshaVere narrates the second *Parable* text from the standpoint of adolescent resentment, embarrassment, even hatred, toward the mother she was never allowed (and never allowed herself) to know. Believing instead that "she never really needed us [herself and her Uncle Marc], so we didn't really let ourselves need her" (*Talents*, 405), Larkin has other ideas about the price that has been paid for her mother's utopian desires and designs. The careful "compilation" of her mother's and father's writings belies her stated indifference; so does her stubborn unwillingness to embrace the rigorous optimism of her mother's success. Larkin's choice of her mother's final words – "I know what I've done" – resonates both triumphantly and darkly. The daughter refuses even to watch the first departure of Earthseed members to outer space, much less participate in the future unfolding before her eyes: "I was not on any of the shuttles, of course. Neither was Uncle Marc, and neither of us has children" (405). The narrative and the genealogical line ends here, she asserts smugly, as she shifts blame for an alienated childhood from the safe but benighted Uncle Marc to her courageous mother. We are left doubtful that Larkin can grow up; she notes with unwitting self-incrimination that, "Somehow we – or at least I – *never paid much attention* to the growing Earthseed movement. It was out there" (397, emphasis added). Despite her two advanced degrees in history, Larkin cannot see where history is taking her mother's movement. Her most succinct judgment, "Just nonsense!" (380), persists even as she recounts the launching of the first Earthseed ship to the moon, so prejudiced is she by the safety of the anachronisms Earthseed is supplanting, and by the memory of the person(ality) of the mother whose care and upbringing she missed.

This come-too-late heroine exposes the extent of the festering psychological wound in her admission that large portions of America embrace her mother's vision for a better society "among the stars." But Larkin's persistent portrayal of her mother as a power-hungry zealot betrays an immature view of power, one promoted by the logic of opposition that informs her version of American history and politics. Interestingly, Octavia Butler herself confesses to sharing this view for a time, as she records in an interview appended to the 2007 edition of *Parable of the Talents*:

> I hadn't liked Olamina when I began *Parable of the Sower* because in order for her to do what she was bound to do, she had to be a power-seeker and it took me a long time to get over the idea that anyone seeking power probably shouldn't have it. I had to remind myself again and again as I strove to write *Sower* that power is only a tool like any other tool – like money, like knowledge, like a hammer, even. It's the way tools are used that's important.... I knew this of course, knew it intellectually. I had to come to know it emotionally before I could write the novel.[36]

At the same time, Butler observes, the death of her own mother in 1996 opened the way for that emotional acceptance. After years of struggling with the first 150 pages of *Talents*, the story "began to live and move" only then: "I don't know why [my mother's] passing somehow inspired the situation between Olamina and her daughter.... In a sense, it was my mother's last gift to me." The last gift Lauren's mother left is, ironically, that she dies in childbirth, freeing her child, this extraordinary girl, from the adolescent battles playing out so painfully in Larkin's narrative, which dead-ends in her stubborn affiliations to the past, family, and national histories.

The closest Larkin gets to freedom is through her composing and inhabiting DreamMasks, a virtual-reality medium in which she can "live the adventures" of anyone she pleases, trying out different identities. Her childhood scenarios are the typical fantasies of life with lots of money; of adventures involving "spies, embezzlers and saboteurs"; and, significantly, of a childhood with different parents, "parents who cared about me and didn't wish always that I were another person ... All I had was the usual child's suspicion that I might be [adopted], and that somewhere, somehow, I might have beautiful, powerful 'real' parents who would come for me someday" (327). In addition, her adopted name, Asha Vere, affiliates her with the heroine of the Christian America DreamMasks – Asha is the heroine who saves people, and "*made* them return to God" (327). This is the wrong kind of power, but Larkin insists on retaining her cartoon-heroine name, and never realizes the power that her mother offers out. That power promises the self-envisioning, self-actualization and social integration that Larkin clearly and desperately seeks, and which has already transformed much of American society.

Larkin's conservative affiliations, formed by the teleological rhetoric[37] of a society passing away, actually offers her a kind of false nobility in caution and passivity. Like many of her fellow Americans, clinging to the paternalistic protectionism of President Jarret and his ilk, Larkin settles for compromise. In the classical bildungsroman, this is an important and positive step for the hero. Here, society itself is growing up and beyond that hero. At novel's end she is quite literally missing the boat, yet still describing her mother's story as "narrow" (405). Given this story of arrested development, the novel's conclusion is deeply ironical, ending not with Larkin's judgment, but with the recollection of Olamina's declaration that "I know what I've done.... I've helped them to the next stage of growth" (405) – and she clearly presumes that this is hardly the end of that development. Where Carter's Marianne and Butler's Larkin remain in the *unheimlich* of a post-apocalyptic doom, Olamina and her adherents find the *heimlich* elsewhere, anywhere where the endlessly expanding and accommodating Earthseed can disperse its agents of change, "away from the chaos and destructiveness into which they have fallen and toward a consuming, creative long-term goal" (410).

"YOU HAVE TO LEARN TO USE ALL YOUR SENSES; IS THAT WHAT HE SAY": NALO HOPKINSON'S SIXTH SENSE

Nalo Hopkinson's *Midnight Robber* (2000) has not received extended critical treatment, but this novel is a spectacularly successful instance of a speculative bildungsroman narrative. This novel is about survival and education out of passivity and obedience to outmoded ideological and political structures. But the text attempts not only to recover the present by reviewing the past, but also to recover the future. *Midnight Robber* achieves a vision of an ideal social connectivity and communality by means of a nonlinear temporal structure alien to the classical bildungsroman form. As in Octavia Butler's *Sower*, the Hopkinson bildungsroman functions as a narrative path to the image of the chronotype, and to a new mark of futurity. Her deft achievement is the interweaving of three apparently disjoint sets of tropes: African mythology, African-American history, and the World Wide Web. In a speculative tour-de-force, Hopkinson offers a future world in which a multi-dimensional shift makes possible the interanimation of all three historical frames. The result: a narrative world that is ultimately, as Bakhtin puts it, "saturate[d] with time ... the fullness of time in it."[38] This interanimation of historical dimensions also means that Hopkinson's heroine, Tan-Tan, can succeed where Larkin cannot.

We meet Tan-Tan at about age nine on Toussaint, a planet to which all individuals of African-Americans descent, with whatever mix of bloods, were invited in order to create a utopian world that redeems their slave history: "All the bloods flowing into one river, making a new home on a new planet" (18). As if following Octavia Butler's vision of a diverse and inclusive utopia "beyond the stars," Toussaint is populated through a second Middle Passage, this time a journey to freedom. The planet celebrates this journey annually with Carnival-like parties that feature elaborate costumes symbolizing aspects of their history: "Long time, that hat woulda be make in the shape of a sea ship, not a rocket ship, and them black people inside woulda been lying pack-up head to toe in they own shit, with chains round them ankles. Let the child remember how black people make this crossing as free people this time" (21), from a corrupt Earth to this utopia.

In this world of the near-future, Tan-Tan's first real teacher is not human but her *eshu*, an implanted "earbug" that functions as an artificial intelligence (AI) personal "genius" and guardian, and connects her to a vast network system. This "Granny Nanny web" involves nearly all citizens on the planet, integrating each individual with the community through various modes of social connectivity. This model of integration takes its name from the spider-like figure of the African god, Anansi, who traditionally controls "the realm of opportunity and potentiality and the concomitant risks and perils involved in such situations. As such, his residence is at the crossroads … A powerful ally and a hard teacher, Eshu should always be cared for and respected."[39] In *Midnight Robber*, the *eshu* is a conscious "being" who participates in a historically inflected electronic web that holds the collective memory of Toussaint's African and African-American histories.

More of a mother to Tan-Tan than her own mother, who "would look in on Tan-Tan once a day and pat the tiny shoulder, just a little bit too hard" (48), the *eshu* is also a gentle and honest teacher:

The eshu showed her more pictures of old-time Earth Carnival: the Jour Ouvert mud masque, the Children's Masquerades. When Nursie came to fetch her for breakfast, Tan-Tan was tailor-sat on the floor in the dark, still in her Robber Queen costume, staring at the eshu screen and asking it questions from time to time. The eshu answered in a gentle voice. (30)

The care of Tan-Tan's *eshu* breaks off when her father, Antonio, murders a rival lover to his wife. Instantly condemned to life imprisonment, Antonio escapes (with underground assistance) through a "dimension veil," with Tan-Tan in tow, arriving at an exile planet, New Half-Way Tree. This new world is a dystopic version of the planet Toussaint paradise, "the way a shadow is a dark version of the real thing, the dub side … like a ripe Maami apple in one fold of a dimension veil" (2).

Both babes in these literal woods, Tan-Tan and Antonio are met by a bird-like creature named Chichibud. The so-called *douen*[40] is their mentor in bush survival, and Tan-Tan, by far the better pupil, begins her new education in this alien terrain. Like Lauren Olamina's father, and Marianne's before him, Antonio is too tied to the past to be successful in this new world. Despite being warned that "You must learn to live in this place, tall people, or not survive" (100), Antonio, having "had enough of the lesson" (103) on the dangers of the bush, falls asleep drunk during his watch, nearly getting them all killed by wild creatures. "I know this bush," scolds Chichibud, "not you. You ignorant, you is bush-baby self. If you not going to listen when I talk, I leave you right here" (107). Tan-Tan, on the other hand, asks questions, learns the ways of her guardians, whose social organization, ethic of care, and principle of communal interest over self-interest contrast with the degraded societies and degenerate behavior of most Half-Way Tree humans, all in exile from the Toussaint community.

For all that, Tan-Tan's cultural and personal history comprise a rocky soil for these seeds of new wisdom. Whereas she recognizes that *douen* knowledge is more relevant to her physical survival than anything her parents could (or did) teach her, her psychological survival is another matter. Her father's attachment to her is more than paternal. As she grows older, her father sees in her more and more the figure of her mother, Ione; it is only a matter of time before he comes to her bed. At age nine she is forced into a years-long incestuous relationship resulting in two pregnancies, the first aborted. The second one, though, is not. On her sixteenth birthday, Tan-Tan kills her own father in self-defense during the last in a series of rapes. She is left not only pregnant again, but psychologically abject, and a different set of survival skills are needed. Chichibud, again, becomes her teacher. Immediately after the murder, her bird-friend comforts her – "Papa Bois see what really happen in that room, Tan-Tan. He ain't judging you" (172) – and to protect her from sure punishment among the New Half-Way Tree humans, he brings her to his own hidden community, the Kabo Tano tree, "a Papa Bois, the daddy tree that does feed we and give we shelter. Everyone douen nation have it own daddy tree" (179). A daddy tree who only gives, never takes or attacks. Tan-Tan herself can scarcely believe what she sees, an entire community literally entwined throughout the branches and living symbiotically off its water system and fruits. Although at times "She ain't think she could take much more strangeness" (183), she accepts the invitation to live "*With we*" (the asterisks denote speech in the *douen* language). Thus isolated from all human beings, Tan-Tan gradually reorients herself among these gentle and humane, although not uniformly friendly, creatures. The *douen* are themselves abused by the exiled Half-Way Treers, regarded as a sub-human and inferior race, an echo of the slave history the humans share. Recognizing this, the birds invite her to "Come in peace to my home, Tan-Tan. And when you go, go in friendship" (179).

Rescued from a probable death sentence by the humans in Half-Way Tree, she learns how a race of proud and intelligent creatures have learned to survive and work with, but also to surpass, the incursion to their planet of human beings who regard themselves as "masters." Tan-Tan learns, first of all, how both to *see* and to *experience* differently: "I go show you how to make the bush your home for the night," says Chichibud (101); "Every noise you hear in the bush mean something. Bush Poopa don't like ignorance" (103). She learns "lessons in yelling and stick throwing"; she learns the *douen* language. When Tan-Tan finds herself separated from her *douen* sister Abitefa, she panics at first; then remembers, "calling back to mind Chichibud's lessons. *You have to learn to use all your senses; is that what he say*" (223) (emphasis in the original).

The most important lessons the *douen* teach her relate to responsibility and trust. When unwittingly she and her *douen* sister betray that trust, revealing their whereabouts to the vengeful humans, the *douen* hold her responsible. The entire douen community abandons and destroys their Papa Bois – not just their home but the actual, natural infrastructure of their community. A double-shame now becomes threefold. But Tan-Tan's salvation lies in a *douen* verdict of her crime: not "an eye for an eye," but this: "*When you take one life, you must give back two*" (174) (emphasis in the original). She slowly comes to understand that the two lives she must "give back" are not only her child's life but her own. The compensation for killing her tormentor lies not in either her shame or her punishment, but in reclaiming herself and claiming her child.

Tan-Tan's recovery is tracked through a series of interpolated narratives that are actually newly composed legends of the Midnight Robber. In one parable, entitled "Tan-Tan and Dry Bone," the girl wanders in Duppy Dead Town, where "people have one foot in the world and the next one already crossing the threshold to where the real duppy-them living" (198). Inhabiting this psychological purgatory, Tan-Tan feels only "the pain of knowing what she is, a worthless, wicked woman that only good to feed a duppy [dead spirit] like Dry Bone. How anybody could love she? She don't deserve no better" (202). Dry Bone is Tan-Tan's negative daemon, "[he] was she sins come to haunt, to ride she into the grave" (205).

Tan-Tan must literally carry Dry Bone, who appears as an emaciated old man – a displacement of the father who raped her: "and is like she pick up all the cares of the world.... She feel the weight of all the burdens she carrying: alone, stranded on New Half-Way Tree with a curse on she head, a spiteful woman so ungrateful she kill her own daddy" (201). Nearly strangled by Dry Bone's embrace and his demands for food, she feeds him and her own emotional abjection: "And all she working, she could hear Dry Bone whispering in she head like knowledge: 'Me know say what you is, Tan-Tan. Me know how you worthless and your heart hard. Me know you could kill just for so, and you don't look out for nobody but yourself. You make a mistake when you pick me up. You pick up trouble'" (203). When a passing turkey buzzard flies over, seeking his own meal, he coaxes Tan-Tan to give up her burden. The girl argues, "I is a evil women, and I must pay for my corruption by looking after Dry Bone." The bird advises differently:

> I ain't know about you an any corruption, doux-doux.... You smell fresh like the living to me.... If a man attack you, child, don't you must defend yourself? I know this, though: I ain't smell no rottenness on you, and that is my favourite smell.... Like Dry Bone not the only monkey that a-ride your back, child. You carrying round a bigger burden than he. (206)

The buzzard refers her to Papa Bois – "He could look into your eyes, and see your soul, and tell you how to cleanse it" (207) – something she has heard from her guardians, but not yet accepted. The parable closes, however, with Tan-Tan's compliance with this advice.

Only at this point does the traditional Carnival disguise that has so appealed to Tan-Tan since her childhood make sense: The Robber Queen, even "scarier" than the legendary Robber King who steals children that "make too much mischief" (48). Taking on the persona of the Robber Queen, she can begin fighting the Robber King, "[t]he man with the golden wooing tongue" (48) – that is, her own father Antonio, who robbed her of her sense of moral, psychological, and physical integrity. Tan-Tan begins to journey back toward human society – not as herself now but as the Robber Queen, a traditional Carnival truth-teller and avenger of wronged justice. The Robber Queen "visitations" become legendary among the New Half-Way Tree humans, and Tan-Tan begins to hear exaggerated tales of her own "supernatural" interventions. These are, it turns out, the sources of the interpolated narratives. New Half-Way Tree children begin dressing up like her, and create avenger-type games in which the Robber Queen is always victorious. These games project an agency Tan-Tan does not yet have, but she is stirred by the imagined possibility of wilful action and justice done.

The imaginative promise of the legendary Robber Queen invests Tan-Tan with a self-righteousness long lost to her, but reanimated as she is forced to face off with her father's New Half-Way Tree wife, Janisette. While her stepmother has pursued her through the bush with the intention of arresting her, Tan-Tan realizes Janisette was not only aware of Antonio's sexual abuse, but gave her stepdaughter the weapon for stopping it: a hunting knife for her sixteenth birthday. After the months-long ordeal that has corresponded both with her pregnancy, her adoption into, and then exile from, a *douen* home, Tan-Tan finds her own voice. Indeed, her very body becomes a site of transformation, even transfiguration: "Is like a spirit take [Tan-Tan]. A vengeance had come upon her, it was shining out from her eyes strong as justice. Not one of them would dare try and prevent her" (244). At this moment of justice, Tan-Tan becomes who and what her experience among the *douen* has made her: *someone*, not the child raped by her father, not the abject adult who can only blame herself.

> She was, *somebody* was speaking out loud. Words welled up in somebody's mouth like water. Somebody spoke her words the way the Carnival Robber Kings wove their tales, talking as much nonsense as sense, fancy words spinning out from their mouths like thread from a spider's behind: silken shit as strong as story. Somebody's words uttered forth from Tan-Tan's tongue. (325)

In the showdown with her stepmother, she declares that "for the first time, I defend myself, Janisette." And at that moment, "Tan-Tan knew her body to be hers again, felt her own mouth stretching, stretching open in amazement at the words that had come out it. Is she, speaking truth; is truth!" (325–326). With the revelation of Janisette's motivated birthday gift, even her gang of supporters recognize the justice of Tan-Tan's self-defense. Tan-Tan tastes her vindication, and can make peace with her own history[41] and with the new life she is carrying.

The multidimensionality of this text makes itself felt at this moment in a surprising way. Tan-Tan's baby – her son and brother – suddenly emerges as an active character, along with the voice of one to whom, we realize only now, we have been listening all along: Tan-Tan's *eshu*. Reluctant to be born into such a degraded world, Tan-Tan's baby is being coaxed out by the *eshu*, whose speaking is signaled in the text by bold typeface. And just now, recognizing the identity of this character who has been *telling* this story all along, the novel's *opening* words make sense: "Oho. Like it starting, oui? Don't be frightened, sweetness", coaxes the *eshu*, "is for the best. I go be with you the whole time. Trust me and let me distract you little bit with one anansi story" (1). We learn that Tan-Tan's cyber-parent[42] has pursued her through the dimensional shift for the nine years since her father abducted her. Furthermore, we discover that this *eshu* does not exist as an artificial implant in the body of this nearly born child. Up until now all Toussaint citizens are injected at birth with the "nanomite solution that would form [their] earbug" (48), literally embedding the technological link to Granny Nanny (or Anansi, this "web"). But in a convergence of events, the instantaneous coincidence of Tan-Tan's impregnation with the *eshu*'s discovery of her in the "other dimension" causes an actual physiological mutation in the fetus:

When Granny Nanny realise how Antonio kidnap Tan-Tan, she hunt he through the dimension veils, with me riding she back like Dry Bone. Only a quantum computer coulda trace she through infinite dimensions like that, only Granny Nanny and me, a house *eshu*. And only because Tan-Tan's earbug never dead yet.... We try to contact your mamee [Tan-Tan] when she find she nine years ago, but the nanomites growing she earbug did calibrate wrong for Nanny to talk to them across dimensions. Eight years it take Granny Nanny to figure it out ... She instruct the nanomites in your mamee blood to migrate into your growing tissue, to alter you as you grow so all of you could feel nannysong at this calibration. You could hear me because your whole body is one living connection with the Grande Anansi Nanotech Interface. Your little bodystring will sing to Nanny tune, doux-doux. You will be a weave in she web. Flesh people talk say how earbugs give them a sixth sense, but really is only a crutch, oui? Not a fully functional perception. You now; you really have that extra limb. (327–328)

This baby's body has incorporated not only the genetic information from its parents, but a new "virtual" genealogy that connects its nervous system up directly with the World Wide Web. This baby is the first naturally born cyborg, and he will inhabit a wholly new "time-space regime."[43] Tan-Tan gives birth, in other words, not only to a form of utopian body, but to a revised image of futurity.

 With the *eshu*'s promise of a new kind of life for its host, guided by a virtual web connecting all the threads of Tan-Tan's personal, tribal, and more recent national histories, the baby acquiesces to be born. This child is itself an image of a chronotype, a new being who brings with him, as Haraway predicts for such a monster-child, "worlds whose fibers infiltrate deep and wide throughout the tissues of the planet, including the flesh of our personal bodies."[44] The ending-as-birth in this novel, in contrast to the previous texts considered in this chapter, proposes an embodiment of a new model of human being, who is a conscious witness to his own birth. The *eshu* thus approves of Tan-Tan's decision to name her baby "Tubman," signaling a renewal of the liberatory struggle for personal and social consciousness, and inhabiting, as Haraway envisions, "less the domains of 'life,' with its developmental and organic temporalities, than of 'life itself,' with its temporalities embedded in communications enhancement and system redesign" (12). The "stem cells" for Hopkinson's imagining of the cyborg-child carry the hybrid information of known and unknown beings, offering to the contemporary bildungsroman a hero, and a world, which (again like Haraway's cyborg) "must be read, too, with the mixed, unfinished literacies" (14) that speculation is able to teach us.

"A WORLD IN THE MAKING": THE BIRTH OF THE SPECULATIVE BILDUNGSROMAN

In this chapter, I have examined feminist authors' recent efforts to rewrite a literary form long associated with the endorsement of male subjectivity. The Butler and Hopkinson novels in particular cultivate a feminist speculation that opposes the epistemological authority of tradition and ideology. The structures of sense-making imposed by culture have typically made nonsense of women's experiences, and offered her nowhere for her aspirations. In inventing formal and rhetorical disruptions to the traditional bildungsroman, these authors wrench open the closed-loop comedy of its conclusions. These contemporary texts are radically open-ended, privileging the *process* of history rather than a culminating verbal icon representing an alleged social ideal. The symbolic content of this revised form is the *scandalizing* of narratives of sameness, both in exposing the lie of a "culture of no culture" – and by creating a narrative of development that may, in fact, leave the scandalizing heroine – think of Lauren or Tan-Tan here – alive and kicking at the end.

In this context of a scandalized ideology, one common feature of these feminist bildungsroman texts stands out. The utopian moment of the classical bildungsroman is *marriage*, the symbolic fulfillment of conservative bourgeois ideals and thus, the conclusion of the hero's ideal. These novels pervert that narratological centering around marriage and replace that symbolic event with *rape*. In all but one of the texts mentioned above, the heroine is raped; the exception is Butler's Olamina, who prevents one only by stabbing the man who attempts it. Obviously this event violently ruptures the genre's traditional, civil ideal, as symbolized by consensual and sanctioned sexual union in marriage. The rape symbolizes instead the violent reality of each society's (dis)placement of women and girls under patriarchy.

Furthermore, these novels' association of rape itself with marriage is even more scandalous: recall that Carter's heroine is raped and *then* married off. Tan-Tan's incestuous rape is similarly associated with a perverse kind of marriage: as she contemplates aborting this "monster child" seeded by her father, she also

felt for the gold ring she had knotted into a corner of the dhoti she was wearing. Antonio's wedding-band. The one he had give her for her ninth birthday.

All those years of wearing it, and every time her hand had brushed it, it had propelled her back to that birthday night, to Antonio touching her, hurting her, to the smell of liquor on his breath. (237)

A moral and sexual ideology that allows men the privilege of rape-as-power and condemns women to the abjection of accepted guilt is the cultural setting for these bildungsroman heroines' "quests." That is scandalous. But their ordeal consists not simply in surviving physically, but psychologically: the ordeal is surviving the scandal. The figure of the Robber Queen is thus exemplary. Marianne, Lauren, and Tan-Tan are transgressors, and for much of the narrative, seen as "guilty" in some way – often more by others than by themselves. Tan-Tan's ordeal is far more traumatic, for she accepts a "guilty as charged" judgment before any "trial" has occurred. Her experience is only slowly revaluated, thanks to the nurturing *douens* and their "Papa Bois," who "see what really happen in that room" (172). As Haraway reminds us, the feminist modest witness cannot be innocent.[45] In her willingness to be "inventive," to engage different ways of being and knowing, to intervene in ideological structures that act as a prison, Tan-Tan becomes herself, for a time, a scandal. It is through Tan-Tan's performative inventiveness, through her narrative fantasies of the Robber Queen, that her scandalousness is actually affirmed as a life-positive force.

As Bakhtin predicts, the emergence of a "new man [sic]" means that "the organizing force held by the future is therefore extremely great here – and this is not, of course, the private biographical future, but the historical future. It is as if the very *foundations* of the world are changing, and man [*sic*] must change along with them."[46] The "changed" or mutated modest witnesses who *are* these novels' hero/ines (including Tubman) map paths to a more speculative version of the future, the imagining of new dimensions, spatial and even temporal, of human history. The "necessary future" that Bakhtin identifies as the "sense" of the genre is no longer a future envisioned as an "assimilation of time."[47] Rather, these postmodern texts propose provisional futures that emerge from the integration of necessary change, time in process. The hero/ine's development does not fulfill the outline of a social ideal. Rather, it participates in a "process of becoming" synchronous with the alteration of an ossified social ideal. The goal and symbolic content of the bildungsroman is an ideal of an ongoing invention and intervention. As the heroine achieves a "differential"[48] consciousness, the narrative of sameness or reproductive futurism is mutated by a generation of difference.[49]

If this is the case, then the replacement of a conclusive marriage by the female hero's actual or near-rape, and by the expectation of a baby, either not yet born or in the very *process* of being born, is structural revision worth pausing at. "Reproductive futurism" is a model of futurity that Lee Edelman rejects in his provocative 2004 study, *No Future,* by challenging the "paramount value of futurity" so closely associated with our "investment in the Child as the obligatory token of futurity," and the "fantasy of meaning's eventualization."[50] The divestiture of such tokenism also means the barring of "narrative movement toward a viable political future." The task of narrative is to queer every attempt at an optimistic futurism, such that energies of vitalization ceaselessly turn against themselves, "narrative realization and derealization overlap[ping]." There can be no "promise" in the figure of the child, he argues; we are promised only what "the queer, in the order of the social, is called forth to figure": the death drive. In the exposure of the queer, he concludes, faith in either "the consistent reality of the social" or of the social subject[51] must be abandoned, along with all political "sides," committed as they typically are to futurism's "unquestioned good."

This pointedly anti-utopian position actually aligns closely with Carter's grim narrative: the "promise" of a birth is no guarantee of a thriving or sustainable future. Consider Marianne who, literally "stranded" at novel's end, is expecting nothing; her self-nomination as the "tiger lady" betokens a return to or – to use a term with more neutral connotations – an *arrival* at an inhospitable state of nature. But the conclusions of Edelman are figured otherwise in the Butler and, especially, the Hopkinson texts. In *Parable of the Sower,* we are permitted to hope for the future Lauren imagines in an outer space "well out of the shadow of [our] parent world" (83); although *Parable of the Talents* tells us that the future does not lie with her biological offspring, Larkin Olamina-Bankole. If anything, Larkin is an abortion of futurity, rejecting the mission supporting Earthseed's brave new world. If Larkin feels abandoned, she is: her mother's was a necessary commitment to a future demanding other kinds of affiliation, other forms of family and community. In fact, whereas these two novels tell us little about the event of Larkin's birth, the publication of Lauren's Earthseed tracts on the "world-wide-web" is described, as previously mentioned, as "like watching a birth" (*Sower*, 391). But the texts themselves are more appropriately described as sown like seeds, to be cultivated toward "a consuming, creative long-term goal" (*Talents*, 410). The sower, rather than the birther, stands a better chance in Butler's vision of futurity; while both roles trope the notion of a "generative" future, the possibilities of seeds taking root, and developing into plants that become established and proliferate, is more suggestive. This image holds more promise than a wholesale investment in a single child. The gesture of textual dissemination closing *Parable of the Sower* is akin to the not-quite-traditional *envoy* that concludes *The Female Man*.

Tan-Tan's child is thus a truer offspring of Lauren Olamina, an *envoy* in his own right, capable of moving multidirectionally as his life moves forward. Reconfiguring the disability of Lauren's hyperempathy, Tubman possesses a unique ability to attend to the entangling dimensions of reality – because he himself is such an entanglement of human, nonhuman, and posthuman worlds. The figure of the unprecedented Tubman, therefore, is no simple "token of the future," but rather a token of the *present* as conceived by Bakhtin's notion of the chronotype, a token of the fullness of time, a "pregnant moment"[52] – an always arriving. Tubman marks an *emergent* future. Edelman's promotion of a side "outside all political sides" – a position comparable to earlier claims for the *neutrality of utopia* – is a political and historical dead end. But Lauren had it right, when she *almost* said, but repressed, this remark to her father: "I think *your* world is coming to an end, and maybe you with it" (emphasis in the original). Tubman emerges already conscious of his entanglements in time and in space, even in his unique body. This "monster-child" is the "queer" child never previously conceived (of), with an "extra limb," and a literal sixth sense.

I have discussed some of the plot adjustments required by these novels' revision of the classic bildungsroman. But there is a significant alteration, too, of narrative mode and voice. Because of female protagonists' motivation in *yearning* rather than in *assimilation*, the speculative bildungsroman de-links the association between the traditional bildungsroman and literary realism. The transparency of the bildungsroman's original goals requires not only the compromise, or integration, of the hero to a specific vision of society, but also a compromise to a certain version of literary representation. Earlier female bildungsroman texts are characterized as at best "offer[ing] a limited possibility for female autonomy while simultaneously critiquing the societal expectations that constrict women"[53] and at worst "portray[ing] a world in which the young woman hero is destined for disappointment"[54] or even suicide. Released from the *imperative* to compromise, the scandalous protagonists of the Butler and Hopkinson novels discover an imperative to reinvent both self and community, with direct effects on each novel's obligation to adhere to realist proscriptions of style and form. *Jane Eyre* is darkened by the uncanniness of the gothic mode to express this girl's yearnings and drives; so here, the "realism" of these narratives must be expressed involving science fiction, fantasy, and even virtual game tropes and scenarios.

Finally, these novels represent an increasing complexity of voice. Carter's *Heroes and Villains* maintains a standard third-person narrative voice. With Butler's *Parable of the Sower,* we find a first-person narration, as well as a journal-style text interpolated with the narrator's accounting. The sequel, *Parable of the Talents*, recasts Olamina's journalistic accounting through a framing device that shuttles the reader between the temporal fields of Olamina's present to her daughter's, and thus triggers the ironical reinterpretation of Olamina's accomplishments, and our understanding of Larkin's own arrested development. But in *Midnight Robber,* Hopkinson employs an unusual combination of third- and *second*-person voices, which together craft our reading and understanding of Tan-Tan's journey, first, and then of the queered child's. The *eshu*'s comprehensive perspective not only opens and closes this text, but interpolates the narrative in between with legends of the Robber Queen, and with the history of Toussaint.

All these stories, we learn at the end, are designed to distract Tan-Tan's baby enough to ease its passage into the world, but we "hear" these several voices in *Midnight Robber* through text that is distinguished by different typefaces. Toussaint's characteristic *patois* is in a normal font – although its entanglements of English, French, and African lexicons and syntax are unfamiliar enough to require a period of adjustment for most readers. The *eshu* communicates through the neural networks of the baby, who is "a weave in she [the Granny Nanny/Anansi] web" (328). This communication is signaled to the reader by a bold typeface. *Douen* speech is marked by asterisks, as previously noted. In Butler and in Hopkinson, in other words, we see an emergent *heteroglossia* take over the very typography of the text, extending to the actual page the multiplicity of languages, interpolated stories, and nonlinear temporal structures throughout. Hopkinson's narrative in particular literalizes Lucy Sargisson's proposal that the utopian space is one in which "[n]ew and inventive languages can best be imagined and deployed … as can different social, sexual and symbolic relations."[55] Hopkinson gives us a full sense of a new reality; the invention and intermingling of these languages leaving visible the spaces between, whereby the heroine and her child – even we ourselves – might stake out the ground for new individual and social identities and new models of affiliation, community, and home.

CHAPTER 2

"With no guarantees, of course"
The art of the possible

Two things significantly distinguish human beings from the other ani-mals; an interest in the past and the possibility of language. Brought together they make a third: Art. The invisible city not calculated to exist.

— Jeanette Winterson[1]

WINTERSON IN THE WORLD AND OTHER PLACES

Where *is* that elsewhere that is the home to which one truly belongs? Is it somewhere? Is it nowhere? Or is it nowhere that becomes some-where in the spaces of the imagination? These questions have haunted Jeannette Winterson from the outset of her remarkable career. Winterson writes of her mother in *Oranges are not the only fruit* (1987)[2] that "she had all the longing of an exile for a place where she could never return. Like other exiles, her longing grew a narrative of its own. Her desire told itself as memory" (166) — as retrospect, that is; never future aspiration guiding present action. Winterson is, although in fact adopted, her mother's daughter and holds her own longing close. For all her expressed devotion to Virginia Woolf, Jeanette Winterson has rarely appeared interested in the exact location and dimensions of "a room of one's own." She pursues instead a space of desire with fluid boundaries and unexpected dimensions. Her characters discover these, sometimes by searching for them and sometimes by heedlessly bump-ing up against the ways in which experience limits desire and identity alike. The author longs for a space that lets desire flourish, rather than atrophy and fester; that space is her own, clearly post-Romantic as well as post-modern, art.

Winterson's pursuit of freedom through imagination and the "work" of art dates from that inaugural novel, which traces the life of a fictionalized Jeanette moving through, against, and finally, transgressively out of the fiercely circumscribed space of her adoptive parents' rabidly evangelical and moralistic household. The claustrophobia of that original adoptive home is countered in Winterson's fiction by the freedom of "the world and other places" (the title of a later short story collection), the freedom of spaces *elsewhere* from home. The events surrounding the appearance, blurring and/or disappearance of those boundaries are the stuff of her novels' fantastical plots. Her conception of utopia is not an end-state erotic paradise; nor is it simply a weary Romantic's acknowledgment of the essential irony that romance, that reality, and that our relationship to both reality and romance, *must* continually change.

In this chapter, I map out Winterson's own movement toward a definition of utopia on a path that paradoxically narrows and broadens as her career advances. In what I believe was her first great novel, *The Passion* (1987), she explores both the nostalgia for the space she never quite owned – the childhood home – as well as the places and spaces one discovers in adulthood. A more recent work, *The PowerBook* (2000), discovers yet another felicitous geography for sex, romance, and mysteries of identity: the expansive cyberspace which the author accesses by opening up her laptop computer, her PowerBook.[3]

"ANOTHER CHANCE": NARRATIVES OF DESIRE, *THE PASSION,* AND *THE POWERBOOK*

The structuring of utopian narrative as a journey gives *The Passion* its narrative shape, but irony determines the weather on the voyage. The novel's hero, Henri, a foot soldier and favored cook in Napoleon Bonaparte's army, seeks from the beginning a place where he belongs. His "ideal" place turns out to be a prison island to which he is condemned for a murder of passion. A seemingly strange place to find freedom, the island – "always [a metaphor] of the heart"[4] – represents the most important of the imaginary counterspaces of this novel, with a geography whose topographical features are situated not through longitudinal or latitudinal lines determined by coordinates of space and time, but through the coordinates of desire and ecstasy, along the body and the psyche, where the spaces of imagination and reality blur. But the journey is ultimately a negative one; Henri refuses to leave his near-solitary confinement on an island prison even when given the opportunity. Pointing toward a persistent trope I will trace throughout this study, Henri ends up shipwrecked, although willingly. He discovers, he believes in, his freedom to love and desire in the endless realm of fantasy that solitude offers him. The hero's commitment to solipsism is, however, clearly a form of madness, as his friends warn him. This kind of island paradise is a trap, a lotus land. And it is a frequent temptation in Winterson's novels.

By the time Winterson composes *The PowerBook,* her sense of utopia is self-consciously plastic and expansive. Desire is not merely written on the body, although the joys of lust and particularly lust fulfilled are there, always, in her work; it is written through the body. It is, in short, the narrative impulse of her fiction. The room of one's own is prefigured in Henri's island. Elsewhere that "metaphor of the heart" becomes the pleasure-palace that is the realm of art, where the logic of reason and the logic of desire meet and mold word and form into endlessly changeable narratives of possibility. This "no-place" of fiction and fantasy is the most necessary and sought-after real estate on the map, a utopian space where what is possible can be staged again and again. In an author so attracted to a world without coordinates of time and space, who privileges the present moment with Paterian intensity, what could be more attractive than cyberspace, a "wilderness" (91) or nowhere that is everywhere simultaneously? And what would cyberspace offer? Theoretically, freedom, infinite possibility, an "electronic frontier" that "suggests the possibility of a vast, unexplored territory."[5]

"In the space between chaos and shape," Winterson remarks in one of her short stories, "there was another chance."[6] In *The PowerBook,* cyberspace is a kind of utopian horizon where the sexed body is loosened of its proscriptions, where one can "literally" lose his or her body:[7] "I know about disguise" (16), says a crossed-dressed character in the novel's opening fantasy section. "Even my body is in disguise today. But what if my body is the disguise ... I use to hide myself?" (17). Free of the body in cyberspace's virtual reality, Winterson can enjoy, as in a foreign country, "relief from identity" (52), the chance to explore "millions of possible worlds" (63) as one "scroll[s] into another self" (120). And she explicitly describes this drifting, shifting dimension of the imaginary offered by cyberspace *as* utopian. One refrain throughout the novel is: "What I carry back from those other worlds to my world is another chance" (64, 236, 270), and that "chance" is the continually receding horizon that utopia offers. Echoing the utopianist's cry of "demand[ing] the impossible," Winterson remarks elsewhere that "[o]nly the impossible is worth the effort" (65).

The PowerBook opens by employing a very old novelistic device, in only one more variation: the narrative "frame," which begins here with an email communication:

It's night. I'm sitting at my screen. There's an e-mail for me. I unwrap it.
It says – *Freedom, just for one night....*
Just for one night the freedom to be somebody else....
You say you want to be transformed.
This is where the story starts. Here, in these long lines of laptop DNA. Here
we take your chromosomes, twenty-three pairs, and alter your height, eyes,
teeth, sex. This is an invented world. You can be free for one night.
Undress.
Take off your clothes. Take off your body. Hang them up behind the door.
Tonight we can go deeper than disguise. (3–4)

As in her earlier novels, Winterson obscures the sex of her interlocutor:
it is a "coordinate," but "This is a virtual world." In the story that follows,
therefore, coordinates and borders are unreliable landmarks as "Jeanette,"
a figure of the author herself, is "gone interactive" (31) with a nameless
email correspondent, with whom she coauthors, and cohabits, this story.
In a virtual world emptied of boundaries and expectation, invention rather
than irony motivates setting and plot: "This is a virtual world. This is a
world inventing itself. Daily, new landmasses form and then submerge.
New continents of thought break off from the mainland. Some benefit
from a trade wind, some sink without a trace. Others are like Atlantis –
fabulous, talked about, but never found" (73). Which will they inhabit?

With the chapter headed "New Document" – nearly all chapter headings
are terms or commands relating either to word processing or to email – the
first of many windows is opened onto this interactive fantasy space, and
their love story begins. They meet by accident, when the partner that each
is with – in the other woman's case, her husband – recognize each other as
long-lost friends. Thrown together as their partners reminisce, "Jeanette"
and the unnamed woman talk, attract, touch, ditch their partners for a
hotel room and for lovemaking. Over the course of the story, they separate, and find each other again, in Paris, in Capri, in London.

In the intimacies of her lover's body, "Jeanette" seems to find her real –
and I use the word "real" intentionally – utopia:

In this space which is inside you and inside me I ask for no rights or territories.
There are no frontiers or controls. The usual channels do not exist. This is the
orderly anarchic space that no one can dictate, though everyone tries. This is a
country without a ruler. I am free to come and go as I please. This is Utopia. It
could never happen beyond bed. This is the model of government for the world.
No one will vote for it, but everyone comes back here. This is the one place
where everybody comes. (205)

That "attic room" was "[o]ur private world. Our promised land" (236).

This is the most clearly articulated description, certainly in this novel if not in all of her work, of Winterson's conception of a utopic state. It is a not an eroticized place merely; it is Eros itself – "the one place where everybody comes" (205) – which Winterson has spent her career thus far persuading us is the very center of our human being. While her utopia is experienced physically, a mapping of desire and sheer lust along the body, she reaches that utopia through an exploration of the psychic economy of human love, every instance of which "Jeanette," as the author's fictional persona, sees without irony as "a dramatic enactment of the wild, reckless, unquenchable, undrainable love that powers the universe" (223).

Winterson's virtual topography of desire is her promised land, or so she hopes as the novel opens, a utopian counter-space that permits the kind of mobility her mother could never dream of, and offers the possibility of transformative, ecstatic experiences that probe the limits of her own identity. Winterson participates in a popular postmodern approach to subjectivity, proposing, according to Paulina Palmer, that "the creation of the self [is] through fantasy and desire."[8] In other words, subjectivity is created through the interplay of the real and the fantastic – and the narrative space that is Winterson's text is precisely the field for that interplay.

And yet ... as in so many utopian texts, the reach of irony doubles back to overshadow its characters and reader. The surprising desire for this woman overwhelms "Jeanette," alternately filling her and emptying her. *The PowerBook*'s account of these continuously shifting emotions, ranging from ecstasy to abjection, becomes a frustrating, wrenching narrative. As writers on love from Sappho onward show us, the tension between presence and absence, fulfillment and desire, is what inspires, or at least creates the occasion for, many works of art, in all its romantic irony. Winterson puts it this way: "What keeps the tension is the tension itself – the pull between what I am and what I can become. The tug of war between the world I inherit and the world I invent" (248). This is the tug felt as well by every writer in the utopian tradition, who is forced to return, like their own characters – More's Hythloday, Swift's Gulliver, William Morris's Mr. Guest, Winterson's Henri in *The Passion*, or her own fictionalized self in *The PowerBook* – to live henceforth in a world charged with yearning.

The utopian aspects of cyberspace, a *virtual* reality, are similarly incommensurate with the body's demand for physical fulfillment. Anne Balsamo notes that "what these VR encounters really provide is an illusion of control over reality, nature, and especially over the unruly, gender- and race-marked, essentially moral body."[9] Although the border between the imaginary and the real is radically fluid in this novel, this much is clear: what blocks access to Winterson's utopia is her lover's belief only in real time and space. "Then she [the lover] made a speech. I suppose you can guess the lines. Inside her marriage there were too many clocks and not enough time. Too much furniture and too little space. Outside her marriage there would be nothing to hold her, nothing to shape her. The space she found would be outer space. Space without gravity or weight, where bit by bit the self disintegrates" (45). We can hear Jeanette's skepticism ("I suppose you can guess") in her description of the lover's words as clichéd speech. But in fact, the lover does understand quite precisely the kind of utopic and ecstatic space that so appeals to Winterson: "What I carry back from those worlds to my world is another chance" (64), she argues. But the lover is too afraid and will not, possibly cannot, take that chance, and one night she disappears: "There were no e-mails for me. You had run out of the story. Run out on me. Vanished.... Here I am like a penitent in a confessional. I want to tell you how I feel, but there's nobody on the other side of the screen" (73).

Through all these comings and goings – real, virtual, and imaginary – Winterson pursues her own permanent utopian island that will close the gap between them. The more she searches, the more she realizes that she has already found it – in the storytelling itself:

> I was typing on my laptop, trying to move this story on, trying to avoid endings, trying to collide the real and imaginary worlds, trying to be sure which is which.
> The more I write, the more I discover that the partition between the real and invented is as thin as a wall in a cheap hotel room....
> When I sit at my computer, I accept that the virtual worlds I find there parallel my own. I talk to people whose identity I cannot prove. I disappear into a web of co-ordinates that we say will change the world. What world? Which world?
> It used to be that the real and the invented were parallel lines that never met. Then we discovered that space is curved, and in curved space parallel lines always meet. (107–108)

Exploring her own sense of a geography with "the usual" coordinates of space and time, Jeanette insists that "What exists and what might exist are windowed together at the core of reality" (129), like multiple windows of her computer screen. But unlike a computer, the human imagination does not just keep windows open, but actively seeks connections. The artist and storyteller will invent landscapes of desire, of which cyberspace is only one. She will raise a telescope to her mind's eye, seeking the horizons where desire directs her. She invents tropes of transit that move toward the ever-dissolving and emerging horizons. She is at the very fold or "part(ition)ing" of real and alt-real: "Our real lives are elsewhere. Art finds them."[10] There, Winterson proposes, wherever that might be on "the map," is our home; meanwhile, she dwells at the very border of romance.

FINDING ROMANCE HERE, THERE, AND ELSEWHERE

Jeanette Winterson makes romantic obsession seem, if not necessarily inevitable, inevitably necessary in order to be truly alive. Not everyone accepts the openness to risk that obsession requires, but it may be that no one knows him/herself well unless at least once the risk is taken. Obsession ferociously heightens subjective experience, as love paradoxically engulfs the subject and frees her; defines and obliterates her; opens up the universal, even as love entombs her. Julia Kristeva, a clear influence on Winterson, tells us that "Love is the time and space in which 'I' assumes the right to be extraordinary. Sovereign yet not individual. Divisible, lost, annihilated; but also, and through imaginary fusion with the loved one, equal to the infinite space of superhuman psychism.... I am, in love, at the zenith of subjectivity."[11] Romance is the infinite space and endless time Winterson seeks but as Kristeva implies, that utopia lies only within the world of fantasy, as we see negatively in *The Passion*, but far more positively, if still tentatively, in *The PowerBook*.

Critics have described Winterson as narcissistic, but they miss her point: over and over again, the grandiose claims love makes, upon body and upon spirit, are claims she provisionally accepts, even though, novel after novel, the lover at the center of the text confesses his or her incompleteness.[12] The constant return to the subject itself marks a very real obsession. But if Winterson writes "more realistically" about obsession, it is not because her writing has much to do with conventional fictional realism. That is rarely her mode, which tends instead toward outlandish genres such as the fairy tale; modes like magic realism; images and tropes of the grotesque. The *extra-vagance* of such modes is precisely wherein lies her unique form of realism, which has nothing to do with the nineteenth-century version: "If prose-fiction is to survive it will have to do more than to tell a story.... Fiction that is a modern copy of a nineteenth-century novel is no better than any other kind of reproduction furniture."[13]

The epistemological dimension of Winterson's redefinition of literary realism parallels Su's discussion of contemporary postcolonial writers' rejection of "the simplistic form" of realism: "The novel is not, then, realistic by virtue of replicating or imitating historical events; rather, the realism of the novel is linked to its capacity to force readers to reassess what they observe in their daily lives."[14] Winterson's writing insists on the "reality" of imagination and the blurring or even subversion of ideological categories, such as gender. It has to do instead with transgressing conventional narrative tropes in order to *more* realistically (re)present what Kristeva calls the indissoluble knot (*noue*) of the symbolic, the imaginary, and the real that ties together the experience of love. That space around and between the entangled threads, Kristeva suggests, is the space of narrative itself: "the story" of a love, of loving, that must necessarily stand outside the experiencing of love itself. Winterson's work is always already about art and love, and the art of loving, an *ars amatoria* that persistently returns to the problem of narrative space.

For Winterson, narrative space can be a utopian space, an endless imaginary realm of limitless possibilities. "I cannot give my position accurately," writes the *PowerBook* narrator, "The coordinates shift. I cannot say, 'where', I can only say, 'Here', and hope to *describe* it to you, atom and dream" (247). As suggested earlier, such a space can only be ironical. Winterson's characteristically extravagant fiction reflects the tug of war mounted by desire's rapturous attraction to another, and irony's knowing expectation of retreat in a struggle that neither lover wins. Hope itself is thus troped in Winterson's fiction as a vision of salvation that quite "literally," only *time will tell*. And so Winterson closes this novel with a chapter ordering us, as on a computer, to "SAVE":

> I dipped my hands in the water [of the Thames]. Liquid time.
> And I thought, "Go home and write the story again. Keep writing it because one day she will read it."
> You can change the story. You are the story.
> No date line, no meridian, no gas-burnt stars, no transit of the planets, not the orbit of the earth nor the sun's red galaxy, tell time here. Love is keeper of the clocks.
> I took off my watch and dropped it into the water.
> Time take it.
> Your face, your hands, the movement of your body …
> Your body is my Book of Hours.
> Open it. Read it.
> This is the true history of the world.

If there is any progress in this pilgrim's journey through the multidimensional geography of this novel, it is registered in the generous and psychically risky gesture at the end: the offer of another chance to build another web or set of coordinates that will present the absent one once more. "The promise," Jeanette writes toward the end of the novel, "is that the world is always beginning again. No accumulations of the past can stop it. Another day. Another chance. Does nobody believe this?" (270).

Winterson's dependence on this faith in art – "There will be a future. We believe in our unreality too strongly to give it up" (20) – is what irritates many of her critics,[15] although they are likely less sure of their judgments after the author's nervous breakdown and suicide attempt in 2008. Winterson herself puts it this way, before that crisis:

When we let ourselves respond to poetry, to music, to pictures, we are clear-ing a space for new stories about ourselves.... If we can fictionalise ourselves, and consciously, we are freed into a new kind of communication. It is abstract, light, changeful, genuine. It is what Wordsworth called 'the real solid world of images'. It may be that to understand ourselves as fictions, is to understand our-selves as fully as we can.[16]

Coming out the other side of that crisis, she still has not abandoned what David Lodge so acutely and so early recognized as a radically Romantic poetic which made available to her "new imaginative territory" (*PowerBook*, 26) in the world of fiction, offering "millions of possible worlds, unactual-ized, potential" (63). For Winterson, the desire of the body and the imag-ination are the same: "Art," she observes, "is cellular."[17]

"WITH IRONY": ART AND DESIRE IN ATWOOD'S SPECULATIVE FICTION

Art is not the fulfillment but the maintenance of its promise. – Josh Cohen[18]

Margaret Atwood likely concurs with Winterson's remarks about the counterspaces created by art and storytelling, and their relationship to what she, too, regards as lodestars of human existence: love and freedom. Atwood likely shares as well the utopic imperative art offers, that "work" of reading, seeing, and critiquing. It is not likely that she is very sanguine about Winterson's "promise [that] the world is always beginning again" and that "no accumulations of the past can stop it" (*PowerBook*, 229–230). While equally attentive to the complex web of filaments connect-ing love, freedom, and the rare spaces where these can coexist, Atwood's political sensibility makes her more attentive to what Winterson called "external figurings"[19] that interfere with our imaginative capacity; that is, for Atwood, "context is all." With a caustic wit and an incisive and skeptical political sensibility, her inquiries into the relationships between art, society, and "utopia" typically arrive at possibilities darker than Winterson's: that art may be hijacked and put to the service of deceptive and false visions of utopia.

Whether faithful or skeptical, what is at stake for both authors is nothing less than a defense of human freedom – indeed, for Atwood, of humanity itself. As the author observes in her 1989 speech, "Writing Utopia," "the Utopia-Dystopia as a form ... challenges us to re-examine what we understand by the word 'human', and above all what we intend by the word 'freedom.'"[20] And she goes on to mention that one of the central "concerns" of this form is "relations between the sexes." Whereas sex in utopia typically "goes for a sort of healthy-minded communal sex" or else opts for a bland arrangement that is "sexually neutral," dystopias "usually exhibit some form of slavery or, as in Orwell, extreme sexual repression." Either way, the character of sex in these places reflects the character of the impulse either to harmonious order or to tyranny that utopia and dystopia represent: "Neither are what you'd call tolerant, but both are necessary to the imagination."[21]

What also becomes apparent in her essays as well as her novels is that a world without an authentic respect for art generally is not a world worth living in, the worst kind of human dystopia: "A society without the arts would have broken its mirror and cut out its heart. It would no longer be what we now recognize as human."[22] For that reason, imagining such a world through art and storytelling is itself a critical intervention, and Atwood's speculative fiction consistently and urgently concerns itself with the danger of allowing art to become irrelevant or "useless" in a technology- and profit-driven, deeply masculinist culture such as our own. Of the speculative novels that Atwood has written, including *The Handmaid's Tale* (1985), *Oryx and Crake* (2003), *The Year of the Flood* (2009), the first two in particular attend to Atwood's growing interest in the uses and abuses of art, not simply by individuals but also by powerful corporate and political interests.

Atwood is of course particularly concerned with the capitalist ideology of our own culture, in which "absolutely everything is a consumer good." Too few realize, she observes, that "our technological inventiveness is generated by our emotions, not by our minds," and thus dismisses the critical function of the arts which "tell us how and what we feel, and how and what we feel determines what we want."[23] Such a dismissal is part of the dismal setting of *The Handmaid's Tale*,[24] in which the free exercise of art of any kind, of counter-narratives textual or visional, is forbidden by a

brutally theocratic government that uses the tools of art for its own purposes. The cunning Gilead leadership perverts the play of language and
the symbolic order with the duplicity of its own intentions. The political
abuses of art are a disturbing and overlooked theme in this novel; the
creative arts as such are not simply devalued but repressed as a decadent
expression of individual freedom and critique.

What art becomes instead, under these circumstances, is an expression
of social pathology, at worst, and a trivialized time killer at best. And as
Offred gets used to the layout of her new Commander's home, it is the
remnants of the creative that strikes her: functional objects – chair, table,
lamp – and moving on to the more ornamental: "There's a rug on the
floor, oval, of braided rags. This is the kind of touch they like: folk art,
archaic, made by women, in their spare time, from things that have no
further use. A return to traditional values. Waste not want not" (7). This
perception of art's particular utility in Gilead is enhanced by Offred's
perception that she is now herself a similar sort of domestic ornament, a
mark of the Commander's status, in fact; worth keeping only for her utility as an incubator, as a "national resource" (65). Her valuable recyclable
materials are simply the body parts involving childbirth (we learn later in
the novel that hands and feet are deemed unnecessary, thus the parts of
the body to be beaten as punishment for handmaid infractions). Those
resource materials, at least, are "not being wasted."

What is being wasted, of course, are all the facets of her intellectual and
emotional individuality, no longer of "any use"; the nonmaterial effluences
of her recasting as a handmaid – her personality, memory, emotions, free
will – remain behind in her continuous, inchoate apprehension of desire.
Having remembered the adage "Waste not want not," her next thought is
not "What do *I* want?" but rather "*Why* do I want?" (7; emphasis added).

Offred's account, however, remarks on two forms of artistic activity in
Gilead, both belonging to the "domain" of the Commander's wife. One
activity is knitting scarves, which are reputedly sent to the Gilead guardians, the Angels, posted at the Front; the other is gardening. With a per-
ceptiveness sharpened by a growing sensitivity to irony, Offred glimpses
a connection between a "woman's" craft, like knitting, and the social
pathology enforcing the uselessness of women:

I can hardly believe the Angels have a need for such scarves; anyway, the ones
made by the Commander's Wife are too elaborate.... Fir trees march across the
ends of her scarves, or eagles, or stiff humanoid figures, boy and girl, boy and
girl.... Sometimes I think these scarves aren't sent to the Angels at all, but unraveled and turned back into balls of yarn, to be knitted again in their turn. Maybe

it's just something to keep the Wives busy, to give them a sense of purpose. But I envy the Commander's Wife her knitting. (13)

But there's more to it than just filling time, Offred realizes later in the narrative, and she reinterprets the boy-and-girl pattern produced by Serena Joy: "[knitting] away at her endless Angel scarves, turning out more and more yards of intricate and useless wool people. Her form of procreation, it must be" (154). This creativity thus serves a basic "wish-fulfillment" function of art: making present what is absent, what is, in Gilead, most "wanting" and most "wanted." The more Serena Joy "turns out," like a machine, the figures of children she is unable to produce herself, the more apparent is the psychic function of her creative art, so appropriately domestic in nature.

Indeed, as Offred muses, she recalls that both of these themes, women's devalued time and women's fertility, are present in those paintings she used to admire in museums:

There's time to spare. This is one of the things I wasn't prepared for – the amount of unfilled time, the long parentheses of nothing. Time as white sound. If only I could embroider. Weave, knit, something to do with my hands. I want a cigarette. I remember walking in art galleries, through the nineteenth century: the obsession they had then with harems. Dozens of paintings of harems, fat women lolling on divans, turbans on their heads or velvet caps, being fanned with peacock tails, a eunuch in the background standing guard. Studies of sedentary flesh, painted by men who'd never been there. These pictures were supposed to be erotic, and I thought they were, at the time; but I see now what they were really about.... They were paintings about boredom. But maybe boredom is erotic, when women do it, for men. (69)

A certain fullness of time, and a certain fullness of body: these are the things wanting in the women's lives. Offred recognizes that men's artistic representations of women, in paintings, in photographs, have always idealized women "not in use," useless, but beautiful and, of course, alluring, infinitely desirable.

Gardening is the other artistic pursuit available to Serena, and that too is explicitly connected in Offred's mind with the "female function," procreation – but also with (barely) repressed desire. There's "something subversive about this garden," Offred notes, "a sense of buried things bursting upwards, wordlessly, into the light, as if to point, to say: Whatever is silenced will clamor to be heard, though silently. A Tennyson garden, heavy with scent, languid; the return of the word *swoon.*... Goddesses are possible now and the air suffuses with desire" (153). What's also repressed, and what "bursts upwards" often enough is the anger at the psychological as well as physical emptiness, a barrenness that is of the mind as well as the body. Offred observes Serena guillotining the heads of flowers:

She was snipping of the seedpods with a pair of shears. I watched her sideways as I went past ... She was aiming, positioning the blades of the shears, then cutting with a convulsive jerk of the hands. Was it the arthritis, creeping up? Or some blitzkrieg, some kamikaze, committed on the swelling genitalia of the flowers? The fruiting body. To cut off the seedpods is supposed to make the bulb store energy. Saint Serena, on her knees, doing penance. (153)

Can it be a coincidence that both knitting needles and garden shears are the weapons of desperate women in this novel? In an Atwood novel, surely not. We learn that jealous handmaids attack pregnant ones by stabbing them with knitting needles in the stomach; we know that Offred "coveted" (153) the shears, fantasizing later of stabbing the Commander in the neck with them.

Textiles and gardens in the Gileadean context reflect Serena's frustrated desire to be fully integrated into the Gilead ideal of communal fruitfulness – but the artful symbolism of "the Ceremony" is a periodic reminder of the gap between the ideal and the real, and the violence wrought with the tools of Serena's art – needles and shears – is a reminder that the Gilead utopic vision is not yet at hand. This point is emphasized later, when Offred yearns "with a force that made the ends of my fingers ache" (156) to hold the fashion magazines the Commander offers her during an illicit night visit. Recalling how "infinitely discardable" such magazines, with their displays of women sculpted by the arts of fashion and cosmetics, seemed in the time before, "a device to fill in empty time while I was waiting for Luke." But now she realizes this time was not empty, but filled precisely by representations of desire urgently felt by Offred:

What was in them was promise. They dealt in transformation; they suggested an endless series of possibilities, extending like the reflections in two mirrors set facing one another, stretching on, replica after replica, to the vanishing point.... The real promise in them was immortality. (157)

For Offred, the art of cosmetics (denied to her, of course) is also a mark of freedom, an unhampered expression of desire, a masquerading of one's "real" body in the fantasy version of it, the better version. In a certain sense, Offred herself might be considered a form of Gileadean art, an "artful" substitute for the infertile Wives of the Commanders. She in fact plays an entirely scripted role in Gilead's only real form of "creative" cultural work: its composition and regular staging of its Ceremonies, Birthings, Particicutions, Salvagings, Prayvaganzas – all of them performance art pieces, as obscene as any piece of pornography in their display of a sexualized ideology of male domination and power worship.

Denied embroidery, knitting, cosmetics, or any other sort of "pig ball" to keep her mind running, Offred does in fact create her own work of art, as elaborate and in the end as powerful, as Gilead's own work of staging a new American utopia. That work is the narrative that she produces, a semi-fictional autobiography and *bildungsroman*, of sorts. For Winterson's "Jeanette" as for Atwood's "Offred," the art of storytelling and/as the art of love ultimately focuses the heroines' attention. The art of the possible for Offred exists *only* in narrative, in her telling and retelling of her story, of Luke's story, of Moira's, Nick's, her daughter's, and her mother's. But the likelihood of inventing truly "new stories about ourselves" that offer a new and liberating kind of communication, as Winterson proposes, seems questionable. The only "new kind of communication" Offred discovers is irony.

As I have argued elsewhere,[25] *The Handmaid's Tale* is pervaded by irony at every level, and numerous scholars before me have explored various aspects of the multivalent irony of the novel as a whole, from its satiric nature, to its layered narrative structure, and to the irony of the novel's plot, which Lois Feuer describes as "the irony of the 'woman's culture' [becoming a] totalitarian nightmare." Numerous scholars have written about Offred's discovery of the "multiple possibilities of language" without mentioning verbal irony as a linguistic term.[26] Whereas Winterson's "Jeanette" can believe in the possibility of new and mobile subjectivities in and through the invention of new (self-)narratives, Offred rarely achieves any epiphanies in her narrative, a fractured, second-life bildungsroman of sorts. In the state of unfreedom in which Offred lives, her sense of self is rather at a nadir of abjection and self-recrimination.

Herein lies a critical difference between Winterson's and Atwood's conception of utopian hope. Although fantasy plays its part, Atwood is much more interested in how an individual's experience of hope plays out, as it were, in the complex context of the present, with the severe political and moral challenges (those external figurings) of the here and now. Much depends on *choice*. Atwood's remarks on "female bad characters" are instructive of her own method generally:

But female bad characters can also act as keys to doors we need to open, and as mirrors in which we can see more than just a pretty face. They can be explorations of moral freedom – because everyone's choices are limited, and women's choices have been more limited than men's, but that doesn't mean women can't make choices. Such characters can pose the question of responsibility, because if you want power you have to accept responsibility, and actions produce consequences. I'm not suggesting an agenda here, just some possibilities.[27]

Of herself, Offred reveals her own inattentiveness to political developments leading up to the takeover by Gilead, as well as her cowardice in the face of risk. "Dear God, don't make me choose" (285), she begs; and realizes at that moment that she has "resigned" herself "freely, to the uses of others. They can do what they like with me. I am abject" (286). It is also arguable (and has been argued) that equally reprehensible from a political standpoint is her complicity, even to the end, with a romantic vision[28] – and a fantasy romance narrative that allows her to "trust me," Nick's final offer of freedom. If Offred's tale has shown anything, it is that love is not the "keeper of the clocks." Margaret Atwood might allow that "desire" *is*, although her work is characterized by a cool acknowledgment that malignant forms of desire, realized through exertions of will, power, and the politics thereof are more likely to mark the moments of historical advance than the benign and joyful forms of desire, realized through love, art, and other forms of individual expression.

"THE ART OF THE POSSIBLE": CELLULAR ART IN *ORYX AND CRAKE*

Atwood's exploration of the possibilities of art continues in her celebrated "speculative fiction" novel, *Oryx and Crake*,[29] and this exploration links the two novels in surprising ways. In *The Handmaid's Tale,* Atwood speculates on an imagined revival of a neo-puritanical condemnation of art, and the deliberate defacement of creative expression of any kind whatever. This novel is a disquieting look at what happens when ideological manipulations threaten art's capacity to envision desire, create possibility, and embrace freedom, individual and social. In *Oryx and Crake*, Atwood broadens that perspective, closely scrutinizing a generalized cultural demeaning of "the arts" as such. *Oryx and Crake* carries on an often explicit debate about the relative values of art and technology in creating a better future and, indeed, a better humanity. The effect of this in the novel is to clarify Atwood's ironical vision of the clash of human desire for power and for love, and how easily these desires are perversely fused. The central figuration of this clash in *The Handmaid's Tale* is frankly represented in Offred's alternately submissive and resistant behaviors, allowing herself to be subjected to the monthly performance of "The Ceremony" while increasingly risking her life in "grabs" at love and a sense of freedom, during her night visits to Nick. We are continually reminded of "real" versus "not real" forms or expressions of desire; "reproduction" – whether of art, furniture, flowers, or people – is a central trope and as we have seen, Offred becomes increasingly keenly attuned to the ways in which this conflict exposes Gilead's pathological efforts to "reproduce," not just the children who will become its future citizens, but also the ideology into which those children will be indoctrinated.

Reproduction(s), both true and false, of life and of liberty alike constitute the central trope of *Oryx and Crake*, and its narrator, however different his circumstances are from Offred's, finds himself similarly "reduced." Like Offred, the hero's narrative is retrospective and ironical, nostalgic and self-disparaging. His tale, like hers, swings between abject despair of the future, and a yearning hope for the discovery, or recovery, of meaningful community, if only with one individual. He, like her, discovers in the frank recollection of his own personal history the unwitting and irresponsible role he played in the broader historical catastrophe that he survives and from which he now suffers. And Jimmy, too, is a "word person" (64), prone to recalling and free-associating off words, creating wordlists, making up and then revising stories he tells himself and the so-called children of Crake (genetically engineered humans who are immune to the virus that wipes out the rest of humanity). The effort keeps him sane and reassures him of the reality, however appalling, of his personal history and very existence.

This novel's setting later in the twenty-first century advances Atwood's speculations regarding the perversion of sexual ideology within a dystopic social imaginary. The earlier novel conceives of social control through a brutal repression of sexual desire and a rescripting of men's and women's social roles through control of sexual and "hence" ideological reproduction. This later novel imagines a world so technologically sophisticated that "natural" desires are regarded as irrelevant. "Nature" itself – from plants to the smallest microbes to animals and then human beings – is manipulated through bioengineering. New creatures are being invented, hybrid animals developed through gene-splicing, and their names invented through word-splicing. The enhancement of the human body is the focus of the scientific community in which Jimmy grows up, with his father working at a company called OrganInc., which gene-splices different species of animals together to form hybrids – rakunks, snats, wolvogs, pigoons – and Jimmy himself takes his first job writing marketing materials for "AnooYoo," a firm that creates creams, foods, pills, anything "to make you fatter, thinner, hairier, balder, whiter, browner, blacker, yellower, sexier, and happier.... Hope and fear, desire and revulsion, these were his stocks-in-trade, on these he rang his changes" (248). His new employers insist that people seek perfection "in themselves": "They like to hear about the before and the after ... It's the art of the possible. But with no guarantees, of course" (246). Thus, Atwood knowingly extends Orwell's *Brave New World*, which she characterizes as a "hedonistic ersatz paradise ... where absolutely everything is a consumer good and human beings are engineered to be happy."[30] The ascendancy of this "art of the possible" – born of what Ulrich Beck calls the "technological imagination"[31] – occurs at the expense of the "traditional" arts, effectively appropriating the connections between desire and creative embodiment, and between power and (re)production, both sexual and artistic.

"*Watch out for art*" is a quip by his childhood friend turned scientific genius, the eponymous Crake. The remark takes on significance to Jimmy only after Crake's death – after, in fact, the apparent extinction of humanity by a viral holocaust that Crake unleashed. As the apparent sole survivor, Jimmy, now self-nominated "Snowman" (as in "the Abominable"), begins to see the consequences of society's devaluation of art in favor of science. He can see how his own ineptitude and lack of interest in the world of "the numbers" effectively alienates him from the dominant class of society: the scientists and technicians of genetic engineering, "our people" (27), by his father's lights. And he can see, although he does not put it this way, that the greatest form of "contemporary art" *is science*. Jimmy's father is a "genographer" working to create "pigoons," engineered pigs designed to grow multiple and "foolproof" human organs for transplantation and "spare parts" (23).[32] The genographer moves the family into one of the high-security walled communities or "Compounds" protecting the technical class from "*the Pleeblands*," where those unfortunates not employed by the monolithic OrganInc reside. The walls of the corporate micro-utopia of the Compounds ensure the invisibility of "the pleebs" in the unnamed city (but very possibly Boston),[33] where things were "unpredictable," "risky," and chaotic. The Compounds are "the same idea" as medieval castles, Jimmy's father says, "with high walls and drawbridges and slots on the ramparts so you could pour hot pitch on your enemies"; "'So we are the kings and dukes?'" concludes the child; "'Oh, absolutely,' said his father, laughing" (28).

His mother's dissenting voice challenges the deepening confusion between natural and artificial, real and unreal, "science fiction and science fact" (27).[34] "Why knock it?" asks her husband, but she does, descending into a depression caused by a sense of moral hypocrisy and powerlessness to prevent the ethical collapse she foresees. Her eventual defection from the Compound labels her a "traitor" – not just of the Corporation and "the country," but of her hapless young son, for whom she leaves this unhelpful charge: *Don't let me down.* Jimmy grows into a normal enough but disaffected teen, interested more in laying women than cultivating any "useful" intellectual talent. His rudderless life is thus directed for him, and after graduation he ends up – not being "a numbers person" – at the arts-oriented Martha Graham Academy ("named after some gory old dance goddess" [186]), an institution that only verifies his social irrelevancy among an elite class of technocrats:

The system had filed him among the rejects, and what he was studying was considered – at the decision-making levels, the levels of real power – an archaic waste of time.... Who was it who'd said that all art was completely useless? Jimmy couldn't recall, but hooray for him, whoever he was. The more obsolete a book was, the more eagerly Jimmy would add it to his inner collection. (195)

The Academy is simply a holding place for similarly unmotivated young people, its mission having suffered a "kind of attrition – this erosion of its former intellectual territory" (187). Thus, the classes in music, dance, acting, filmmaking, and visual media are generally regarded by Compound residents like Jimmy's father as comparable to "studying Latin, or book-binding: pleasant to contemplate in its way, but no longer central to anything, though every once in a while the college president would subject them to some yawner about the vital arts and their irresistible reserved seat in the big red-velvet amphitheatre of the beating human heart" (187).

Tapping unwittingly into the vein of Wilde's ironical epigrams (*"All art is quite useless"*) and of Burne-Jones's declaration of unrepentant aestheticism (*"The more materialistic science becomes, the more angels shall I paint"*), Jimmy begins to apply himself. He majors in the art of words, called "Problematics" (nicknamed "Spin and Grin") with classes in "Applied Logic, Applied Rhetoric, Medical Ethics and Terminology, Applied Semantics, Relativistics and Advanced Mischaracterization, Comparative Cultural Psychology." While touting its graduates' "Employable Skills," the Institute's "risible degree" prepares Jimmy only for a trivial life, "Window-dressing ... decorating the cold, hard, numerical real world in flossy 2-D verbiage.... The prospect of his future life stretched before him like a sentence; not a prison sentence, but a long-winded sentence with a lot of unnecessary subordinate clauses" (188). Nevertheless, or perhaps consequently, Jimmy develops "a strangely tender feeling" toward old words such as *"wheelwright, lodestone, saturnine, adamant ...* as if they were children abandoned in the woods and it was his duty to rescue them" (195). This metaphor comparing words to parentless offspring of the imagination resonates backward and forward in the novel: looking back, Jimmy sees himself abandoned by his parents, both literally (by his mother) and figuratively (by his father). Looking forward, he will find himself, years later, dutifully rescuing the nonbiological, orphaned off-spring of the eponymous "Crake."

Crake's career develops entirely differently from Jimmy's,[35] although as adolescents they spend the same countless hours together watching snuff films or porn, and playing complex online games with titles such as *Extinctathon*, foreshadowing Crake's later aspirations. After high school, Crake enters the elite Watson-Crick Institute, where the next generation of scientists, the real leaders of this twenty-first century world, are trained. Compared to Martha Graham, located in the Pleeblands, dismally down at the heels and "behind the times," Watson-Crick is "a palace," with "exten-sive grounds" exhibiting genetically altered plants, flowers, and even "liv-ing" rocks or "neoGeologicals" (200). In fact, the Institute is a palace of art, housing not only first-class contemporary artworks, but also the living artifacts of the future. Jimmy, on his first visit, feels "more and more like a troglodyte" (201), an historical anachronism along with the arts he studies.

Crake's research, on the other hand, is the future. His unit is called *Paradice*: "What we're working on his immortality" (292). Crake consid-ers "how much misery" could be saved through genetic alternations that would eliminate sexual competition – programming "only pair-bond[ing] for life, like gibbons," or else "total guilt-free promiscuity," behaviors that "would always succeed," mankind could eliminate the "torment" and vio-lence that precipitate from "biological mismatches" (166). Whereas the Pill of the twentieth-century controlled reproduction, "the Project" of the twenty-first begins with the invention of the "BlyssPluss Pill." The "elegant concept" behind this pill: it immunizes users against all sexually trans-mitted diseases, "prolong[s] youth," and provides "an unlimited supply of libido and sexual prowess, coupled with a generalized sense of energy and well-being" that also "immunize" users against malignancies, such as jeal-ousy and violence, that develop from "frustration and blocked testosterone" (294). Advantageous secondary effects of the pill are not only the quelling of unfulfilled desire, sexual or otherwise, but reduction of populations and resource consumptions. These "large-scale benefits" to "society as a whole" extend beyond local or even national communities: "on the planet.... it was going to be global" (294). Unlike Winterson's Jeanette, who regards lovemaking as a kind of utopia of complete inclusion, Snowman considers the flip side of utopia – its exclusions, the ones who are not allowed in: "for every pair of happy lovers there was a dejected onlooker, the one excluded. Love was its own transparent bubble dome: you could see the two inside it, but you couldn't get in there yourself" (165).

During this period, Jimmy and Crake begin their debate regarding art, science, desire, and freedom. Jimmy is skeptical of this vision of "'a bunch of hormone robots,'" and he wonders, as his mother did before him, about the skewed ethics grounding these technological interventions into both the physical and psychological nature of human life. Jimmy wonders about "free choice" and about what would happen to the "inspiration" that biological "mismatching" provides poets and artists: "' – think Petrarch, think John Donne, think the *Vita Nuova*'" (167). When Crake returns with "Wouldn't you rather be fucking?" (167), Jimmy is successfully goaded: "'When any civilization is dust and ashes,' [Jimmy] said, 'art is all that's left over. Images, words, music. Imaginative structures. Meaning – human meaning, that is – is defined by them. You have to admit that.'" Crake does not, arguing that "'the archaeologists are just as interested in gnawed bones and old bricks and ossified shit … They think human meaning is defined by those things too.'" He goes on to describe art as "amusement" akin to masturbation, "'whack[ing] off over doodling, scribbling, and fiddling'" (168).³⁶

Continuing on this metaphoric trajectory, Crake suggests that art "serves a biological purpose," and compares art to the mating call of a male frog, who is successful if he has "'the biggest, deepest voice because it suggests a more powerful frog, one with superior genes.'" Small frogs achieve this art of the body by "'[positioning] themselves in empty drainpipes … as a voice amplifier, and the small frog appears much larger than it really is…. So that's what art is, for the artist … An empty drainpipe. An amplifier. A stab at getting laid'" (168). Crake is describing a form of what Snowman later thinks of as "art of the body," along with the snuff videos and pornography he used to watch with Crake in high school; those films of brutal killings and brutal sex also represent an artful fulfillment of desire, for power and for sex: "the Body had its own cultural forms. It had its own art. Executions were its tragedies, pornography was its romance" (85). And Crake's genetic sculptures, the Crakers? The utopian body, according to Crake. These figures are not only designed to be perfectly attuned to their environment (their body temperature, for instance, is set for the now tropical climate of the North); they are also designed perfectly, if extravagantly on Crake's part, for "guiltless sex," devolved into animals simply fulfilling a transient appetite.

Indeed, their creator designs them with animal-like adaptations in mind: both male and female genitals turn blue ("a trick of variable pigmentation filched from the baboons" [164]); the males offer flowers to the females ("just as male penguins present round stones, said Crake, or as the male silverfish presents a sperm packet"); the males perform "a sort of blue-dick dance, erect members waving to and fro in unison ... suggested to Crake by the sexual semaphoring of crabs"); the male not chosen for copulation leaves "with no hard feelings left," and the female and her chosen ones (four of them) "go at it until the woman becomes pregnant and her blue colouring fades. And that is that" (165). With a vulva specially designed to be "ultra-strong ... extra skin layers, extra muscles," women never suffer from these "hormonally robotic" serial copulations. Revising the Gileadic ceremonies, Atwood's Crake "gets it right": there is never a sense of violation, no possibility of rape, never any violence or despair from sexual mismatchings: "Hoorah for him," thinks Snowman dejectedly, as he listens to the Crakers' "noises off": "There's no more jealousy, no more wife butcherers, no more husband-poisoners. It's all admirably good-natured: no pushing and shoving, more like the gods cavorting with willing nymphs on some golden-age frieze" (168).

These designer humans are literally a type of "cellular art," the embodiment of Crake's vision of human perfection. "Useless" passions bred out, the Crakers are undeniably beautiful, happy and childlike, "amazingly attractive, ... each one naked, each one perfect, each one a different skin colour – chocolate, rose, tea, butter, cream, honey – but each with green eyes. Crake's aesthetic" (8). Later we get further details: "Each is sound of tooth, smooth of skin. No ripples of fat around their waists, no bulges, no dimpled orange-skin cellulite on their thighs. No body hair, no bushiness. They look like retouched fashion photos, or ads for a high-priced workout program" (100). Although each body is a work of art, the Crakers are psychologically "artless," incapable either of deception or invention, incapable of unpacking metaphor, taking every word literally. Given his dismissal of the creative arts generally as akin to the misalignment of sexual urges, it is not surprising that Crake also eradicates the desire, and hence the ability, to create art, to (re)produce "unreal" worlds, images, or ideas. "Watch out for art," Crake had told Jimmy regularly: "'As soon as they [the Crakers] start doing art, we're in trouble.' Symbolic thinking of any kind would signal downfall, in Crake's view. Next they'd be inventing idols, and funerals, and grave goods, and the afterlife, and sin, and Linear B, and kings, and then slavery and war" (361). Morality itself, Crake understands, requires imagination; so does "hope": fearing death, of which only human beings among God's creatures are aware, mankind is "doomed by [the] hope" that "they can stick their souls into someone else, some new version of themselves, and live on forever" (120). Without the ability to "imagine their own deaths," the Crakers will have no need for hope, no need for the creative arts' "maintenance of its promise," but only the near-mechanical fulfillment of a periodic instinct for procreation.

Atwood's awareness of the generic tradition in which she is working in this novel surfaces in Snowman's efforts to associate his situation with something meaningful.[37] Ironically, however, he blames Crake for creating of Snowman himself a version of Frankenstein's monster: "'Crake!' he whimpers. 'Why am I on this earth? How come I'm alone? Where's my Bride of Frankenstein?'" While at his father's wedding to a colleague after his mother's defection, Jimmy had "wanted to be himself, alone, unique, self-created and self-sufficient" (176). No wonder he was attracted to Crake, who aspires to the same condition – and in doing so, both commit themselves to what Braidotti calls a *masculine standpoint,* of which "[s]eparation and autonomy are ... the central features": "In the feminist analysis, this detachment and objectivity are connected to the fantasy of self-generation, of being father/mother of oneself, thus denying the specific debt to the maternal.... It is a form of flight from the feminine."[38] Now, ironically close to that state, Jimmy/Snowman contextualizes his sole survival – discounting the children of Crake – as parallel to the setting of so many "last man" narratives,[39] facing what looks like the end of history itself, even as he searches desperately for "better ways of occupying his time. *His time,* what a bankrupt idea" (40) (emphasis in the original). One of the ways of being nowhere that Snowman considers, because he is out of time (his broken, faceless watch stands as a Carteresque symbol of that), is to write an account of his times, "accounting for" himself as a way of understanding and evaluating:

He could emulate the captains of ships, in olden times ... doomed but intrepid, filling in the logbook. There were movies like that. Or castaways on desert islands, keeping their journals day by tedious day.... He too is a castaway of sorts. He could make lists. It could give his life some structure.

But even a castaway assumes a future reader, someone who'll come along later and find his bones and his ledger, and learn his fate. Snowman can make no such assumptions: he'll have no future reader, because the Crakers can't read. Any reader he can possibly imagine is in the past. (40–41)

Snowman's hopelessness is born not only from his singular solitude and yearning for community, but from his paralysis in a present which is, as even Snowman recognizes, "beyond the end" of history, the scientists having evidently brought about the near extinction of humanity: "He too would like to be elsewhere. No hope for that: he's up to his neck in the here and now" (162). Like Winterson's mother – and indeed like his precursor, Offred – Snowman "had all the longing of an exile for a place where [he] could never return," for whom "longing grew a narrative of its own" and "desire told itself as memory."[40] And like Offred, he fantasizes most about the past, drawn to memories of past lovers he always let down ("What did he want?" he asks himself [259]) – and particularly to his own relationship with the eponymous Oryx, a former child sex-slave whom both Crake and Jimmy had seen in a sex video, and with whom both fall in love. Years later, in the corporate bunker Crake has named Paradice, she appears as Crake's lover and companion, and eventually Jimmy's seducer. Jimmy's failure with all these women betokens his own failure of imagination, thanks to a careless narcissism that has exiled him from much of humanity long before this.

Although Jimmy's form of narcissism carries peculiar risks of its own – self-absorption, inattention, casual failures of imagination and of responsibility to oneself and others – Jimmy's introspective stance now allows him to discern his own culpability for the way of the world, reflecting ironically that it is "discouraging how grubby everyone gets without mirrors" (8). Crake is another story: as in Mary Shelley's precursor novel, the scientist's more dangerous variety of narcissism epitomizes the hubris of a deeply masculinist and materialist ideology of science, technology, and capitalism that devalues all that is not itself. This includes the devaluation and de-meaning of women, of the vast "class" of pleebs, and of the arts: pornography and sexual slavery (such as Oryx's) are nothing more than a kind of benign entertainment; the pleeblands nothing more than breeding grounds for (human) lab animals; art nothing more than a stab at getting laid.

As in *The Handmaid's Tale*, the gendered nature of this usurpation is at the heart of the novel's thematic tropes as well as its plot. Toward the opening of the novel, as Snowman considers how he will live among the Children of Crake, he compares himself to one of the "European colonials" of the past:

running plantations of one kind or another.... Rubber plantations, coffee plantations, jute plantations. (What was jute?) They would have been told to wear solar topis, dress for dinner, retrain from raping the natives. It [the behavioral guide written for newly arrived colonials] wouldn't have said raping. Refrain from fraternizing with the female inhabitants. Or, put some other way ...

He bets they didn't refrain, though. Nine times out of ten.

"In view of the mitigating," he says ... trying to remember the rest of the sentence. (4–5)

The near-complete ideological seizure of society by corporate science is directly compared to *rape*, of nature on the one hand (as in *Frankenstein*), and of the moral imagination on the other, including the creative arts. The coupling of Oryx and Crake at the center of this brave new world is indicative. Oryx is a child educated in and by a state of sexual slavery, perhaps the most abject version of rape; Crake is an ultra-gifted scientist whose early work on the "BlyssPluss" pill essentially enslaves men and women *to* sex while also sterilizing them. His later work effectively takes over procreation from men and women entirely, and makes of him a new god, with his self-selected new goddess, and his "new race" of human creatures. Of course, these creatures are a more perfect version of Victor Frankenstein's, whose "real life" as a form of human monster disastrously exemplifies not only the human need for love, sexual companionship, and social acceptance, but the human vices of prejudice, hatred, and violence. Crake does his best to do away with all of that, only to produce creatures who seem less "human" than Frankenstein's intellectually ambitious, morally sensitive, and emotionally passionate creature. "In Paradise," Atwood muses elsewhere, "there are no stories, because there are no journeys. It's loss and regret and misery and yearning that drive the story forward, along its twisted road."[41] Frankenstein's creature spends his entire life's journey motivated by yearning – and ends it telling his story; Crake's creatures seem to lack such yearnings, and to journey nowhere unless they are actually led.

The technological realm of the novel is clearly male, with its "dukes and kings" and finally its Prime Mover, "Crake"; the natural realm is purportedly left to the female – namely, to Oryx. Her own history as a childhood sex slave and, until her death at the hand of Crake, her "elevation" to being sole caretaker or "mother" of the Crakers, solidifies her subaltern position in the pre-epidemic period of the novel. Her fate as a child was dictated by her pimp, known only as "the man with the watch," who kept track of her "valuable" time. Her posthumous fate is dictated, quite literally, by another man with a watch, Snowman, whose broken timekeeper serves as a purported communication device between himself, and Crake and Oryx, who lie rotting in Crake's compound, Paradice. Whereas Crake, according to Snowman's elaborate and fanciful hagiography, hands down the Laws, God-like, and names his creatures, Adam-like, Oryx creates nothing, but "is" the spirit of nature "herself." Her role before her death was to teach the Crakers of the unity of the natural world – in particular the animals, which are identified as *her* children.[42]

In contrast to the infamous *Island of Dr. Moreau*, in which, Atwood observes, the "[female] locale [of the island] becomes the site of a moral breakdown that is specifically sexual," *Oryx and Crake* locates moral breakdown squarely in the highly advanced society driven by corporate science. As Atwood points out, "There is no Mrs Moreau on the island"; the Crakers' motherless birth, recalling the monstrous birth of Frankenstein's and Moreau's creatures, only foregrounds the ways in which Atwood takes up Mary Shelley's own precocious vision of science replacing the maternal body with its own inventive, technological method of artificial procreation.[43] Moral recovery is offered, ironically, in Snowman's confused and manipulative interactions with the gentle children that Oryx once tended.

"OH HONEY, YOU'RE MY ONLY HOPE"

Unlike Winterson's hopeful "pilgrim," traveling faithfully toward the utopia of love, Snowman wanders through much of the novel without aim or hope; "He has no maps anymore" (150), and he is losing all sense of orientation: "He searches his mind for some lesson or long-lost chart that would tell him [whether "fat" from a pigoon "is a carbohydrate"]: he knew that stuff once, but it's no use, the file folders are empty" (151). At the same time, Snowman associates the multivalence of words with the lost richness of "the time before," and his retrospective narratives deny any hope for salvation into community. His hope finds no place to anchor itself; even Offred manages to cultivate hope in her pursuit of romance's fulfillment of sexual desire and the need for companionship and community. Gradually Snowman's solitude erodes his own abilities to either remember, or to imagine, and words themselves gradually dissociate from their meanings and connotations: "From nowhere, a word appears: *Mesozoic.* He can see the word, he can hear the word, but he can't reach the word. He can't attach anything to it. This is happening too much lately, this dissolution of meaning, the entries on his cherished wordlists drifting off into space" (39).

Although Snowman has no maps, he does recall the way back to Paradice, Crake's "bubble-dome," where Jimmy had been an employee (chief of advertising) and "one of the angels guarding the gate, in a manner of speaking" (151). By the time this visit to Paradice takes place, it is a paradise lost, in ruins, its god-like Creator killed. His "children" remain, recalling H. G. Wells's docile Eloi more than Frankenstein's creature, living in an "edenic" tropical setting near the beach, and taking in the inventive myths and legends celebrating Crake and his female companion, Oryx. For a long while, the Crakers do not recognize the fictionality of these stories, composed – a bit like Frankenstein's creature himself – out of functionally "dead" human narratives from the Bible, history, myth, and legend. The Crakers take these stories as literal truth; although as time passes, they seem more doubtful, as Snowman falters in his narrative ingenuity.

At just this time, the Crakers also develop in unexpected ways, not only demonstrating a sense of initiative, but also the impulse to make art, despite Crake's efforts to root out either impulse. As Snowman returns from Paradice, he discovers the Crakers have created a "grotesque-looking figure, a scarecrowlike effigy," with a head and "face of sorts," and a "ragged cloth body" (360). They are singing: "Ohhhh.... Mun.... Is that *Amen?* Surely not! Not after Crake's precautions" (360). And when the Crakers finally see him arrive, they surround him:

> "We knew we could call you, and you would hear us and come back."
> Not Amen, then. Snowman.
> "We made a picture of you, to help us send out our voices to you."
> Watch out for art, Crake used to say. (361)

This moment of art's first creation among the Crakers is uncanny for several reasons. As Snowman recognizes, it represents a return of the genetically repressed; but Snowman is not entirely surprised, given his knowledge that Crake had been signally unable to eliminate "hard-wired" dreaming and singing from his new race. The resurfacing of art marks a kind of intellectual evolution for the children of Crake. They enter into a culture of their own that includes a concept of "real possibility," expressed through willfully directed action, and through works of art representing desire. Touchingly, once their desire is fulfilled, the absent Snowman made present in reality, and not just in art, the Crakers dismantle the effigy, reminding Snowman, with heavy irony, of the *sparagmos* of mythical heroes.

This scene also marks Snowman's recognition, after spotting from Paradice an unusual column of smoke, that beyond all expectation and hope there are other human beings – three of them, he learns from the Crakers – like himself left in the world. The morning following his return to the beach, Snowman awakens into hope, and fear, imagining what might be:

He can't relax into the sound [of the Crakers' therapeutic "purring"] as he knows he should, because he's rehearsing the future, he can't help it. His mind is racing; behind his half-closed eyes possibilities flash and collide. Maybe all will be well ... On the other hand, these new arrivals could easily see the Children of

Crake as freakish, or savage, or non-human and a threat.... But why imagine the worst? (366)

He awakes into "rapture; there is no other word for it. *Rapture.* The heart seized, carried away, as if by some large bird of prey. After everything that's happened, how can the world still be so beautiful?" (372). This seizure – a rapture, not a rape – is inspired by his imaginative projection of the self into a future where he might be "reborn" into a community of people "like him." The final lines of the narrative propose into a new, if unpredictable, beginning for history:

> From habit he lifts his watch; it shows him its blank face.
> Zero hour, Snowman thinks. Time to go. (374)

Snowman does not drop his watch into a river, as Jeanette does; but his watch reminds him, as it does her, that change can only happen, and hope only be fulfilled, by risking another journey. He could stay, and live in the past and in a desolate present; or he can decide: time to go. Jeanette's exhortation applies here as well: "The promise is that the world is always beginning again. No accumulations of the past can stop it. Another day. Another chance. Does nobody believe this?" (*PowerBook*, 270). Snowman is no more sure of his belief than Offred is, when she steps into the van. But the *hope* of another chance, however risky, makes the picture of a presumed death-in-life worse than being shot dead by fellow survivors of the viral plague, or, for the heroine of the earlier novel, hanged by Gilead's Eyes. As the voice of hope for Offred is Nick, the voices of hope and despair alike for Snowman come from the haunting memories of the women of his life: his mother ("*Don't let me down*" [374]); Oryx ("*Oh Jimmy, this is so positive. It makes me happy when you grasp this. Paradice is lost, but you have a Paradice with you, happier far*" [(308)]); and other past lovers ("*Oh Jimmy, you were so funny*" [374]; "*Oh sweetie ... You're doing really well*" [238]).

In Atwood's grim images of a society in which imagination is degraded and art devalued, Atwood expresses her fear that a cultural (r)evolution spurred only by the utilitarian, profiteering interests of capitalism and by the power interests of a deeply masculinist social ideology will end only in the worst, dystopic scenarios. And yet, while Atwood is no "romantic" in comparison to Winterson, she does propose in these novels that there is not simply a "role" for art but a need for the work of imagination so basic that even the genius Crake cannot eradicate its physiological expression in his creatures' dreams, which are clearly themselves instances of the "art of the body." Without the "play"[44] of imagination within and among individuals, Atwood cannot imagine an historical trajectory forward. And while "Desire is what is real" in Winterson, notes Burns, "more so than historical events or material objects,"[45] desire in Atwood is realized through historical events and material objects. Thus, whereas Winterson favors the "reality" of our romantic dreams, envisioning utopia as the ecstasy of two lovers coming together, Atwood's sensibility directs her toward the difficulty of disentangling the romance of the erotic from other kinds of romance – being in love with power, or with oneself, or with a certain image of God. These entanglements of various forms of desire carry a risk that is far more than simply "emotional": the reality of these other desires takes forms such as the tyrannized body politic of Gilead and its obscene ceremonies and rituals, or the perversely engineered bodies and sexual rituals of the Crakers. "*Romance,*" says a horoscope announcement in Atwood's most recent novel, *The Year of the Flood* (2009),[46] "may take strange forms – illusion and reality are dancing together right now, so tread carefully!"

Indeed, generically speaking, *Oryx and Crake* is itself, surprisingly enough, a postmodern "scientific romance," a form Atwood discusses in her introduction to the 2005 Penguin edition of *The Island of Dr. Moreau*, to which this novel clearly owes much. There, Atwood points out that for Wells, the term "'romance' is more helpful than 'fiction'" because it frees the writer from merely "the known social life": "a romance could deal with the long ago and the far away. It also allowed much more latitude in terms of plot. In a romance, event follows exciting event at breakneck pace."[47] Atwood also outlines Northrop Frye's generic analysis of romance, enumerating such structural features as "a break in ordinary consciousness, often – traditionally – signalled by a shipwreck"; "Exotic climes are a feature, especially exotic desert islands; so are strange animals"; "Boundaries between the normal levels of life dissolve; vegetable becomes animal, animal becomes quasi-human, human descends to animal." Finally, according to Atwood's summary of her one-time teacher's rubric, "the protagonist is often imprisoned or trapped, or lost in a labyrinth or maze, or a forest that serves the same purpose.... A rescue, however improbable, restores the protagonist to his or her previous life and reunites him or her with loved ones."[48]

The connections should be obvious: Snowman is not literally shipwrecked, but he is metaphorically, and as we have seen, he makes the connection himself. The "exotic clime" is there, thanks to abrupt climate change worldwide. Certainly we have the strange animals, created by geneticists even more irresponsible than Dr. Moreau, who at least kept his beasts confined to an island and did not mess with viruses. The Crakers and Moreau's creatures are parallel in their hybridity; the boundaries between human and animal are unclear, and each "race" gradually tends toward its origins – Moreau's victims to their animality; Crake's to their humanity. And finally, there is the protagonist, not trapped, but "lost"; not "rescued" exactly, but stepping out of the forest in order to reenter what is left of human society, whether to a renewed life or to death, he has no idea. Tread carefully indeed, in this Paradise.

From *The Handmaid's Tale* to *Oryx and Crake* to *The Year of the Flood*, Atwood consistently warns that some dreams are "overly optimistic projections of [one's] own mind.... How many sailors have been wrecked in pursuit of islands that were merely a shimmering?" (*Flood*, 165). As in Chapter 1, we see this author utilizing traditional forms to contemporary ends, and Atwood's manipulations of the "scientific romance" into what she has called a "speculative fiction" are such that she might add the term *speculative romance* to the repertoire. The critical distinction of the speculative romance from its precursors is simply this: as in the *speculative bildungsroman* described in the Chapter 1, the *speculative romance* will not rest in the generic certainty of social integration; in all of these novels, there is precious little "society" left and an uncertain faith, if not outright skepticism, in historical progress. Disrupted too, therefore, is the alignment of individual and social integrity.

Whereas Atwood notes that every novel begins with this question, "What if?" her sense of her own speculative project is to confront what she regards as an oncoming "perfect storm" in human history: the confusion of rationality and passion, of morality and egoism, of technology and art. "The *what if* of *Oryx and* Crake is simply, *What if we continue down the road we're already on? How slippery is the slope? What are our saving graces? Who's got the will to stop us? ...* It's not a question of our inventions – all human inventions are merely tools – but of what might be done with them."[49] What if, in other words, there is no "promise" in the future because we live, now, in an age of general "immiseration"[50] and threat? As I have argued implicitly throughout this chapter, "responsibility" – both individual and corporate, local and global – may be Atwood's great subject. Her recent speculative fictions, Janus-like, look backward and forward, speculating on the obscure motives and even obscurer consequences of what has happened already; speculating too on what, in a possible future, clearly *could* happen based on the footprints left by individual, as well as by corporate, national, or global bodies. The protagonist of a speculative romance would live in just the temporal hinge where, to recall Winterson's trope from *The PowerBook,* "what exists and what might exist are windowed together at the core of reality" (129).[51] In a speculative romance, there can be no conclusive ending. Atwood has commented that "I like to leave the endings open"; but of *Oryx and Crake* she says, more specifically, "I don't know what Jimmy's going to do, what he should do."[52]

Thus, the final chapter of *Oryx and Crake* is entitled "Footprint," an obvious double allusion, as commentators have noted, both to *Robinson Crusoe,* and to the legend of the Abominable Snowman, whose name Jimmy appropriated after finding himself in the new wilderness of the post-apocalyptic era. As "Snowman" follows the unexpected footprints of other surviving humans, he imprints his own "good foot," as "a signature of a kind," next to the largest of the strangers' footprints. His footprint is the beginning of an archive of his journey toward a hoped-for new beginning; as a symbol of his hope and will to join the future. But never, in Atwood, is anything guaranteed. With characteristic irony, the narrative observes that "As soon as he lifts his foot away the imprint fills with water" (373). In addition, the other, "bad" foot, severely infected "like a shoeful of liquid fire" (374), has hobbled him, and appears as likely to actually kill him as not. So much for happy endings, although clearly Atwood has, as DiMarco observes, "guide[d] readers to contemplate seriously the ethical implications of particular choices"[53]; as with Offred, so with Snowman, as the reader follows his footsteps on the mental journey through the past and present, and watches him begin taking a stand on the careless role he has played in this manmade biological holocaust.[54]

From the moment Snowman entertains an imagined reunion with other survivors, his sense of romance is aroused not by any personal sexual urges but by the desire for community. He is an "exile" no longer, because he has imagined a story with the possibility of an ending, and in doing so chosen a future – although he has been warned: "Tread carefully." Desire, as embodied in the imaginations of artists, scientists, politicians, and so many other "creators" of society, comes to be associated in both Winterson and Atwood with experiences of romance that are both sexual and cultural. In Winterson's novels, this "dance" traces the boundaries of the lover's island, "always a metaphor of the heart," whether the blessed island exists in reality or not: the vision will always be there. She avoids the dark possibilities of Atwood's vision, where such an island might well be simply a "shimmering" illusion of safety on the way to drowning; or the darker political possibilities of the dance, which is as likely as not to trace the boundaries of a fool's Paradise.

The risks of treading in the world of romance, whether erotic (Winterson), scientific, or speculative (Atwood), are critical and necessary to both authors. Neither can imagine a world with any shred of political freedom, moral sense, or human happiness that does not require the work of the imagination, a "space between chaos and shape," to recall Winterson, in which "there was another chance." For characters Jeanette, Offred, and Snowman alike, the possibilities of language and narrative art themselves create a fragile utopic space, a textual "art of the possible" that promises to revise history, again and again, by offering "possibilities, tiny peepholes," even if the audience is itself under "reduced circumstances" (*Handmaid's Tale*, 21), and even though life may well end instantly in a blast of gunfire. The prospect of a new community, whether simply a couple or a new group affiliation, does not close the text, but opens it to the possibility of hope: another chance, another reader, another space where dialogue between "one imaginer and another"[55] can take place.

For these authors, hope is aesthetic, political, and ethical in its projection of an ideal community, although Atwood's statements on art, narrative and otherwise, reflect her fears for an historical trajectory that seems hell-bent "on destroying itself, and the biosphere along with it, because it seems unable to check its own greedy and aggressive behaviours."[56] From this, Atwood observes, emerge "the [narrative forms] utopia and dystopia, which have proved over and over again that we have a much better idea about how to make hell on earth than we do about how to make heaven." Nevertheless, provoked by what she sees as a war against the arts by leaders of contemporary culture, "politicians among them – [who] have done their best to finish [art] off," Atwood can write a defense of art as fervent as Winterson's:

But it is still the human imagination, in all its diversity, that directs what we do with our tools. Literature is an uttering, or outering, of the human imagination. It lets the shadowy forms of thought and feeling – Heaven, Hell, monsters, angels and all – out into the light, where we can take a good look at them and perhaps come to a better understanding of who we are and what we want, and what the limits to those wants may be. Understanding the imagination is no longer a pastime or even a duty, but a necessity; because increasingly if we can imagine it, we'll be able to do it.[57]

Even here, Atwood cannot resist acknowledging the double-edged sword that is the imagination: source of visionary creativity in the arts and sciences; source of dangerous projections and misguided illusions of power. Yet like Winterson Atwood remains staunch in her defense of humanity's imaginative capacity to express "something that is true to itself" and to reveal thereby "the full range of our human response to the world – that is, what it means to be human, on earth. That seems to be what 'hope' is about in relation to art. Nothing so simple as 'happy endings.' … An approach to perfection, if you like."[58]

The rapture of experience recognizes the necessity of "the other," although Atwood remains ultimately more interested in the moral dimensions of individual character and of political entities than in the Wintersonian raptures of ecstatic sex. Yet for both authors the "approach to perfection," while never completed, is always offered; the promise never fulfilled, but maintained. There are, as Atwood's Crake ironically observes, "no guarantees," but art's promise of community, backed by an investment in the values of the imagination and sympathy, remains the single most critical article of faith in the canon of these two authors.

CHAPTER 3

Archives of the heart
Inventing history at the edge(s) of time

> *Our ancestors. Our belonging. The future is foretold from the past and the future is only possible because of the past. Without past and future, the present is partial. All time is eternally present and so all time is ours. There is no sense in forgetting and every sense in dreaming. Thus the present is made rich. Thus the present is made whole. On the lagoon this morning, with the past at my elbow, rowing beside me, I see the figure glittering on the water. I catch sight of myself in the water and see in the distortions of my face what I might become.*
>
> – Jeanette Winterson[1]

In Chapters 1 and 2, I have examined feminist speculative texts that focus on the way art complicates and re-presents historical and identity consciousness, always moving us toward a mobile standpoint that yearns toward emergence rather than stasis. There are, of course, urgent formal implications. In introducing the notion of *speculative standpoint*, a type of feminist standpoint, we could continue the ongoing critique of the classical bildungsroman's strong political commitment to the perfect integration of the (male) individual into (Western) bourgeois society, and to the alignment of personal and communal histories. The contemporary texts investigated in Chapter 1, instead, radically rewrite the conventional bildungsroman's representation of the nature and production of knowledge, and therefore, the relationship of its hero/ine to that knowledge. The ideological center of gravity is shifted. Chapter 2 then focused on how contemporary authors consider the work that *they* do – the "work" of art – as the kind of intervention that resists a monologic historical narrative. Like the novels of Chapter 1, these texts open onto dimensions of time and space that offer different worlds, counterspaces as Tom Moylan has coined them, in which the established understanding of our human nature might be reconceptualized, and the trajectory of our personal and communal histories recalibrated.

This chapter extends the discussion of nonlinear history(-ies) and narrative strategies by adding exemplary texts by Ursula LeGuin and by the formidable Doris Lessing to the work of Winterson. As variable as the structural and tropological experimentation may be in each novel, there is a certain similarity among them. Each attends to what Lessing, in her peculiar novel, *The Cleft* (2007),² names "parallel Lines of Memories" (28), bridged by narrative connectors pieced out of personal and communal histories. When the scaffolding for such bridges comes from materials at hand, however, the stability of the structure proves questionable: with each time-bridge, the entirety of this universe changes or evolves, just as each unique joining of two sets of DNA reconfigures two bodies into a third. Indeed, as we have seen, the field of genetics emerges as an alternative figuration of historical evolution, and textual play with tropes of "reproduction" is ongoing.

The possibilities for rewriting history appear more open to Jeanette Winterson, whose novel, *The PowerBook*, holds out a cheerful vision of "a new kind of communication" that is "abstract, light, changeful, genuine." Whereas Atwood (re)creates an historical document simply too ironic for us to leave with any confidence in "another chance," Winterson, as we have seen, can claim without irony that "Our real lives are elsewhere. Art finds them."³ Her more recent *The Stone Gods* (2007) is set at various historical moments at the opposite ends of history, each approaching or even reaching the final edge of human history. This chapter's readings of *The Telling, The Cleft,* and *The Stone Gods* revolve around the common lineage of each human "being" in natural *and* in cultural histories. Mother and father contribute two strands of genetic information, the recombinant connections made randomly. But nature and culture offer another set of evolutionary possibilities: the joining of Mother/Nature and Father/Culture creates a nonrandom affiliation of metaphorical fields that have almost invisibly (that is, ideologically) influenced the trajectory of our human affairs. These novels therefore conduct a genealogical study consisting in teasing out more than one dimension of "genetic" lineage, and challenging a more or less "closed-system" conception of human nature as so much "hard wiring." In its place is drawn an open system in which there are choices – call it "free will" – that intervene in a fatal(istic) outcome. Such a conception gives birth to new ways of being and knowing, evolving memes that promise a future not doomed to repeat "the same old story."⁴

"FOOTSTEPS ON THE AIR": DEMANDING THE IMPOSSIBLE IN *THE TELLING*

In Ursula LeGuin's *The Telling* (2000), a Terran woman named Sutty arrives from Earth at Aka, a planet that has been riven by a civil war initiated by a corporate-controlled, technocratic neo-Terran regime. Like all "converts" the Corporation fervently follows a path of presumed cultural advance by so privileging science and technology that indigenous ways, such as arts and poetry and the spiritual practice of "Telling," are criminalized as primitive and corrupt activities. As one in a long line now of literary travelers, Sutty is both a historian and anthropologist, sent to observe without judgment or prejudice the ways of the Akan: "Look, listen, notice: observe" (9). Her particular task is to explore their literature and language; as the novel opens, she has so far fared badly in this task. While trained in the ancient Akan language, no one she meets in the main city knows (or admits to knowing) that language. The texts and manuscripts she had hoped to see are officially destroyed. Sutty finds herself (unprofessionally) irritated by the "endless aggression of propaganda" from the Corporation; there is "nowhere to get away from [it]" without simply isolating herself in her apartment, "shutting out the world she'd come to observe" (9).

Officially, the customs of the time before no longer exist. Unofficially, the new Akan leaders know that these ancient texts and the traditional ways still exist, somewhere. Sending Sutty to find that place, the colonial government hopes she will lead them to the undiscovered site of the Lap of Silong, where it is alleged many old texts and artifacts have been hidden. Sutty quickly gains the trust of these rural Akan people and begins to understand the depth of their diffuse spiritual sensibility. There is no absolute god; the Akan word for *god* is "without referent. No capital letters. No creator, only creation" (102). There are no rules, no authoritative texts, and, Sutty believes initially, no concept of absolute truth. With an academic's commitment to interpreting and categorizing, Sutty struggles to define this original Akan sensibility. No term seems fully accurate until she decides on "The Telling," capturing her first central insight: Akan spirituality is based not simply on perception and attentiveness, on acts and on words, but on the *sharing* of all those things in narratives that are preserved, as with many colonized peoples, *orally*. The communal experience of telling is critical, not only for transmission of knowledge and of individual as well as social identity. Telling is critical for "experience" itself: "perception seemed to involve description – telling about the place, or the act, or the event, or the person. Talking about it, making it into a story" (104). This Akan outpost is an "invisible web" (158) dependent on, and productive of, intersubjective engagement.

The task of narrative is to *make* an event (or act, place, etc.) meaningful, although Sutty never hears a definition of what the meaning is or should be. Gradually she apprehends this is a "religion of process" in which "[c]onclusions led to new beginnings" (103), not to doxa that become the basis for all decisions or policies. The adherents who come there are continuing a lifelong pursuit of textual reading and telling, with a gradually accretion of meaning around each narrative. It would be incorrect, Sutty realizes, to call these tellings "interpretations," as that implies a fixing of meaning that is alien to Akan sensibility. Akan consciousness itself – both personal and national – is explicitly archival. Although the *maz* or spiritual leaders tell the same stories over and over again – the Aka audience has heard some of them since infancy – there is never any sense that that story is "done," that it is "just" history. "The telling never stopped" (97). These narrative threads are the very stuff of the "invisible web" that is this postcolonial Akan outpost.

In a revision of Plato's Cave parable, Sutty is forced to reorient her notions of history and reality simultaneously. Having been led to the Lap of Silong, the supposed repository of the remnants of Akan literature and writing, Sutty enters this "dream of darkness, strangeness," finding not a single huge cave but a dense network of them, "endless bubble chambers interconnecting, interfacing, dark walls, floors, ceilings all curved into one another seamlessly, so disorienting that sometimes she felt she was floating weightless. Sounds echoed so they had no direction. There was never enough light" (194). These "caves of being" (195) do not offer second-degree projections of reality. They are illuminated to reveal "round rooms full of words, where the Telling lay hidden, in silence." She finds countless thousands of documents in every conceivable format, from illuminated manuscripts to bound books to vellum, parchment, loose sheets, all rescued from the corporate colonizers. "All the poems in the world were here" (197), she realizes. The Telling is a kind of *poesis*: a continuous making.

History may be anchored by these treasured archives, but because of the Telling, neither past nor present can be fixed into any master narrative. And the future: there is no expectation the future will be the "same old story." Rather, the future is figured by an image Sutty sees everywhere in both their poetry and philosophy, their legends and mottos: the "twice-forked lightening tree," a trope of the necessary divergence of every ontological or epistemological position. What is most valuable about the thousands of texts in the archive is not that they represent "one way" of thinking; they do not "prove" anything. They are, each one of them, "glances" and "glimpses" of a truth or reality that changes with every telling, and with every listening. Both the one who tells *and* the one who listens are speculators. This is speculative standpoint.

Sutty is an historian but even faced with the evidence, she often disbelieves what she sees. The real plot of this novel is not the history of the Akans, in fact, but Sutty's reorientation through her own discovery of unfamiliar and unknown categories of reality. The Akans regard knowledge as a "gift" (243) and "the gift is lightning" (250). Knowledge, the gift, the lightning: all are "forked," multiple in their possibilities. And in this, the last is first, as it were: the gift of extravagant knowledge is offered to a "half-witted" individual who kept trying to teach Sutty a particular exercise pose: "He gestured, Up! Up! ... Finally, whispering, 'Up – like this – see?' he took a step onto the air. He brought the other foot up on the invisible stair, and then climbed another step up the same way.... He was standing on air" (137). Although she watched him being helped down "two nonexistent steps to the floor," she spent the days and weeks that followed wondering how it could happen, persuading herself it did not, but still seeing "in her mind's eye ... those two callused, muscular, bare feet stepping up the absent mountain." She debates whether the air would feel "cool" or "resilient" on one's feet.

As an historian she could describe the event, but not "explain" it, although from that moment she "paid more attention to the old texts and tales that talked about walking on the wind, riding on clouds, traveling to the stars ..." (139). These are glimpses of dimensions and outer spaces that Sutty did not yet know how to accept, but the novel closes with the promise that she will, someday, likely step onto the air. As she begins negotiating with representatives of her own and of Akan Corporate governments, she knows she is seeking a way of returning both to a basis of reciprocity, exchange, and true open-mindedness among nations and communities: "Those were the intangible, incalculable stakes. The money burned to ashes, the gold thrown away. Footsteps on the air" (264).

THE CLEFT: THE FIRST SEXUAL (R)EVOLUTION, OR, "FOR THE LUST OF KNOWING"

What Lessing shows is that no one knows what evolutions are necessary ... we only know that movement is the key. – Jeanette Winterson[5]

Lessing's writing over her long career has brought many surprises, and her allegiance to feminism is famously querulous, as is Winterson's. But the oddity of her most recent novel's account of early human evolution into sexual dimorphism sets many readers back on their heels. There is little that is appealing about either the males or the females in this tale, who are reduced to more or less cartoonish versions of masculinity and femininity. The novel appeared in print only about three months before the announcement that Lessing would receive the Nobel Prize for literature, when The Swedish Academy cited her 1962 novel, *The Golden Notebook,* as the most famous work from "that epicist of the female experience, who with skepticism, fire and visionary power has subjected a divided civilisation to scrutiny."[6] But, *The Cleft*'s "oracular essentialism,"[7] as the reviewer from *Ms.Magazine* put it, seemed inexplicably out of step with the keen intelligence for which the author was being celebrated. There were warning signs. Lessing has never sat comfortably at the table with contemporary feminists; neither has Winterson, who had nevertheless asserted back in 2001 that Lessing should "lighten up. It was your generation of feminists, the 70s, the golden age of the women's movement, that gave us the really damaging, batty stuff; all men are rapists, all sex is power, pornography is abuse, marriage is a crime. And what about separatism and political lesbians? Thank God those days are gone."[8] Even as Lessing predicted that *The Cleft* would make many people unhappy, she made no effort whatever to explain or justify her clearly intentional provocation.

Feminist readers are rightly put off that a writer as rugged as this one might endorse the epigraph from Robert Graves that "Man does, woman is." Who would not bristle at the suggestion that without the miraculous intervention of the male of the species, we females would still be lolling about in bovine contentedness? Any reader might smile at Lessing's remarks, in the foreword of *The Cleft,* about the "lack of solidity," instability, and "erratic"-ness of men compared to women, and nod assent at her speculation that perhaps men were an afterthought to the creation, first, of women. But the same reader would likely raise her eyebrows at the description of women as "endowed with a natural harmony with the ways of the world." She might find, as *Spectator* reviewer Olivia Glazebrook did, the reduction of women and men to "nags versus cads" a proposal "too silly to take seriously." Julie Phillips concurs: in the end, "[Lessing's] view of male and female is bafflingly banal." John Leonard, reviewing for *Harper's Magazine*, grants Lessing a little more gravity, seeing Lessing's characterization of early women and men as stereotypes deepening into archetypes: "relentlessly, she grinds us down to acquiescence.... Only children and terminal naifs believe in such fantasies as free will or liberal humanism or existential psychology or historical determinism or the Holy Ghost or the Enlightenment." Although Leonard praises the novel's brutal skepticism regarding individual agency, he does not contradict the novel's apparent conclusion: the more things change, the more they stay the same.[9]

If acquiescence to an incorrigible biological determinism were really the "take-away" from *The Cleft*, it would be easy to leave the novel behind as a thin and unfortunate effort. But this conclusion underestimates badly the ongoing provocativeness of this author. Roberta Rubenstein's approach is one of few to make sense of this novel's crux, which she describes as a contrast between "linear and circular modes of cognition," formalized as "the uni-directional unfoldings of history," and *myth*, or the "nonrational, the suprarational and synthesizing level of mental activity" on the other. This "central tension and energy" of Lessing's writing accounts for her characters' "often contradictory orientations toward experience and the nature of reality."[10] That is, this "tension" catalyzes the irony that permeates so many of Lessing's works. In this novel, only irony explains the crass jokiness of the names "Clefts" and "Squirts"; how is it possible to read that, or write that, "straight"? It also explains the unpleasantness of the vision of women's discovery of sexuality as purely functional. Remarking on the "uselessness" of the boys' breasts, which feed nothing, and their genitalia, which cannot give birth, the women infer, with a sense of dawning knowledge as they watch spawning fish, that "that's what they [the Squirts] were for." So much for romance, we think to ourselves. But romance, as well as history, *is* the subject of this novel, not just the emotional sort of romance, but also the literary sort. Lessing's real concern is not about "what really happened" because at no point is this version of human evolution believable, even to the Roman historian who is presenting this story. Her concerns are the shifty interconnections of history, romance, and myth – presentations of cultural memes almost as fundamental to our makeup as any genetic information contributed by our progenitors.

The narrative comprising the novel, *The Cleft*, represents a scholarly project completed by an aging Roman senator and historian living in the time of Nero. He sets out to write a history based on "[a] mass of material accumulated over ages, originating as oral history, some of it the same but written down later, all purporting to deal with the earliest record of us, the peoples of our earth" (6). Earlier historians had taken up this project but abandoned it, he tells us, in part because these documents apparently reveal the priority of the female sex in human evolution, an assertion so "inflammatory" as to cause predecessors to lock up these materials "with the other 'Strictly Secret' documents" (7). As noted at the opening of this chapter, this common structural trope is a first clue toward Lessing's intentions for this novel. From *The Last Man* (1826) to *The Handmaid's Tale* (1985), to speak only of speculative fiction, the discovery of a "hidden cache of documents" sets up a representational fiction of a storytelling situation.[11] This framing has the effect of destabilizing epistemological groundings, either proleptically, as in Shelley's novel, or retrospectively, as in Atwood's. These temporal shifts blur the boundary lines between reality and fiction, report and romance, history and myth. And so *The Cleft* turns out not really to be about the civil war between women and men, as its narrator proposes; it becomes about the impossible tangle of epistemological truth claims. Moreover, the historian's excavation of historical "facts" leaves us with Lessing's skeptical proposal: that a progressive "historical evolution" in human, and especially sexual, relations is frustrated by the obscurity of our origins, an aporia which, from time immemorial, storytellers have filled in with stories of their own and in their own self-interest. As Winterson puts it, what you cannot remember, you invent.[12]

The narrator's introduction begins with a simple factual statement: "I saw this today" (3). He sketches out for us a scenario of young lust between two of his house slaves: "these were no longer children: it was enough only to see them together to know her crossness, his sullenness, were not the result only of a very hot afternoon" (4). Crossness turns to "coaxing," then to pleading as he turns his back to her, returning to the slaves' quarters "at the end of the garden": "I did not need to watch any longer. I knew she would find an excuse to hang about ... I knew too that these two would spend tonight together, no matter what he would have preferred" (5–6). From the "fact" of what the historian sees, he moves quickly to speculation (he stops watching) and to musing that this "little scene seems to me to sum up a truth in the relations between men and women." Only then is he moved to return to a "great pack of material which I was supposed to be working on" (6), the "unwieldy mass" of documents that someone before him had entitled "'The Cleft' – I did not choose this title" (7).

His own choice is revealed later, but in leaving the old title for now he acknowledges the many "cleavings," a resonant and ambiguous word over which this historian will puzzle: the cleaving of women and men, heroes and villains (or, "us" and "them"), "then" and "now," sea and mountain, dreams and realities, fiction and fact. Each of these is introduced in the "relating" of Maire, the only Cleft whose interview, by an even earlier historian, is transcribed here. Maire explains that their name, "the Clefts," memorializes the rocky valley that distinguishes their bit of island coast, with its "clean cut down through the rock" and "deep hole" underneath (10), bearing such a resemblance to their own bodies' reproductive features. These Clefts were, according to the documents, lethargic creatures, half-way between fish and human behaviorally, often found sunning themselves like sea cows. The Clefts spend "many days … doing nothing," are "calm and reflecting" (78), "lazy and languid" (79), enervated "shapeless Thing[s]" (80) who live in caves and pluck fish out of the sea.

The innocence of the Clefts' prelapsarian, even pre-Edenic existence as an insular "community of dreaming creatures" (33) comes to an end with the unwanted introduction of these "new people" (102–103) among them. The inexplicable dropping of the first male infant or so-called Monster is met with surprise and repulsion toward the strange "lumps and bumps" of the boy's genitalia. As more males are born, the nature of psychic disruption provoked by the presence of males to the Cleft "herland" is profound. Some stirring of curiosity among the Clefts is the most positive of these developments. Beyond that, however, the evolution of their emotions seems less benign. Anticipating a birth is eventually no longer a pleasure for the mothers: "we were afraid, and when one of us saw that the babe was a Monster, she was ashamed and the others hated her" (13). The women find themselves thinking "critical thoughts" (68), as they compare each other "in their minds, each idea with a shadow" (88–89), something both present and absent. They develop an us-and-them sentiment, "Cleft and Other" (102), which takes the form not only of suspicion but of shame, and also of disgust.

As if inevitably, therefore, the original event marking male and female congruence is not some imagined "social contract," but – once again – a rape. Overtaken by their desire, a group of "squirts" seize a young woman, run her all the way back to their home, and enjoy a mass rape. Was it seaweed stuffed hard into her throat to stop her screaming, or the serial violation that killed her? No one said. But the reward for "their flaccid squirts" was an intimation of shame, prompting them purposely to suppress the telling of the event. While there is no developed morality, an inchoate apperception of wrongdoing gathers into a sense of enmity: "an idea with a shadow," hosts and hostiles. The othering of males and females has begun on both sides but, following the old adage, history is written by the victors. A masculinist idea(l) concurrently casts its shadow: the other(ed) woman.

Throughout the dozen-plus pages of her recorded narrative, only recently deciphered out of an ancient language, Maire proves a reluctant interviewee. Because she and her kind are the object of unprecedented inquiry, she is sensitive both to how she herself construes the story of the

Clefts, and how the Clefts are themselves construed. In the "informative" passage chosen by our narrator-historian, Maire opens with a querulous correction of her interrogator:

Yes, I know, you keep saying, but what you don't understand is that what I say now can't be true because I am telling you how I see it all now, but it was all different then. Even words I use are new, I don't know where they came from, sometimes it seems that most of the words in our mouths are this new talk. (7)

Even more perceptively, Maire associates the new words with "a new kind of thinking [which] began like everything else when the Monsters started being born" (8). Speculation itself, in short, is born, as the Clefts begin to think about what this means, not just "now," but for the future, for what might happen.

The new language, in other words, brings with it a new sense of time. The Clefts' original sense of time was as an undivided "eternal present" (31). Maire's inability to locate an "original" time confirms this: "No, I cannot say how it started. That is not our story" (10); "How we thought has never been part of our story, only what happened" (11). She perceives that the ability even to say "what happened" is mediated by the evolution of the "new talk" (7) and vocabulary of the males. Her own name, she notes, is "one of the new words," but "We didn't think like that, no, we didn't, that every person had to have a name separate from all the others" (11). Cleft language had been transparent, a mark of their prelapsarian nature, expressive of presence only. It is not even clear that this language was "verbal" as such: the senator notes that "their songs are not histories or stories but a kind of keening, sounding like the wind when it sighs and murmurs" (32) – a form of "natural" speech, whereas "the songs of the early men," according to the historian, "were histories, of a kind" (41).

These divisions are reflected in the erosion of their own linguistic transparency. With the introduction of the "new talk," language takes on the function of dispersion, to distinguish and divide, to express "an idea and its shadow," as Maire poignantly puts it. The new words cleave the I's from the we, us from them, and the story "in our records," which "is known," from the other party's. The Squirts give the Clefts names, the "Maire" whom we have met, and "Astre." The shift from "we" to "I" marks the emergence of a new kind of awareness: the birth of self-consciousness, and self-admiration, with words now available to describe their distinctions from the Monsters, and from one another: "*Beautiful* – you taught us that word and I like to use it. I am beautiful, just like The Cleft with its pretty red flowers" (12). Maire herself clearly regrets the story she is telling, and not just because she has "a bad feeling" about the early treatment of the Monsters (although she still regards their bodies – "you" – as repugnant). She regrets there *is* a story to tell, after "a new thing began" (17). We hear resentment toward her obviously partial interviewer, who interrupts frequently to question and doubt:

I agree, it was strange we never thought to wonder what was happening on the other side of the Eagles' Hills. You always talk as if we are stupid, but if we are so stupid how is it we have lived for so long, safely and well, so much longer than you … Our story goes back and back, you tell us so, but your story is much shorter. But why should we have moved about and looked for new things, or wondered about the eagles? What for? We have everything we want on this part of the island – your word for it, you tell us it is a large island. Well, good for you, but what difference does that make to us? (13–14)

The Roman historian, assessing Maire's account, is more generous than his predecessor: "I believe the birth of the Monsters was the first bad or even disturbing thing to have happened to them" (32), particularly as the most profound consequence is the loss of the power to self-generate: "we, the Clefts, lost the power to give birth without them, the Monsters – without you" (21). The integrity of their bodies' self-generative functionality as well as their perfect communal accord are lost with the transparency of their language.

This also means that the nature of Cleft historiography has changed. Before the sexual divide, their history was constructed by consensus, consistent with their sameness. "What I am saying now is not part of this kind of recording," she remarks; " [the story] is told first among ourselves, and one will say, 'No, it was not like that,' or another, 'Yes, it was like that,' and by the time everyone is agreed we can be sure there is nothing in the story that is untrue" (9). Only then is the story preserved by "the Memories" – chosen Cleft children who receive and pass down that story "as it was told to them" (8). Maire reports that the Clefts' first serious disagreement – ever – was over what details of "the first monstrous babe" should be passed down to the Memories: "what was the point of the story if it left bits out?" Maire now suspects that "a lot was left out," an accusation no pre-Squirt Cleft would have made, and she falls back to "what we all know," just the facts: "no one wanted to feed the Monster.… That first Monster babe had a bad time" (18). The story she is being prodded to tell now she understands to be a product of the males' "kind of recording": "that is how we became Hes and Shes, and learned to say I as well as we – but after that there are several stories, not one. Yes, I know what I am telling doesn't add up to sense but I told you, there are many stories and who knows which one is true?" (20–21). What has been lost is the clear internal logic of the Clefts' pre-Monster history. With the Squirts' appropriation and revision of Cleft history ("our story") that logic is disrupted. No wonder that Cleft history sounds either like nonsense or invention to the Squirts.

Although he seems empathetic,[13] this unnamed Roman historian is a craftier storyteller than he lets on. As he finishes the transcription of Maire's account, he begins to discredit it as a "smooth tale, told many times" – a tale that is "not untrue" but "useful" (21) – even though earlier this interview is described as so "informative … I am putting it first" (7). He "spares" the reader "too unpleasant" details, unable (or refusing) to "bring myself" to "reproduce that other fragment here" (21). Yet this suppression of "raw and bleeding" details that "I don't think it would have been easy to fake" (24) tantalizes the reader, leaving to one's imagination the "ingenuity of the cruelties thought up by the Old Females" (21), the "revolting, sickening truth" (23). In a betrayal to his claim of objectivity, he recommends to those who might take offense at even this version, that they "start the story on p. 29." If *we* flip to page twenty-nine, we too will skip entirely the only direct transcription of a Cleft's voice. Thus, although the Roman goes on to "establish my credentials here, right at the beginning of my story," his own motives are divided, as he gives with one hand what he takes away with the other. Loftily declining to reproduce the entirety of Maire's statement, he characterizes his own version to be "speculative, but … solidly based on fact." Early claims of good faith are compromised by obfuscation, judgmentalism, acknowledged fabrication of details and unacknowledged contradiction: "I shall make [their eyes] blue because of the blue sky and blue seas" (78); "They probably had brown eyes" (170); "The long hair [of the Clefts] is my invention" (44).

Concealing his own name, which remains "dark" (24), further erodes our trust. Claiming that "what kind of man I am" is not "really of importance in this debate" (6), he interrupts the narrative continually with personal and professional observations that *reveal* what kind of man he is: a cuckolded older gentleman, either too tired or too humiliated to do anything about his young wife's deceptions other than patronizingly warn her to "be careful" with the powerful political friends she has made through his connections. Of his children he reports little, except for a memory of overhearing a childhood discovery of sexual difference. To his daughter's exclamation, "Why have you got that *thing*," his son announces "[b]ecause I am a boy … and what he is saying dictates a whole series of postures" (thrusting his pelvis out; pushing his erect penis down and letting it spring up).

The interpolations also tell us a great deal about his sense of historiography and historical change.[14] The historian does not explain his preference for the title *Transit* rather than *The Cleft*, although in retrospect that preference reflects his interest in evolution and movement in space.[15] His methodology is organized around the discernment of "parallel Lines of Memories," not only the differing narrative histories offered by Clefts and Squirts, but also the lines that bridge those histories to our own. He thinks often, therefore, about the nature of time itself, as well as the nature of narrative:

> We Romans have measured, charted, taken possession of time, so that it would be impossible for us to say, 'And then it came to pass' ... for we would have the year, the month, the day off pat, we are a defining people, but then all we know of events [among Clefts and Squirts] is what was said of them by the appointed Memories, the repeaters, who spoke to those who spoke again, again, what had been agreed long ago should be remembered. This historian has no means of knowing how long the Clefts' story took to evolve. (101)

The speculative nature of his enterprise – with "no means of knowing" such a great deal – frequently trips him up. There is evidence of the "discovery" of fire in the documents, evidently; "we easily look back now," assures the historian, and see the Squirts sheltered during a thunderstorm and watching lightening spark brush fires. Reminded of "something familiar" in the "frisking," "leaping," "flashing down from the clouds," and in the strong currents of their river, "we" can see the helpless Squirts "suddenly" – like a bolt of lightning – knowing that fire can be tamed, and doing so. But perhaps, he self-corrects, "'suddenly' is not right, perhaps it should be 'slowly'. What causes these changes where something impossible then becomes not only allowed, but necessary? [And] *why?*" (105). Good questions he cannot answer, beyond further conjecture and admission that "this historian, previous historians and all future chroniclers" face, "brought to a stop" by records that are "crabbed and cracked and faulty" in the telling. He seeks "some kind of tale, with that internal logic, not always perceived at once, that seems a guarantee of verisimilitude" (136). Verisimilitude is by definition, however, not truth.

The evolution of a story is not random. Whereas the Roman doubts aspects of the Squirts' written histories, he positively discredits the Clefts' oral histories, as if these were more easily tailored and corrupted: "We all know that in the telling and retelling of an event, or series of events, there will be as many accounts as there are tellers.... Whose version of events is going to be committed to memory by the Memories? So, at last, the tale, the history is finished, to the point where no one will actively dispute it"

(136). His problem: there is the version of the "Old Shes," and of Maire, whose version "[w]e may be sure that Old Shes would not agree with"; and there is the version forwarded by "us," "the boys," whose "records were full of anecdotes, sharply remembered events involving the Old Females, who certainly would not agree with one single word agreed on by us" (137). In saying so, he contradicts an early assurance that he would produce a narrative *both* communities, male and female,[16] could agree with.

His interpolations are laced with thoughts about the "interested" constructedness of history itself, and also about the dubiousness of historians' truth claims. Given the nature of the discrepancies in a set of historical accounts, he wonders whether any such account is more like "rumour" than a factual story, "[a] tale expressing some kind of deep psychological truth" (142).[17] He suspects the male insistence of "priority [over female] was a later invention" (29), an intervention in the Clefts' history of female priority, and their communal Memories of reproductive independence. Yet the Roman is no different from his professional forbears, connecting *his* version of Squirt history to the future of the Empire he has served. He sees in the Squirt leader, Horsa, "an ancestor of us," with his/"our" "need to conquer [what we see] … what we know is there we have to know too" (216). That ambiguous, tautological statement, with its elision of risk and surprise, leads to this ironically shortsighted forecast of Roman history: "Why should there ever be an end to us, to Rome, to our boundaries? … I sometimes imagine how all the world will be Roman, subject to our beneficent rule, to Roman peace, Roman laws and justice, Roman efficiency" (216). Many centuries later Joseph Conrad's Charlie Marlow has a similar thought, imagining early Britain colonized by the brute force of Roman legions. But Marlow sees nothing benign or "beneficent" about a ruthlessly "efficient" overpowering of a land (hardly a "civilization," presumably) of natives whose inferiority is proved by their inability to defend themselves. The Roman historian, anticipating Marlow again, glimpses a Roman empire weakened by the needs to conquer and "have"; he nevertheless "secretly" deems the ancient Horsa, with his urgent "need to know that other wonderful land," to be a Roman. "One of us. Ours" (217).

The Roman's claim to "separation and autonomy" as an historian is subverted by his attention to, and identification with, early human males, themselves drawn to the females like moths to a flame or, more dramatically, to the mouth of a volcano. The eruption of Vesuvius prompts the Roman to think again about The Cleft, and to muse on these landmarks' similar histories. Both explode, killing bystanders with "poisonous fumes" and "a noxious powder" (rock-ash and gas, from Vesuvius; bone-ash from pulverized remains of Cleft sacrifices). Symbolically the landmarks are inverse images of one another, like the sexual genitalia: one is phallic, the other vaginal. The reported implosion of The Cleft leaves questions "that in their own way are as difficult as the ones we ask over the great volcano, which we must assume will one day blow again ... the outburst of Vesuvius tells us we may not assume permanence for the coastlines of islands or even the islands themselves" (259). The exact location of The Clefts' island has never been determined, pointing to "impossible origins" not only of our sexuality, but also our speculations.

The same indeterminacy marks the origin and conclusion of the narrative itself. After the close of his history, the Roman had "not expected to say any more on this subject" (258), but he offers one final speculation on the parallel between the explosions of The Cleft and of Vesuvius. The Roman's own story aligns with Horsa's frustrated tale of "'longing', 'wanting', 'dreaming'" of "that other shore I saw there, gleaming like a dawn" (250–251). His own speculative "shouts into the past" (251), however, are questions for which "there need not be answers" (251). This is a gloomy reprise of his earlier characterization of history as "whispers from the past, the immense past, voices that repeat what has been said by other voices." He surmises earlier that historians must ask questions based on "what we know, what we have experienced – and our questions disappear as if they were stones dropped into a very deep well" (170–171). At least in that case, through "the process of listening" (136), something may be heard; the well itself is a resonant image of "sources" and of the aural echo chamber through which sound is transmitted. Now, the simile shifts. He expects nothing to come back: his questions are compared to "throwing stones into the sea" (251), lost forever, without expectation of response. With a final maxim of "Let it be," he stops listening for history's answers, and stops writing.

It is tempting to ask why the narrator-historian wrote this story in the first place? No historian's motivations are innocent – he admits that – but his story settles nothing. By the end of "my story," we are left to understand that this "history" is no such thing, only a fictional reconstruction of remnant, corrupt texts whose content sounds admittedly implausible – more like myth or legend, thinks the Roman, "attractive hazy fables" that account for impossible origins: "our own [national] history ... too bursts forth out of myth, with Aeneas" (26). There is no epic hero in this story, however. The Squirts' first effort at nation-building utterly fails. Within sight of this "other shore" that their leader, Horsa, dreams of reaching, they are blown back to their starting point. Led home in disgrace, Horsa is given nothing short of a severe scolding by Maronna, leader of the Clefts and possibly his mother. She stands screaming at him, "so full of anger, while he stood there, limp, guilty, in the wrong," failed in his journey and in his responsibility to several young boys who had come with him, and perished. This humiliation leads to a moment of tender embrace, indeed a spark of love, the historian imagines: "There, in Maronna's arms, loved and forgiven, somewhere in Horsa's restless mind had started the thought: Tell her about the wonderful place I found, yes I will. She'll want to see it too, I am sure of it. She will understand, yes, she'll come with me, we'll go together, I'll make a ship better than any we've made, and we'll land together on that shore and …" (258). A hopeful vision of another voyage to a better place, to a place of romance, and a new home and community for the couple rises up: "together on that shore and …"

These are the final words of the official history. The romance ending is tempting … but would Maronna, just scolding him for foolhardiness, leave everything she knows for his dream? The narrator intrudes one last time to get the last word, and to snatch that temptation away. The ellipsis is ambiguous: and … what? Endless bliss? Doubtful. Another chance? Success? Or another shipwreck? The Roman's own final intervention is a betrayal of history, although he probably would concur now with a statement from Jeanette Winterson's *The Stone Gods* that "Stories are always true … It's the facts that mislead" (53). What the Roman produces is not a history book but a locked "archive of the heart." This expression too is from *The Stone Gods,* to which I will turn momentarily; its tropological usefulness here has to do with etymology. The word "archive" specifically refers to a repository of *public* or institutional records (from Greek *arkheion*, repository of official records, from *arkhē*, government). An archive of the heart is thus something of a contradiction in terms. Yet it is an apt term for this narrative. These documents are archived public records, long suppressed for (sexist) ideological reasons. The Roman historian's excavation and reconstruction of (male, textual) transcriptions of (female, oral) Memories, point over and over again to a "deep psychological truth" about Rome, and about the historian himself. While musing on the weak manipulations of predecessors to contain a narrative of social and sexual origins and thereby justify a logical (and dubious) claim for male priority ("Man does, woman is"), the Roman's self-reflexive craftiness and in(ter)vention expose a hermeneutic incapable of displacing, much less breaking free of, his own romantic nostalgia for a utopian island, "an other shore," of sexual and domestic peace. He is shipwrecked.

"SAME OLD STORY": *THE STONE GODS*

The Stone Gods (2007)[18] reprises many of Jeanette Winterson's common themes: her attention to the desires of body and imagination, and to romance, sexual and literary; to the facts and figurations of history, evolution and stasis, repetition and echo, parallel lines of memories. There are other common tropes: the creation of "new words" for new worlds; the presence of "monsters"; the lure of an "other shore," a horizon of desire, and the apprehension of being lost on the voyage, shipwrecked, yearning for home. They share a gendered view of the degradation of the contemporary world, charging a masculinist technocracy responsible (although never made accountable) for the uses and abuses of technology. They share a curiosity about what non-gendered society might look like, and how the evolution of humanity might be described not simply in terms of a biological economy that organizes our "natural history," but also in terms of libidinal, moral, and political economies that give birth to the more purposeful movements of our political and personal histories.

The setting of *The Stone Gods* lies temporally at the other end of the speculative history sketched out by Lessing. Mankind's urgent drive for technological mastery of "Mother Nature" leads to a rocket technology that is "fuel-greedy, inefficient and embarrassingly phallic" (although they have since switched to the more efficient flying-saucer shape). Our species' obliviousness to the risks of overreaching and unseen consequences brings both accelerated climate change and a nuclear war, wrecking the natural and man-made worlds alike ("We had no idea how much effort it would take us to make a bad copy of what Nature had given us for free" [86]). As in *Oryx and Crake*, this third world-war history evolves "naturally" from the era in history, identified as the 1980s, in which "materialism became the dominant value. If you couldn't buy it, spend it ... it didn't exist" (136). Here too, much of the population lives in an area called "Wreck City," another "No Zone" that recalls Atwood's Pleeblands: "no insurance, no assistance, no welfare, no police. It's not forbidden to go there, but if you do, ... it's at your own risk" (151). Yet most so-called Wreckers regard their home as safer, and freer, than the alternative.

The novel opens with the announced discovery of a new world, a blue planet to replace the "run-down rotting planet" (7) of Orbus, a version of our Earth: "the chance of a lifetime. The chance of many lifetimes.... we searched until we found the one we will call home" (4). In the sighting of the new planet, the masters of Orbus find a place "perfect for new life" (6), fulfilling a myth of renewal and rebirth, a "new beginning" for the civilization of "the Central Power" (e.g., the West). Although the narrator tells an interviewer that the move to Planet Blue is "the opportunity to do things differently" (4), the President of Central Powers gives a more likely scenario, one of conquest: "it is understood that any discoveries belong to us. He [the President] compares us to the men who found the Indies, the Americas, the Arctic Circle; he becomes emotional, he reaches for a line of poetry.... – *She is all States, all Princes I ...*" (5). Donne's lines about the universe of desire will echo throughout the novel. But the President, an unlikely lover, clarifies his terms: "Monsters [any indigenous creatures] will be humanely destroyed, with the possible exception of scientific capture" (5). The new government will be democratic; non-democratic powers such as the Caliphate and the Pact members will not be permitted to go "within a yatto-mile ... We'll shoot 'em down before they land.... The way the thinking is going in private, we'll leave this rundown rotting planet to [them], and they can bomb each other to paste while the peace-loving folks of the Central Power ship civilization to the new world" (7).

Recalling Atwood once more, the Central Power itself is the handmaid of a vast gen-tech corporation, "MORE-*Futures*," which has bought out – essentially *is* – the government. Seeing itself as replacing a Reaganesque economics of greed with a new "economics of purpose" (136), it is "not about making money: it is about realigning resources" (136), a linguistic spin that the narrator well recognizes as veiling its real purpose. It is not a free country anymore, she says. "It's a corporate country" (59), one that plans to transplant the rich only in a ship-liner called the *Mayflower*. Spike, a so-called Robo *sapiens* who will loom large in this story, adds that "[y]ou made a world without alternatives, and now it is dying, and your new world already belongs to 'they' (*sic*)" (65). The robot predicts more of the same on the Blue Planet – and indeed, the very first effort to manipulate the environment of that planet technologically leads to the abrupt onset of a new ice age.

Just here the narrator identifies herself for the first time: "My name is Billie Crusoe." Like Jimmie/Snowman in *Oryx and Crake*, she is an employee of "Enhancement Services." She is also a romantic and an anachronism, living in a seventeenth-century farmhouse called "Cast Out Farm" in the middle of cultivated fields. The farm is a retreat from the "hi-tech, hi-stress, hi-mess life" beyond, and it stands like a monument, or like an "ancient ancestor everyone forgot ... a bio-dome world, secret and sealed: a message in a bottle from another time" (11). There Billie can preserve what is valuable (to her only, it seems) from the past:

pen and paper ("Why can't you use a SpeechPad like everybody else?"), and also the beauty and diversity and "life that fills every bit of uncultivated hedge and verge." She describes Cast Out Farm lovingly, as a place of fulfillment and abundance, savoring each detail of its flower and fauna, down to "the frogs [who] wait patiently to be in a fairytale" (12), like enchanted princes released by love. It is a place she feels responsible for, in contrast to the "rest of the world," which gave up that obligation at a high cost: "We made ourselves rich polluting the rest of the world, and now the rest of the world is polluting us" (31).[19] Billie's troublesome criticism of the Powers That Be lands her in exile from this idyll, and forced into a different tale, an adventure romance in which Captain Handsome, a space privateer who will take the first humans to the "brave new world" (46) of Planet Blue, "will defeat the dragon and be offered the kingdom … a vast virgin country bounded by rivers. Dragon, kingdom and … Princess" (47–48).

The novel is comprised of several linked stories of adventure, risk and romance, genesis and apocalypse. These act as the parallel Lines of Memories in the first section of this novel, narrative threads that present themselves as strands of textual DNA: fairy tales; the Bible; *Robinson Crusoe*; Captain Cook's *Journals*; Coleridge's *The Ancient Mariner*; the historical romances of Walter Scott and Joseph Conrad; lines from the love poetry of Shakespeare, Herrick, Wyatt, and T. S. Eliot. The novel has a "refrain" that is picked up from Donne's "The Sun Rising." Moments from contemporary science fiction also rise up – from Joanna Russ's *The Female Man* and Marge Piercy's *He, She and It* to Atwood's speculative fictions. Characteristically, there are also references to Winterson's own work. These threads are so tightly woven into the texture of this novel that its very form functions as an echo chamber, inter- and intratextually.

Indeed, "Echo" is a central trope in this novel. Already at work creating the history of this signal event, the embarkation to Planet Blue, the spaceship crew creates a beautiful fable, "the way all shipcrew tell stories" (50). It describes a series of planets, each a version of Earth – and each one a possible future or a possible past, each a place "real and imaginary. Actual and about to be" (39). This may describe in particular "a planet called Echo":

It doesn't exist. It's like those ghost-ships at sea, the sails worn through and the deck empty … It passed straight through the ship and through our bodies, and the strange thing that happened was the bleach. It bleached our clothes and hair, and men that had black beards had white. Then it was gone, echoing in another part of the starry sky, always, 'here' and 'here' and 'here', but nowhere. Some call it Hope. (51)

In the next episode of the fable, however, following an iteration of the novel's refrain (*"Chanc'd upon, spied through a glass darkly, drunken stories strapped to a barrel of rum, shipwreck, a Bible Compass, a giant fish led us there, a storm whirled us to this isle. In this wilderness of space, we found …"* [51]) the sailors describe finding a nameless white planet. Once ("once upon a time, once upon a time like the words in a fairytale") it held oceans, cities, and life, "naked and free and optimistic." And while in days past it was "a world like ours" (56), now it is a "bleached and boiled place" with "no future" (52), a "white-out" – as if its story itself had been erased.

As in *The Cleft*, Winterson presents a vision of an exploded civilization, covered in the white dust of bones and buildings. Below the charred surface is an "elephant's graveyard" in which, presumably, everything is remembered. In this Dantesque space are the "carcasses of planes and cars" trapped in an endless cycle of melting down and re-forming: "This was the inferno, where a civilization has taken its sacrifices and piled them to some eyeless god, but too late" (52). The captain of the spaceship asserts that this white planet is "where we used to live (55); it is one potential image of our own, contemporary world. While "Hope" is about to be actualized in the voyage to Planet Blue, the narrator, fearing "a repeating world – same old story" (49), wishes that this planet "could sail through space" toward a place, and time, beyond human reach, "where the sea, clear as a beginning, will wash away any trace of humankind" (22). Orbus, Planets Blue, Red, White – each is just one of a series of planets killed or maimed by human beings; Planet Echo is a template for all of them.

This trope of a repeating (his)story, as easily described as "a suicide note" as "a record of our survival" (39), is mirrored by the overall narratological structure of Winterson's novel. It resembles the structure of Russ's *The Female Man* in its fissuring into alternate temporal planes. While Spike reminds Billie often that everything is "imprinted forever by what it once was," that does not mean stasis: for all mankind's attempts to control his universe, she points out, this is not a "uni-verse" in which alternatives do not exist: "the end" has been man-ufactured. "You made a world without alternatives" (65), she points out, but the universe is "neither random nor determined. It is potential at every second. All you can do is intervene" (62).

This call for intervention is what distinguishes this vision of human possibility ("what is impossible sometimes happens" [63]) from the Roman's resignation: what is impossible may simply be unimagined. Billie's advantage over the Roman is being able to learn from an ideal teacher and historian, the Robo *sapiens*. "She" is in fact not a she but only in the form of one to make her more acceptable to humans. The robot "can remember everything – faces, information, numbers, conversation – and they can make connections. These are robots who join the dots. Ask them for advice, and they will give it to you: impartial advice based on everything that can be known about a situation" (15). Spike has no preconceived ideas or concepts; as for gender, it is a "human concept, and not interesting" (63), although she is not blind to the implications of gender in this world. She points out that as a Robo *sapiens* she is programmed "not to overmasculinize data. That has been a big mistake in the past" (145). So are all the decisions made through motives of "greed or power." Her in-human neutrality in all things means that "she can arrive at the best answers. We may not want to hear those answers" (133). Detail matters, Spike elaborates, in reaching any objective decision, "even the tiniest detail can influence a decision" (132). Connecting the dots, therefore, does not mean determining the arc of past events and taking the "logical" next step. Connecting the dots also means connecting them forward, speculating, projecting possible although not necessary scenarios: "the future is not sustainable ... Human beings will have to begin again.... With a pristine planet and abundant natural resources.... [A] hi-tech, low-impact society, making the best of our mistakes here, and beginning again differently" (32).[20]

Furthermore, such foresight is not infallible: when some random event causes an erroneous calculation in which Spike herself participated, the humans send an asteroid, meant to speed up Planet Blue's evolution into a viable habitat, slamming into the virgin planet early. The Robo *sapiens* dispassionately revises the vision of the likely, or even possible, future: Planet Blue is ruined for human habitation for the foreseeable future. The crew retreats to an underground base colony, leaving Spike to "power down." Two things happen, however, that alter the personal histories of Billie and Spike, and possibly human history. Billie makes a sudden choice, willfully intervening in her own history for the first time, not to return to Orbus with the crew. She jumps ship at the last moment to face extinction along with Planet Blue's dinosaurs but also with the Robo *sapiens* with whom she has to her own astonishment fallen in love:

Here is a moment in time, and my choices have been no stranger than millions before me, displaced by wars or conscience, leaving the known for the unknown, hesitating, fearing, then finding themselves already on the journey, footprint and memory each imprinting the trail: what you had, what you lost, what you found, no matter how difficult or impossible, the moment when time became a bridge and you crossed it. (80)

A fairy-tale ending after all? Not likely. Billie celebrates finding "the missing map.... She is the place that I am" (88). But Spike has already told her that "Love is an intervention. Hand over hand, beginning the descent of you. Hand over hand, too fast, like my heartbeat. This is the way down, the cliff, the cave. No safety, no certainty of return" (68). As the anticipation of death, "the hangman waiting" (80), gives "intensity" to Billie's "new life," this narrative veers toward tragedy, a story that "began and faltered.... that ended long before they should" (87). Still, this ending has a potential new beginning of sorts. Imagining someone finding their remains, Billie wonders whether this future (not necessarily human) being would know that "they came from another planet that was dying, and how, on our way to extinction, we traveled here to one new-born?" (85). Even the man-made apocalypse on Planet Blue is an intervention that creates the conditions for a future not possible before.

Well aware of the role of random events in the universe, Spike stages an intervention of her own, throwing out a "shout" to the future, a line of repeating computer code that she sets up to be broadcast into space toward a possible, but not necessary, recognition of some future consciousness, "[s]omeone, somewhere, when there is life like ours" (82). Even over the course of this opening section of the novel, what is "like ours" has also evolved: "ours" now includes the Robo *sapiens* who is becoming more and more "human," who has already evolved a heartbeat that Billie can feel. The Roman historian's notion of history as iteration is countered by Spike's notion of history as variable possibility. Whereas the Roman historian's masculinist standpoint speculates on the origins of a world he already knows and only seeks to explain, or justify, rather than to change, Spike's speculative standpoint acts as a catalyst for invention and intervention: creative connections, bridges of time lying "open at the border, allowing a crossing, a further frontier" (87). Robo *sapiens* is "the future of the world" (64) precisely because she recognizes no master narratives, no moral taboos, and no single destiny: "Every second the Universe divides into possibilities and most of those possibilities never happen. It is not a universe – there is more than one reading. The story won't stop, can't stop, it goes on telling itself, waiting for an intervention that changes what will happen next" (68).

The shout backward to the past is not the only possible direction. In this novel, there are shouts forward to the future: the shout that Billie calls "hope." Either way, or both ways, they echo and whisper, reshaping not only the story of the past, but of the present and future. These time-bridges are characteristically signaled in this novel by the appearance of portals of one sort or another, not an edge, over which one either stands or falls, but a "liminal opening" (146): a gate, a door, or a story – the "true" kind that "lie open at the border, allowing a crossing, a further frontier." Billie looks for those moments that open portals to her past, revealing "imprints from everything [she] once was," but also portals to the future – all her possible futures: "The final frontier is just science fiction – don't believe it. Like the universe, there is no end." The narrator reiterates her hope in novel stories, not those with "a beginning, a middle and an end, but ... [the ones] that began again, ... that twisted away, like a bend in the road" (87).

As she and Spike await death on Planet Blue, Billie thinks about and rejects her vision of "the Maybe Islands," a figuration of a dystopic state of mind that second-guesses past decisions and choices ("If only I hadn't ..."). This backward-looking vision is "a pristine place of fantasy that is really no better than the razor-rocks of misery" (84) because the possibilities one imagines in the past are closed off now: "The Maybe Islands are hostile to human life." Rather than shouts to the past, Spike proposes we message forward: "Now she was coding something different, for the future, whenever that would be. 'A random repeat, bouncing off the moon. One day, perhaps, maybe, when a receiver is pointed in the right direction, someone will pick this up. Someone, somewhere, when there is life like ours'" (82) – when and if history repeats itself on a planet "some call" Hope. But in sending out her radio signals Spike offers another possibility: "Everything is imprinted for ever with what it once was." She calls this "consciousness" (in humans) and cell memory (in computers) – and prompts Billie to realize that while "the universe [may be] a memory of our mistakes" (87), "there is no end" to the story of history. There is no "final frontier": "True stories are the ones that lie open at the border, allowing a crossing, a further frontier" (87).

This moment constitutes one of the novel's many temporal folds, which are troped spatially as well: it is an edge, a border, "as if this were the edge of the world and one more step, just one more step ..." (147). Characteristically for Winterson, this juncture of fantasy and reality, life and death, is troped sexually, a temporal-spatial intercourse coincident with a dying fall: Billie and Spike, human and robot, make love, discovering, as on "a journey on foot to another place" (90), "the unknown and known ... the strange that I am beginning to love" (88). The narrative is "a traveller's tale; I was the traveller" (91); it is also a conquest story of the capture of the "body-beloved" ("*She is all States...*"). As Spike is dying in Billie's lap, she picks up a book that the spaceship captain had given her:

Captain James Cook's *Journals*. This travel story bends us away from the story of Billie and Spike, to another story, of another Billy (*sic*). This Billy is a crew member of Captain Cook's ship, the *Resolution*, which landed in March 1774 on Easter Island. Mistakenly abandoned there by his ship, the distraught Billy is saved by "a shout; a voice that answers the silent place of despair" (105). The shout of hope comes from another abandoned sailor, named Spikkers.

Like the first Billie, this Billy is also "on two voyages at once": "the first of direction and course, and the second unpurposed and untried, if that voyage can be mapped. I do not know any man that has mapped it, for each must make the voyage his own, and record it in the secret places of his heart" (109). Surveying the treeless, stripped "wasteland" of Easter Island, he muses on the way mankind, whether "Civilized or Savage, cannot keep to any purpose for much length of time, except the purpose of destroying himself" (109). Images of destruction from the earlier section of the novel, the red dust of the soil, the exploitation of "an island [once] abundant in all things" (110), hint at Billy's own conclusion that "[i]t is as if, here, everything signifies some other thing: ... even the island, even the world are symbols for what they are not" (112).

Years earlier, Winterson wrote that "all islands are a metaphor of the heart"; here, this new world of Easter Island is so troped again: on this island is captured the loved one, where he is both celebrated ("I will set in the sky and name you") and jealously guarded ("I will hide you in the earth like treasure"). The Easter Island section of *The Stone Gods* is another retelling of civilization's self-destruction, through another form of environmental degradation: the felling of every last tree on the island, and the famous Stone Gods with them. Spikkers too is felled, hurtling from a cliff ("like a star out of its orbit" [115]) and dying in Billy's arms, and we hear the resonances of the earlier account of Billie and Spike. As Spikkers dies, his dream of returning to his native Amsterdam is fulfilled, thanks to Billy's conjuring, in the mirroring surface of a Delft tile, the image of Spikkers' canal-side home: "'Go in,' I say to him. 'Go in'" (116).

This is another temporal fold: at this instant, Billy reports (imagines?) "[a] white Bird open[ing] its wings." He had explained earlier that the soul of a man is not carried within him "like a shadowy shape of himself inside himself," and this is why the soul is "nowhere to be found at death." Rather, the soul is "like an albatross or frigate-bird" that follows the wake of a Ship, "for it does not keep its residence in a man's body, but in his purpose.... And what am I but a Ship in little, and above me the white throat of a winged bird?" (109). This ship is headed to that same

Amsterdam house, where "he [Spikkers] must make ready till I have finished my business here" (116). As Spike dies, Billy recognizes his own journey, unpurposed until this moment.

The third voyage of Billy/ie resonates with yet another narrative: this time, the author's. In the section titled "Post-3 War," we recognize Winterson's characteristic narrative bend toward the hidden story of her own birth. Indeed, one of the most surprising things about this novel should not be: in the end, it is about Winterson's career-long yearning to find what Fredric Jameson, analyzing the romance genre, calls "impossible origins" that are recovered with the achievement of perfect love. Winterson herself is the (barely disguised, in the end) historian and hero of all three stories, seeking the hidden treasure, the knowledge of love embodied in two perfectly joined bodies. Over her career Winterson has told this story again and again, set in different places, times, even dimensions. The paradigm for this novel's utopian world of love ("where every body comes") is figured this time as the womb where, she imagines, she enjoyed absolute maternal love.

But one does, after all, have to be born. In keeping with the voyage trope of this novel, Winterson's birth is described as a "shipwreck, the mewling infant shored on unknown land. My mother's body split open and I was the cargo for salvage.... Shipwrecked on the shore of humankind" (122–123). Prior to that landfall she was "[a]t liberty in my mother's kingdom, at sail on amniotic seas," or, in what we recognize as another resonant figuration, "walking on the inside, weight-free, like a spaceman" (129). The baby is at once a traveler and (buried) treasure, for who can know what a new life will be "worth": babies are "like a safe – no way to see what's inside and no guarantee that the effort will be worth the trouble" (122). Readers of Winterson will recognize how familiar are these persistent tropes of treasure, value, and worth, and especially of gambling, playing the numbers, and risk taking. This voyage to recover what she has lost ("the person whose body I was, whose body was me") is the hopeful work of mapping out a parallel universe in which she lives "an echo of another life": "it's like one of those shells with the sea inside it.... put it to your ear and the other life is there.... I always believed that I would see her again" (124–125).

This investment in her own future, like all investments, is fueled by desire, the spirit of speculation. Her currency is words – "everything signif[ying] some other thing"; her economy is in the careful saving and spending out of her stories, true "archives of the heart" (146), speculations on recovering the treasure she has lost. The economy of Billie's story is not the cynical "realignment" of resources, as the Central Power president put it. Hers is a wholesale (re)investment of resources, emotional and physical, toward the finding of her own lost world, the lines of her stories purposed toward reconstructing "the lost and found/found and lost" that is the "spiral in us," "like a section of our DNA," the story "we can't tell" (125). Thus, the blank simplicity of "the line that is the first line of this story – I was born" (120), as simple yet as complex as "I saw this today." This is the same opening line of the story of Billie's namesake, Robinson Crusoe – "*I was born in the year 1632*" (122). It also resonates within the story of another child, another "precious treasure" who loses first one and the other parent: David Copperfield, too, "was born," and now thinks himself "like the boy in the fairy tale" who "should be able to track my way home again" (chapter 2). These textual allusions comprise Billie/Jeanette's own literary lineage in fairy tales ("Only in stories does the thing come out fortunate and clean, gifted and golden" [122]); in travel and adventure stories; in nineteenth-century bildungsromans such as *David Copperfield* or *Great Expectations*.

Indeed, Winterson sees herself in the figure of Billie, as "a lost manuscript" (127), written in the DNA code of unknown authors. Her story "surfac[es] in fragments, like a message in a bottle, a page here, a page there, out towards an unknown shore"; or like the radio code that Spike has sent out to the future. Through a wide range of textual echoes, Winterson begins constructing temporal bridges to her "lost world," through textual echoes that float like messages in bottles or like "drunken stories strapped to a barrel of rum." However, the apparent directionless tossing of messages over waves eventually reveals a kind of path, and begins teaching her that her story has more directed or purposeful movement. Thus, Winterson's persistent song of herself becomes an epic voyage in its own right, as Billie explains to Spike:

"Loneliness is about finding a landing-place, or not, and knowing that, whatever you do, you can go back there. The opposite of loneliness isn't company, it's return. A place to return."
    "Like Ulysses."
    "Yes, like Ulysses who, for all his travels and adventures, is continually reminded to think of his return." (145–146)

Indeed, the return home is Winterson's archetypal plot, as early back as *Oranges are not the only fruit* (198), and pursued in *The Passion* as well: "I was homesick," Henri recalls, "from the start" (6). Retrospectively, he sees the irony: "And the heaviest lie? That we could go home and pick up where we had left off. That our hearts would be waiting behind the door with the dog. Not all men are as fortunate as Ulysses" (83).

Nostalgia and rapture are the touchstones of her emotional range. But the instant when "time became a bridge" is her paradigmatic chrono-type, connecting and weaving together parallel Lines of Memories. These instants are variously troped as images of "[a] seabird, a space-ship, a signal, speed of light. A shooting star" (129).

As in *The Cleft*, history is a "process of listening." But in this novel, the narrator never *stops* listening. Therefore, her ending holds out a very different promise. The "purpose" of mankind in so many of the novels examined in this book is to destroy. In both *The Cleft* and *The Stone Gods*, we watch landmarks made of rock – The Cleft; Vesuvius; Easter Island gods; the white, red, and blue planets; the concrete kingdoms of the West – all destroyed by mankind's insistence on control, demanded by a specifically masculinist myth of conquest: "*It will proceed as before: the fighting, the killing, the lack, the loss, for power, for envy, for every stupidity that man can devise*" (203). A repeating world – "the same old story" (49). Unlike the Roman narrator who concludes that little has changed or is likely to in our human nature, Billie is assured that many outcomes are possible.

At the end of the novel's third section, "Post-3 War," such an outcome – one of the author's narratological "bends" – suddenly stretches out before us. This Billie, another version of the first two, finds a manuscript lying on a seat in the Underground. The title is *The Stone Gods*. Reading at random, Billie thinks it is perhaps a dissertation on Easter Island; or, no, "a love story ... maybe about aliens. I hate science fiction" (119), rejecting, as we know, "final frontiers" and insisting on horizons. We suddenly realize that this manuscript is the narrative of the world we read of in Part I of the novel: the world that existed 65 million years ago. The effect of this is similar to the complex confusion created by the opening frame of Shelley's *The Last Man*, which asks us to understand the following text not as a memory of the past, but as a memory of the future. Similarly, the status of this text is suddenly destabilized, revealed to be a portal to past, present, and future all at once. The narrator herself feels the effect of the temporal vertigo: "I had a strange sensation, as if this were the edge of the world and one more step, just one more step ..." (147).

Thus in this section, the Billie of "Wreck City" does not simply find the manuscript. She claims that she has written it, and has found it again after leaving it on London's Circle Line, like one of those messages in a bottle. She reveals now to this iteration of Spike that the manuscript is hers, although now, because she *just* dropped it upon finding it again, its pages are "shuffled as a pack of cards." Like Offred's audiotapes, these pages will be reconstructed by whomever finds it next. No matter how she might originally have put the pages together, each person will create the story they want or need: "A message in a bottle. A signal.... A repeating world. Read it. Leave it for someone else to find. The pages are loose – it can be written again" (203).

Once again for Winterson, the art of imaginative writing intervenes in history. But so does love – and it is evident that art and love are essentially intertwined for this author. *The Stone Gods* is another Wintersonian "archive of the heart," a set of private documents and stories made public for the purpose of telling, *sharing* rather than fixing, controlling, or exploiting. The relationship between public and private archives in this love story for the world helps define a conception of love embracing more than a couple or a family, but a community well beyond one's specific place and moment in history. This more extensive form of love is a message broadcast to the future – be it the signal Spike sent in the first section or the intentionally left-behind manuscript in the last. Each message is bridge of time as well, surprising the one who finds it with a portal into her own memory and anticipation and, perhaps, with the discovery of her own new purpose. When, in the final section entitled "Wreck City," Spike invites her to stay rather than "get home" ("What is there at home that you want to get to?"), Billie decides, as she has in all the versions of her character to date, to say "yes" to staying: "the yes answering the yes seems like a creation-call, not a reply I had any right to" (179). But she recognizes the alignment of that moment with other such moments, epiphanic moments when "the universe itself said yes, when life was imperative, and either this can be read as blind and deterministic, or it can be read as the exuberance of a moment that leaves an echo on every living thing forever" (179). Billie insists on "the cosmic *Yes*," echoing another well-known moment of love regained a quest for home. "*Yes, I said, and Yes.*"

The "cosmic *Yes*" resonates through Winterson's universe in ways magnificently minute. It describes the "seconds before" the event of the Big Bang; it also describes the "yes" to life that was "My mother saying yes to my father," like Nora and Leopold. And now, in her own life, "when I picked it up like a radio frequency from a lost star, someone was saying yes to me, such a simple word I could not decode it.... A word that was the lexicon for a new language. A word that would teach me to speak again. The first word, the in-the-beginning word. *Yes*" (179). In other words, every articulation of this purposeful "yes" is a creative moment and an intervention with the potential of putting in motion a new universe of possibilities. The universe can be hospitable. But when mankind insists on having his way – with one another or with the earth – the result is always war, leaving dead, silent victims, who according to the narrator ultimately get "the last word" (197):

> No.
> No more war.

"IS THIS HOW IT ENDS? IT ISN'T ENDED YET": LIFE'S "WINNING NUMBER"

Toward the last pages of this novel, a random event strikes: the recognition of the radio signals that their Wreck City guide (aptly and allusively named Friday) describes as "a message in a bottle – except that it isn't in a bottle, it's in a wavelength" (202). This is the line of code that Spike on Planet Blue sent into deep space in the first section of *The Stone Gods.* The latest iteration of Spike not only is in the right place at the right time to pick up the signal; she is able to decode it, finding an account of a prior human space landing. Spike can also date it, revealing that it originated 65 million years before, corresponding to our calculation of the extinction of the dinosaurs – which we know now were extinguished by the mistimed intervention of the asteroid. This Planet Blue is "a world still forming" thanks to "the intervention of cynobacteria," hosting an atmosphere abundant with oxygen, and thus "a planet receptive to our forms of life." It is very like Orbus, once again, "*with the exception of the dinosaurs, of which we have no record on Orbus*" (202). As the *first* Spike predicted, the one who died in that Planet Blue cataclysm, it took a long time for another version of humanity to evolve that could include, again, the evolution of the Robo *sapiens,* a "missing link" to a better, smarter, more ethical species of human being. Spike is kin, it seems to me, to Hopkinson's Tubman, both beings who evolve quickly beyond "mere" human limitations. The Robo *sapiens'* neural nets are capable of *learning* self-consciousness, defined as "a scale of degrees concerning attention, self-referentiality, self-perception and self-observation."[21] As a model for a new human, Spike bridges the way from a historical reiteration doomed to repeat itself, having reached a sort of historical/temporal tipping point; Robo *sapiens* places humanity on a path that bends away from annihilation.[22]

The novel draws itself together around such choices – risky choices – all taken for the sake of finding one's way home, whether that home is with/in another person ("She is the place that I am"), or on a planet and in a time when humanity is no longer such a feckless presence, gambling away the resources of the earth for its own "economics of purpose." That purpose has led again and again to only one ending. But by leaving her book unfinished ("'this is as far I could go'"), Billie leaves open the possibility of yet another story and another world. At this moment in the text, the narrative unravels its multiple threads and reforms them into the kind of complex echo chamber described earlier. The echo recalls the first Spike and Billie's final hours on Planet Blue, as Billie holds the dying Spike's head in her lap (and only the head – she has dismantled the rest of her body to save power), and finds herself consciously watching the quiet snowfall:

snow fall like Leonids, sparking and starting new worlds that last a second, return, re-form, begin again, I wondered if there is a place beyond this, where the dark dice didn't play, where life itself became the winning number, not gambled away later by people like us who valued life so little that we lost it. (203)

Yet another figuration of the narrative task or purpose of this novel emerges: to spark images of new worlds and happier endings.

Another thread is woven in from the middle Billy/Spikkers narrative, and from the parallel narrative moment in that section: Billy holds the head of the dying Spikkers in his lap, the other islanders celebrating the victory of the "oaf with a stolen prize" who pushed Spikkers to his fatal fall:

And here, on my knees, is the little world I wanted to hold forever, lightly, as the world itself is held in the sky lightly, without threats or fears, without supports of any kind, its own self, a garden of great beauty in a field of stars.... No flag, no territory, no fortress, no claim, but this love. (203)

And a third thread, the thread of autobiography that so characteristically informs Winterson's work. This is not Billie/y, but "Jeanette":

She did love me, for the forty weeks that I was her captive and she mine. We were each other's conquered land.... We were the barter and the prize, what we played for, what we lost. The dark dice, a two and a one, one became two, then two became two ones. A kingdom lost in a single throw. It's risky, but it's our only chance. Come back one day. I'll know it's you. I can track you because we are the same stuff. (204)

In the final sentences of this interpolated passage, the identity of the "she" who is mourned is unclear, the stories seem so close: "*It was the last time we were together; her heart and mine. She did love me, like a star, light years gone.*" Is "she" Spike? Jeanette's birth-mother?

The novel highlights these confusions as matters of temporality, and the narrator proposes that the conventional splitting of time into three parts is incorrect. There are, she submits, only two: now and not now – suggesting again that past and future are not in fact distinct from one another. This perception accounts for the re-emergence on the final page of the novel of a scene that has been only barely submerged: the seventeenth-century farm house that Billie of Part I protected from the development and genetic tampering, with the stream running "through the middle [of the land] like a memory" and the track alongside. This is the house from which she was evicted by MORE-Futures' corporate security. But the "original" of this house – in fact, Winterson's own, real farm house – is imagined here as the place to which her pregnant mother would return again and again, "a place we used to go – her walking on the outside, me walking on the inside, weight-free, like a spaceman." It was a place, away from the press of the world, where her mother went to seek a sense of home and a way to "begin again": "we lean on the gate very often, and she says, 'This is our house,' and I can smell the wood smoke from the fire" (129–130). Unlike so many pre-vious fires (smoking chimneys, bombs and missiles, a nuclear explo-sion, asteroid impact), ignited by wars that destroy each version of our blue planet, this fire is a sustaining one, hospitably drawing in herself with(in) her mother.

On the next-to-last page of *The Stone Gods*, this stream running through the property appears again: "I know this track, this stream, I've been here before, many times it seems, though I can't say when" (206). This is the final time-bridge in the novel, connecting Billie of Orbus/Planet Blue to Billie of Post-3 War and Wreck City, to the author of *The Stone Gods* – and thus to a final version of a possible future in which Billie/Billy does find Spike/Spikkers, and in which Jeanette finds her mother. At this moment, Wreck-City Billie is herself dying, having been shot by secu-rity squads. As her blood drains out, the vision of home appears – and she muses on this wound that was "always there"; like Jeanette's wound, inflicted when her mother left her, a four-week-old infant, at the bottom of a track along a stream, hoping someone would find her. Finding her-self in the same place, Billie drags herself toward the track, where she knew what she would find: the farmhouse, with a fire burning inside. As the darkness behind her "pulls away" – presumably she is approaching her own "tipping point" between life and death – she reaches the gate. She hesitates, knowing she cannot "go back" if she crosses over. But the door opens and "It's you, coming out of the house, coming towards me, smiling … and I knew it would end like this, and that you would be there, had always been there; it was just a matter of time" (206–207). She lifts the latch and goes through. "It was not difficult," the narrator concludes, "Everything is imprinted for ever with what it once was."

Is this the impossible fairy tale ending? No doubt. Billie finds her mother in the visions offered a dying self, just as Spikkers reentered his house in Amsterdam. Yet the narrator claims this story is "true": "True stories are the ones that lie open at the border, allowing a crossing, a further frontier" (87). As Lessing's narrator notes, history is only accessible to one who listens, and so often we do not. But *The Stone Gods* insists that to do otherwise is the biggest risk of all, dooming us to "the same old story" and leaving unbuilt time-bridges to parallel Lines of Memories, bridges that might lead us elsewhere. If, as Tobin Siebers has suggested, one can sustain a faith in the revolutionary potential of repetition, then utopian hope remains through stories like Winterson's; if that faith is lost, as in our Roman historian, then the "nausea" of expecting only ongoing humiliations and failures is all that is left.

"THEIR OWN GENERATIVE PRINCIPLES"

It almost goes without saying at this point that the underlying topic of much speculative and perhaps all utopian fiction is history – but so, too, is the topic of historiography. Mary Shelley's masterpiece, *The Last Man*, is an early and spectacular example in this regard; its grim narrative of the future is spelled out by the Sibylline leaves that the author and her companions stumble over. The leaves of paper are scattered about, shuffled like cards, containing in no coherent order the details not of what *has* happened, but of what *will* happen: writing the future, not only the past – an archive of the future. This literary trope of discovered manuscripts is a narrativizing of memory *as well as* of anticipation. This should remind us of Atwood's *The Handmaid's Tale,* in which appended "Historical Notes," recording a keynote speech at the Twelfth Symposium on Gileadean Studies in the year 2195, reveal that the American social experiment known as Gilead did not survive. We can be relieved to know from these notes that Gilead no longer exists. However, the fragile prospect of freedom promised in Offred's counter-narrative is eclipsed by our eleventh-hour discovery that this entire "tale" is a wholesale reconstruction. These academic historians invest the tale with presumptions, often condescending, about what likely occurred. The tale's narrative is, if not entirely aleatory, molded by a structural logic that was not Offred's, any more than Cleft history is, as it is reconstructed by the Squirts and by our Roman historian.

The novels treated in this chapter expand the critique of "self-generating" knowledge that hamstrings speculative standpoint and discounts feminist knowledge. But they also extend that critique by insisting on narrative strategies that block paths dictated by master narratives. From a generic standing, these novels cannot be "pure" or "classical" versions of any-thing. There is no easy quiescence, nor any easy form of hope. The tra-ditional, narrow sense of an ending is widened by that disruptive "sixth sense" uncovered in Chapter 1: not by any physical sense, but a *sensing* of other temporalities, other pasts, present and futures, not coterminous but coexistent. The narrative denouement is complicated by the possibility of ongoing *renouement* or, better, "entanglement." David Hayman's notion of a "process text" (105) is exactly on target here. The self-thematization of this formal mechanism highlights some texts' resistance to "complacent conventions that see the text as pure product. And [that resistance] remains partly the recognition of the degree to which all texts do indeed contain the germ of *their own generative principles*" (108; emphasis added). Clearly, as Hayman suggests, these new and evolving principles will reshape nar-ratives, and re(de)fine the relationship between narrative and history in any given text: as a *fictional situation*, a process of self-generation implies "the new myth of the text" (107).[23] Narratologically, futurity lies in new textual myths, new metaphors, in hybridity, and in entanglement.

CHAPTER 4

Always coming home, in America
Enacting the romance of community

In a July 2000 interview, Evans Chan was coaxing Susan Sontag into describing her previous (and last) two novels as examples of "historical novels," a generic label she was resisting as too limiting and conventional. "Maybe," she proposes instead, "these novels [*The Volcano Lover* and *In America*] should be viewed as books about travel, about people in foreign places." She continues by noting that she traveled more after her first two novels, and came to value an experiencing of the world "not just in aesthetic terms, but also with moral seriousness.... I want for myself to take in more reality, to address real suffering, the larger world, and to break out of the confines of narcissism and solipsism."[1] In the context of the interview, Sontag is likely alluding to her previous two novels, *The Benefactor* (1963) and *Death Kit* (1965), both of them aptly characterized (and negatively, by many critics) as narratives measuring exactly those confines. The failure of the two earlier novels lies not simply in the belabored feel of their European pretensions but also in the failure of Sontag's (anti)heroes. *The Benefactor* teaches us that the narcissism of Sontag's own celebrated "Camp" sensibility takes one so far and no farther, creating a decadent dystopia of fetishized self-consciousness; *Death Kit* stalls in a similarly solipsistic project. The success of the later two novels is the "break[ing] out of the confines of narcissism and solipsism" in her own fiction, and in her discovery and exploration of her own utopian sensibility.

What does Sontag gain from this correction of her interviewer – and indeed from this acknowledged adjustment in the trajectory of her own fiction writing? A great deal it turns out. Sontag's remark signals a decisive turn, in her later fiction, toward the idea of a community of readers. The metaphor of travel deepens from a merely formal dimension to a psychological and finally ethical dimension. These dimensions come together in Sontag's later fiction, which consciously takes advantage of the travel or quest format so characteristic of the romance and later, the genre of the novel.

But Sontag's fiction moves beyond the novel's "mandate of its own normality"[2] as she employs one of the subgenres she left out of her piece, in *At the Same Time*, on "innovative or ultraliterary or bizarre" narratives. In the 2004 essay, "Outlandish: On Halldór Laxness's *Under the Glacier*," Sontag casts her eye upon the kinds of narratives "that deviate from this artificial norm and tell other kinds of stories." Among these subgenres she includes novels that "proceed largely through dialogue," that are "relentlessly jocular"; novels "with characters who have supernatural options, like shape-shifting and resurrection; novels that evoke imaginary geography."[3] Her catalog of "outlandish" narratives includes "Science fiction. Tale, fable, allegory. Philosophical novel. Dream novel. Visionary novel. Literature of fantasy. Wisdom lit. Spoof. Sexual turn-on." Among the novels she sees as occupying "the outlying precincts of the novel's main tradition," she names *Candide* as the precursor to *The Benefactor*. As with all narratives searching for "best possible worlds," the real journey is, as *The Benefactor* makes clear, a psychological one, although her hero Hippolyte's journey fails for precisely the reason Sontag identifies in a 2000 interview: the protagonist's narcissism and solipsism.

Candide also haunts, in a more complex way, the pages of Sontag's final two novels. This has to do with Sontag's interest in getting "beyond the confines" of her earlier narratives' peculiar claustrophobia, toward a commitment to ethics that is not treated previously in her fiction. With this extension into the ethical, Sontag's later novels become specifically utopian narratives designed to attract a community of readers affiliated to one another by a new social contract. This society is one characterized by a commitment to sympathy, plurality, and to what Sontag refers to as "the exercise of freedom." Sontag's relationship to postmodernism is complicated; her increasingly fervent commitments to art and to a certain moral aestheticism make it difficult to see her as an advocate of postmodern relativism. Yet the recalibration of Sontag's own affiliations translates her fiction from the early anti-bildungsroman narratives into open-ended romances of community that reject "the formal necessity of Utopian closure."[4]

In a certain sense, every novel included in this study thus far is a kind of "historical novel," even when the narrative records the history of the future. Almost without exception, each focuses upon the interactions of personal and national histories by pursuing a position of agency within those narratives. Given the focus in Chapter 1 on bildungsroman narratives, my readings dwelled on the central characters, although to summon to mind now the figures of Marianne, Lauren, Larkin, and Tan-Tan is to realize how vivid is the historical backdrop against which their lives are staged. Chapters 2 and 3 considered novels more interested in the shape of history generally, particularly in (re)producing narratives of historical difference and, sometimes, accounting for sexual difference at the same time. Either way, "the same old story" cannot be a feminist story. It is a way of being nowhere in the negative sense, complacent rather than aspirational, complicit rather than curious and creative, inward-turning rather than outward-turning.

This chapter extends the discussion of history and form in speculative fiction by focusing on two nearly contemporaneous novels that explore the form and function of a particular myth: the myth of American exceptionalism and destiny. Susan Sontag's *In America* (2000) and Toni Morrison's *Paradise* (1998) are certainly utopian texts, although the characteristic time traveling seems to take us into the past rather than the future. The texts are therefore also manifestly historical novels. But the palpable presence of the future disrupts each one. In Sontag's case, the figure of the "author herself" hovers over her story of nineteenth-century European romantics; in Morrison's, the opening line signals that the "end" is already come. Indeed, the openings of both novels collapse temporal levels of the narrative, putting in play the temporal dynamics and the epistemological interrogations characteristic of the texts we have examined in previous chapters. *In America* and *Paradise* are therefore loosely speculative in mode, as well as loosely feminist (although in rather different ways). Both ultimately concern themselves with reflecting back, with a stronger objectivity than the historical "facts" behind them, the myths and projections that have shaped what we know about our past – and therefore what we believe about our present and hope for our future.

More specifically, I argue that both novels investigate American exceptionalism and how a sense of privilege has contributed to the utopian aspirations of this country. More importantly, both novels attend to the ways in which this "privileged" sensibility has distorted those aspirations. The texts do so by following the lives of sets of utopian travelers, particularly of women, whose own personal histories exemplify both the promise and the limits of calling America their "home." Both authors consider the contradictory nature of America's celebrated myth of welcoming all who come to her shores. But Morrison pushes harder on the inhospitableness of America, not just in terms of race but also sexuality, offering a tough-minded critique of the ways in which "inclusiveness" and exceptionalism are at odds with one another, historically, politically, and ethically. Morrison's novel also offers a direct, if more challenging, approach to recovering the utopian dream of an America in which all citizens know themselves to be at home. (This theme is taken up again in her recent *Home: A Novel*, published in 2012.) *Paradise*, she noted, "need not solve those problems [which the novel raises] because it is not a case study, it is not a recipe." However, it is more successful than Sontag's in making visible to us the hopeful possibilities of the future in the vision of a just community. *Paradise* offers (as Morrison says of novels generally) "something in it that enlightens, something in it that opens the door and points the way."[5]

In her award–winning *In America* (2000), Sontag pursues a utopian romance balancing individual and community, intimacy and abstraction. This novel's protagonist is an artist – a diva of the theater. She is what Sontag calls a "striving woman."[6] Maryna Zalenska is extremely work-ful – equally idealistic, equally desirous of love – and persuaded that "work," and especially the "work of art," *can* not only create but transform society. Picking up the tropes of theatricality from her earlier novels, where they are mostly associated with personal theatrics and their erotic efficacy, Sontag presents acting as professional art-work, and the theatre as a uniquely liberating space in which an actor creates herself, and can re-create new aesthetic and social connections with her audiences.

In *In America*, Sontag signals interest in utopian aspirations even before the narrative begins. Its epigraph, from Langston Hughes, reads simply "America will be," announcing that the essence of America – or, at least, the essence of the *myth* of America – is its state of constant transformation into something else: its active futurity, its constant modernity. David Morris reminds us that America "in some sense *is* postmodernism,"[7] yet America's attachment to an anachronistic myth of exceptionalism proves to be, in Sontag's novel, a drag on American progressiveness. Whereas reviewers of *In America* have argued about the novel's problematic status generically because of its "typically" postmodern metafictional devices, one aspect of the issue has been overlooked. The novel, postmodern or not, falls squarely into the formal genre of utopian narrative. In an opening chapter labeled "Zero," to signal a sort of proleptic prehistory to the story, the narrator, Sontag "herself," speaks from the present, as if from the wings of a stage. With obvious references to her own work and allusions to her personal biography, "Sontag" disrupts narratological decorum, "stretching our world" by extending generic narrative boundaries.[8] The narrator describes herself as "so exotic a stranger" (17) to the persons whose lives she will be tracing in this novel; in other words, she is the typical outsider of utopian narrative, like William Morris's "Mr. Guest," who intrudes in order to observe and to record. Like Morris/Guest, Sontag is a time traveler,[9] although in this novel, "traveling back to the past" (19) rather than to the future in order to glimpse the "seeds of prediction" (23) that would determine what America's future, which encompasses Sontag's present and beyond, would look like. Sontag's work, Janus-faced in its irony, looks backward in order to look forward.

What interests Sontag about the work of her latest protagonist is her relation to art, a kind of work with transformative potential. The heroine of this novel is an actual historical figure, a famous Polish actress named, originally, Helena Modrzejeswska, who emigrated in 1876 with her family and a small entourage of friends to the then–frontier town of Anaheim, California. (Anaheim is now, of course, only a few miles from that quintessentially American utopian fantasy, Disneyland.) Having had a "dry run" in a remote Polish mountain, where the cohort would summer in order to "inscribe their own vision of an ideal community" (63), this heroine renames herself "Maryna," and with her husband Bogdan and several other Polish couples sets up an explicitly Fourier–based phalanstery seeking the "unencumbered freedom" (65) they did not find anywhere in Poland. The taste of freedom is what brings them ultimately to California, a so-called Laborer's Paradise (121). Thus she explains her emigration to puzzled friends and stricken fans: "'Since when have you believed in paradise?'" her friend Henryk asks. "'Always. Since I was a child. And the older I get, the more I believe in it, because paradise is something necessary'" (38). And thus she and her friends dedicate themselves to new social roles, no longer as discontented intellectuals but as farmers remaking the land in the image of their bookish utopian blueprint.

Maryna's utopian ambitions take form in the theater, as she realizes the ways in which "work," and especially the "work of art," liberates an actor who can move in and out of identity at will. According to the narrator, "the theatre seemed to her [Maryna] nothing less than the truth. A higher truth. Acting in a play, one of the great plays, you became better than you really were ... You could *feel yourself* being improved by what was given to you, on the stage, to express" (32; emphasis added). For Maryna, the drive is to make this condition of self-improvement and subjective freedom permanent, residing equally in the imagination as in the world, and not a temporary thrill lasting for just a few hours of performance on a Polish stage. Maryna's drive is fully engaged in the theater's promise of futurity, its promise of new identities, and new spaces of performance. Her theatricalized sense of space and action will offer something the "Helena" from the Old World decides she can only discover on "this rude stage" (136), America itself, where freedom is tied closely to the belief that any American can, willfully, "make herself" and become, as we say, a "made" man or woman – one who has "made it."

The association of acting with futurity is essential to the novel's reconstruction of utopian aspirations and potentialities: "Yes," says Maryna early on, "that's what preparing a role is, it's like looking into the future" (48). The Anaheim adventure is clearly another great drama, a rewriting of personal and national history: a freeing from the past and an opening up to the future – a transformation of a social and personal history conveniently joined in the figure of this great actress, long since dubbed Poland's "national treasure." Her insistence on bringing her immediate family and a cadre of devotees along was justified by more than the merely personal. After all, she says, only slightly facetiously, "one can't do plays without other people" (78). More seriously, Maryna believes that her compatriots, "natural pessimists" (223), falsely chain History and Fate together, and that individual Poles including herself are left with too limited a stage upon which to act. Maryna and her husband Bogdan talk about the way in which the Polish people come to believe that failure is a noble thing, justifying a tragic history of national conquest from without, and national underachievement from within. Over and over again Maryna refuses to acknowledge that "the past is a fate" (223) that cannot be escaped; she deems her compatriots' expectation of, and compensatory admiration for, lack of success to be an historical and psychological bondage stalling cultural progress. Even before leaving Poland, Maryna sees the theater as the only possible mode of resistance: "Acting," she observes, "was a program for overcoming the slave in myself" (135). The temporary freedom "on the boards," however, was hardly enough for so ambitious and expansive a personality: "It's a new life, the life I want" (178) she says time and time again, "rewriting the past" (268).

The utopian work that Maryna and company set out to do on arrival in Anaheim, California is not acting, however, but the work of farming, the work of constructing community. As the novelty of manual labor and living off the land wears off and tensions increase within the group, the expansiveness of the rhetoric in letters back home starts to ring false. This highly self-conscious group quickly realizes that the fantasy of returning to pastoral bliss is just that, and they admit to a certain unintended falseness to their efforts. Maryna's eventual lover, Ryszard, accuses her of as much in the theatrical terms that pervade this novel: "Tell me you don't feel you are acting in a play. Tell me that there isn't one Maryna who is kneading dough, … and the other, standing beautifully tall as only you do, who gazes at herself with amazement and incredulity" (206).

Indeed, this ironical self–regard soon prompts Maryna to return to the theater, believing it is a more authentic arena for the enactment of both personal and social progressiveness and personal freedom than scraping out a living on the California hills. The party admit their ineptitude and give up on the enterprise rather quickly.[10] Maryna and company have gotten a little browner, a bit leaner; their hands have developed some calluses. But this kind of labor on the land, however equally distributed, however bracing and healthy, does not advance the horizon of utopia very far. The commune disbands with little apparent regret on anyone's part, and the land in Anaheim, "our Arden" (323), is eventually sold off. The California experience has particularly little direct effect on Maryna, the one who dragged everyone there in the first place, except insofar as it reinvigorates her will to self-invention. What America has offered her already is the sense of a constant Present, a continuous sense of possibility, a constant intuition of the Future. As Maryna's husband notes in his diary, "The Past is not really important here. Here the present does not affirm the past but supersedes and cancels it" (223). Maryna turns away, without nostalgia, from the romantic scheme of the "utopian household," which she has come to view as "so cramped, so ungenerous a stage" (153) rather than as the "perfect setting for a transformation," as she had once described California.[11]

Maryna's own belief in the art and the work of self-transformation on stage crystallizes into a dream to "Make it [her vision of an alternative life] real" (117) on a far grander stage, the wider public stage of expanding America itself. Only then does her project of American self-invention begin in earnest. Removing from mothballs her diva's mask, Maryna will be satisfied with nothing less than the conquering of another nation. Only after abandoning the pragmatic commune work and taking up again the work of transforming herself does she understand the full implications of her musings: "Surely you see," she says in a letter, "that I'm thriving on being stripped of almost all that made me distinctive to others and to myself" (173). For a woman who revels in "impersonating and transforming" (319), this stripping away liberates her from the "slavery," as she put it earlier, of the past, and makes room for the project of *re*making herself in earnest. This cannot take place according to a "blueprint" model for another utopian commonwealth, but according to transformative action on a much wider, a new and constantly changing stage, "this rude stage" (136), America, which she proceeds to tour from coast to coast, from north to south.

And at this work of transformation she labors far more passionately than she does at commune building. She pushes herself to mental and physical limits with a zeal that alarms even her husband who is accustomed to her extravagances. Even he is amazed by her inexhaustible demand for success, her fierce refusal to be limited by the past, and her drive to cultivate a new persona and new audiences. Novelty – or, perhaps better, "modernity" – is more important to Maryna now than any memory of greatness. Make it new. By the end of the novel, "Maryna liked being part of the wave of the future" (330) – and when she is acclaimed, finally, as no longer a great Polish actress, but a great "American" one, she triumphs in her new nobility, not the nobility of failure that fed Polish defeatism, but a nobility of the modern, of the successful.

Tracing the frank failure of the Anaheim farm to Maryna's "self-made" American identity, we might think Sontag denies positive utopian possibilities. In an early interview with Edwin Newman, Sontag mentions "having a kind of disillusionment about the possibilities of community, or even what people are capable of"[12]; Maryna echoes this skepticism when she asks, "Where is the community of friends I believed in?" (304). The novel certainly does reject a naïve view of utopia; indeed, there were hints the commune was doomed from the start – notably in the hovering narrator's suspicion that her cultured protagonists were already too ironical, not a naive "coven of tardy romantics" (10). And there is a more serious charge, against Maryna herself. Her husband, Bogdan, whose diary provides a running counter-narrative to Maryna's increasingly false note of romanticism, remarks that the natural optimism which is characteristic of Americans is rooted in their denial of the past. This fact has a paradoxical effect on the American national character, and he sees that effect in Maryna's exuberance: "The weakness of any attachment to the past is perhaps the most striking thing about the Americans. It makes them seem superficial, shallow, but it gives them great strength and self confidence. They do not feel dwarfed by anything" (223). Maryna's complex heroism brings with it an embodiment of certain quintessentially American virtues – her drive, her adaptability, her faith in the will and in the future. But she also reflects aspects of America that Sontag, in much of the rest of her work, admires least. As the author remarks in a Radio National (Australia) interview (February 6, 2000) with Michael Cathcart, "I am depicting in this book someone who adapts to the United States, to a culture that is both very money–minded and very moralistic."

Maryna's own drive for utopia in this novel is similarly and essentially self-centered; *New York Times* reviewer Michiko Kakutani calls her a "simple narcissist" in his February 29, 2000 piece on *In America*. The heroine's vision of the world has little to do with community, and more to do with a vision of modernity – which for her is itself utopia, a being-in-the-future that takes her from what she was, what she *is*, and allows her to ask herself what she *could* be. In her ground-breaking essay "On Style" (1965), Sontag described the history of art generally as "the history of different attitudes toward the will," a study of "the new ideas of self-mastery and of mastery of the world, as embodying new relations between the self and world." Any single work of art is "the signature of the artist's will."[13] This is an apt description of Maryna's extravagant "way of being" in this new world, with her insistence on paring down experience to nothing but the enacting of modernity, the continuous creation of those "new relations" with the world. But those "new relations" come at a cost to old affiliations and alliances, as we are frequently reminded by the hurt and critical commentaries of her husband, lovers, and forgotten friends.

Thus we hear the more pained meditations of Maryna's husband, Bogdan, who plays a subtle, insistent role in this narrative even as it is overshadowed by Maryna's pursuit of the tantalizing horizons offered by celebrity. While she seeks an authentic sense of personal and national identity in the coupling of her art and her audience, Bogdan's vision of paradise, which is "always being lost" as Sontag says elsewhere, is a more intimate vision of romantic communion that insists on returning to the problem of the body, rather than to the intellectual and the aesthetic. Bogdan's flirtation with homosexual desire seems at first hardly related to the "main story," and yet it runs as an increasingly strong countermelody to the siren song of exceptionalism and ambition that drives Maryna. His journal records "flashes of hope, like flashes of desire. Beginning again. . . . America is supposed to repair the European scale of injury or simply make one forget what one wanted, to substitute other desires" (209). These "other desires," "furtive pinings" staging themselves in "a new theatre of temptations" (209), are rewriting the script of Bogdan's life: "These reincarnated phantoms of endangering desire were already waiting for me. And with them a quiet, firm voice that says, as it never did in Poland, why not? . . . This is America, where nothing is permanent. Nothing is supposed to have fixed, unalterable consequences. Everything is supposed to move, change, be torn down, mix" (210).

Despite Bogdan's appreciation of a new sense of freedom and a hope for an "American" kind of happiness, the journal continues to record an old, imprisoning sense of shame: "Forbidden desire, straining to be liberated by foreignness. A curse of desire" (212). Bogdan feels at home nowhere, knowing that neither Poland nor America is accepting of his particular form of desire. Maryna, meanwhile, feels herself most at home during a long tour performing at American theaters, where indeed "nothing is permanent," and she can stage any and all aspects of her new identity. With Maryna herself off on a trip with her likely lover Ryszard, a dispirited Bogdan, missing his wife at the same time as he guiltily yearns for a male lover, is suddenly gripped by a vision of the enormous falseness of human relations:

My love for M. appeared to me as a great lie. Equally a lie are her feelings for me, for her son, and for the members of our colony. Our half-primitive, half-bucolic life is a lie, our longing for Poland is a lie, marriage is a lie, the whole way that society is constituted is nothing but lies. But I don't see what I can do with this knowledge. (214)

Maryna, on the other hand, celebrates a capacity for happiness supported by her liberating detachment from the past: "Happiness depended on not being trapped in your individual existence, a container with your name on it. You have to forget yourself, your container. You have to attach yourself to what takes you outside yourself, what stretches the world" – including "the joys of hand and mouth and skin" (216). She betrays not an iota of guilt regarding her own dalliances – although, Bogdan notes, "how would I ever know if something transpired between them? I have an actress for a wife" (214).

These differing visions of desire are never resolved, with Bogdan in particular swinging between hope and despair, trust and distrust. *In America* cannot resolve the tug of war between the grip of the past and the reach toward the future. This is a tension Maryna also sees in the American character: "[She] could never understand why in America there was so much suspicion of the arts, even among educated people, and so much antipathy toward the theatre.... Yet there was no end of young women in every American city who thought (or whose mothers thought) they were born for the stage" (352). Yet she harbors no doubts about the centrality of the theater and her role in it, in *creating* desire and the kind of thoughtfulness and regard that can change our relationship to ourselves and to others: "You could do *everything* with the voice ... Your voice rises, effortless, unhurried, and pure – enchanting the whole theatre into reverent silence. Who did not feel proved, then and there, by Isabella's noble plea [in *Measure for Measure*]?"[14]

Is Maryna's self-promotion what Sontag meant by "adapting to America," this unique individualism, tied so closely to will, to work, and to success – and so lacking in loyalty and sympathy to the dreams of others? And what is to become of Sontag's intentions toward recuperating the viability and seriousness of utopia for our own time? In a damning review of *In America*, Carol Iannone describes the novel as the epitome of Sontag's career in its display of intellectual affectation and irresponsible posturing and counter-posturing. No surprise, then, that the reviewer compares the character of Maryna to certain aspects of Sontag herself, both figures "now largely retired from [their] utopian endeavors but still seeking metamorphosis in art."[15] But Iannone misses the import of *In America*'s deeply ironical conclusion. If there is a "utopic sensibility" to be found in Sontag's novel, exposing it requires a shift of the frame by looking away from Maryna's theatrical history and toward the textual staging within which that drama is played out. This novel's form, for all its connections to the theatrical, has a generic agenda of its own, and Sontag's fictional work actively engages it.

In 2001, Sontag identifies the "education of feeling"[16] as the primary aim of novels generally, and certainly this is the case with every one of her own. But Sontag's approval of the novel's sensibility of feeling is reanimated with something more modern: the self-conscious interest in embodiment and display that theatricality offers. Sontag reconnects the novel's role as aesthetic education with her interest in theater's political possibilities for recovering human agency and freedom. If Sontag had believed unreflectively in the twin powers of theater to transform and transcend, she would not have written the closing monologue in the voice of America's most successful nineteenth–century American, Edwin Booth. Complete with italicized stage directions that blur generic boundaries of novel and drama, the monologue seems motivated by an interpretive error on Maryna's part. As they rehearse *The Merchant of Venice*, Booth objects to Maryna's "I feel your pain" gesture of touching Shylock's shoulder. She adds this gesture of sympathy just when Shylock's paradoxical status as insider and outsider is most appallingly on display. In his famous "do I not bleed" speech, Shylock forces each member of his audience to confront the presence or absence of sympathy toward him, to face his or her prejudices and ethical understanding. Shakespeare's genius was to make this a deeply uncomfortable moment for any honest person. Booth thus charges this gesture with inauthenticity. Fear of Shylock's pain would have been a more realistic response, he asserts, for "being in pain is very combustible" (370). To touch Shylock at this moment could never soothe his emotions, but only ignite them.

Edwin Booth should know about the facile underestimations of theater's political and emotional dynamics. We meet him drunk, self-indulgent, and morbid, aware of his brilliance and success, but haunted by historical reality: his brother is the Booth who murdered President Lincoln in the theater: "even a box in a theatre is a stage."[17] While he famously stars in the Shakespearean histories of *Hamlet* and *Richard III*, Booth is condemned to see himself playing a bit part in a singular historical tragedy. This actor's life stands as an ironic critique of aesthetic detachment: is it a mere accident, a coincidence of historical contingency, that one of the most politically dramatic moments of American history is enacted in a theater by the brother of America's most celebrated actors? Perhaps, but in America, the myth of a constant present and the irrelevance of the past obscures the effects of a willful ignorance of the influence of historical contingency. Such willed ignorance, now in the early twenty-first century as then in the late-nineteenth century, as often threatens the ethical and political progressiveness of an idealized American national character as it does promote it.

Maryna's interpretive error may seem trivial, but it is a critical error and a typically American one: the conflation of "willing strenuously and taking for granted" (344) the easy, self-aggrandizing solution. Minor characters like Booth, here, and like Bogdan throughout the rest of the novel, help to correct Maryna's strenuous willfulness. "'Our community is like a marriage,'" Bogdan's journal quotes Maryna as saying; "and suddenly I'm on my guard. I don't mean *our* marriage, she says, laughing. I mean a marriage that's matured by compromises and disappointments and abiding goodwill" (219). Booth invites us, along with Maryna, to find the compromise between the purity of the ideal and the complexity of the real: "Every marriage, every community is a failed utopia," remarks the narrator, "Utopia is not a kind of place but a kind of time, those all too brief moments when one would not wish to be anywhere else" (175) – the kind of moment that Winterson, for instance, would assign to the bed. If Bogdan and Maryna have found compromises within their union, so too have Booth and Maryna: he is her "'husband in art,'" and she is "'as naked [to Booth] as if you were my bride'" (387). Thus partnered here at the end, Booth can gently propose to Maryna that

we can improve the moment. Maybe, I'm not sure, you *can* touch me. I'm not entirely averse to a new piece of business here. I am not so pledged to tradition. And I have an absolute loathing of empty repetition. But I hate improvisation. An actor can't just *make it up*. Shall we promise each other, here and now, always to tell first when we're going to do something new? We have a long tour ahead of us. (387)

The reconciliation of thinking and feeling, intellect and sympathy, self and other, commits Maryna to the sincerity that Edwin Booth requests, delivered onstage in touches of what Jill Dolan calls "gestic moments of clarity." These moments are transformative, even "utopian" moments,[18] insofar as they connect to a "practice of reception" (and *not necessarily* a "program for social action"). This novel ends with the open vision of just such a utopian moment, pointing toward an erotics of art *and* an ethics of art. Through her recreation of these late-Romantic forbears, Sontag proposes to us – the audience beyond Maryna's and Edwin's – a utopic sensibility grounded in desire for the other, in the romance of the couple. Booth's crucial lesson is that the cultivation of *sympathy* should be the highest ideal for an artist who intends to turn an audience from the specter of historical tragedy and toward a cautious intimation of hope.[19] "*Utopia [is] at the horizon of a voyage (travel)*" says utopia theorist Louis Marin,[20] and Maryna may discover her utopia after all, not in cultivating crops, but in cultivating imaginative sympathy. Booth's proposed promise is "here and now, always" (380) to lay bare desire, and the actors' discourse and decisions will inform new, future possibilities on stage.

Gestures of affiliation or sympathy performed willfully, either through art or through political action, stage the best hope for a positively transformative society, as such moments reconnect one individual with another and recall their responsibilities *to* one another. Sympathy urges a common cause, a communality and a communion, an affiliation with progressive possibilities for the self and/in her community. The fragile Edwin Booth, clearly traumatized by his own unique place in American history, is the one who delivers that hopeful message – although it is worth recalling Sontag's own highly criticized appearance in Sarajevo as director of a controversial production of *Waiting for Godot* in 1993. This moment in Sontag's history exemplifies one of the most rigorous biographical instances of the affiliation of Sontag's own political sensibility and political commitment with "an ethical idea" of the theater[21] and indeed, of literature and art more generally. Sontag's insistence has always been on the value of ideas and ideals, even (or especially) in a time that "is experienced as the end – more exactly, just past the end – of every ideal."[22]

What has remained consistent throughout Sontag's career is a continued call for faith in art's fundamental power to change human sensibility. This is the message of Sontag's latest essays and speeches that, like her final novel, exhort us toward a *reconciliation* – her term – of the nostalgic and the utopic in our modern world. This sense of reconciliation, between old and new, real and ideal, pervades her 2003 *Freidenpreis* presentation keynote in Berlin:

"Old" and "new" are the perennial poles of all feeling and sense of orientation in the world. We cannot do without the old, because in what is old is invested all our past, our wisdom, our memories, our sadness, our sense of realism. We cannot do without faith in the new, because in what is new is invested all our energy, our capacity for optimism, our blind biological yearning, our ability to forget – the healing ability that makes reconciliation possible. (*ATST*, 203)

This stance is anticipated in *In America*, in which the complex marriage of Maryna and her spouse Bogdan, and later the "artistic marriage" of Maryna and Edwin Booth, are strengthened by the abandonment of naïve idealism, and by willing compromise to the demanding and endless dynamic of reality and desire. This compromise can only finally be negotiated through the exercise of imaginative sympathy: "If literature has engaged me as a project," remarks Sontag, "first as a reader and then as a writer, it is an extension of my sympathies to other selves, other domains, other dreams, other words [*sic*; for "worlds"?], other territories."[23] Whereas *In America* bothers the idea that America is the utopia of exceptionalism and individualism, it nevertheless does avow a commitment to a fragile utopic sensibility based on an ideal of a sympathetic community, an audience, whether of theater spectators or readers.

TONI MORRISON'S *PARADISE*: MAKING ROOM FOR UTOPIA

Although they are published only two years apart, it is hard to imagine at first glance two more different meditations on American utopianism and national character than Sontag's *In America* and Toni Morrison's *Paradise*. The question of race, for openers, could not be much further from Sontag's overt concerns; there is scarcely any mention of looming wars or national crises. Maryna's self-description as a "slave" to her own history can only resonate ironically against the explosive national histories that set up every one of Morrison's novels. Morrison herself notes that "only African-Americans were not immigrants in this rush to find a heaven. They had left a home. So they're seeking for another home.... Native Americans were being moved around in their home."[24] As the authorial narrator of *In America* points out, these wealthy Polish émigrés choose to flee a national history that enervates their ambition; but traveling in steerage with, say, Irish and fellow Polish peasants, much less sardined in slave holds, is the last thing they would imagine for their pilgrimage to "Paradise." When the hard labor of field work in "our Arden" proves too arduous, most of the group – with the exception of one young, still idealistic couple – returns to the intellectual crafting of plays, journals, essays, and other forms of composition, a mode of work they thought they had left behind.

Yet a juxtaposition of these two nearly contemporaneous novels highlights important concurrences. Both are historical novels, with the shadow of the present insistently darkening the narratives of immigrants,[25] the one set in the "laborer's paradise" of California, the other set in Oklahoma and the West, which, according to Holly Flint, "functions [in the standard American history] all at once as a geographic utopia, a battleground for the American way of life, and an imperial dreamscape" (588). The glimmer of a "more perfect" America in both these novels will be a heterotopic vision in which the obsistence of difference, and not the insistence on sameness, will undergird a notion of freedom, of progress or futurity, and hope. In *Paradise*, as in *In America*, the community is imagined through symbols of its desire and through the revisions of its dominant narratives. The vision of the future is imagined and indeed structured through reenactments of possibility, and through a commitment to the ongoing work of utopia as an ethical project. These two novels are both attending to something about the way we live now.

In Morrison's novel the centrality of human coupling and human community, in *all* its heterogeneous possibilities, figures in two ways: first, within a narrative of sterility that deadens the heart and the history of the utopian town called Ruby; and second within a narrative of regeneration that offers not just a future for Ruby, but a proposal for the progress, if not the "redemption," of America itself. As in Sontag's novel, the vision of a redeemed future rests upon an insistence on love, not only written on the body as human affection, but also figured abstractly as an ethical system of sympathy and care. Such an ethic, they propose, will direct a national body-politic far healthier than the one we inhabit at the moment. But what Morrison offers and Sontag does not is a vision of *hospitality* centered in a particular and robust notion of love. In important ways Morrison's speculation builds off of earlier feminist utopian vision, but she exceeds her predecessors in her frank insistence on the inclusion of all outsiders, including the reader, in that communal vision.

Paradise amplifies Morrison's statement that "all paradises in literature and history and ... in our minds and in all the holy books" are "special places that are fruitful, safe, gorgeous and defined by those who can't get in.... [All] paradises, all utopias are designed by who is not there, by the people who are not allowed in."²⁶ This is in itself not an uncommon point of view, but her way of putting it highlights what she sees as utopia's deepest flaw: its inhospitableness. In fact, *Paradise* is easily recognizable as a contemporary instance in a tradition of female utopian writing Morrison does not mention, a tradition that has at its center the image of "the house" as a sheltering, safe, and free place, bountiful in things quite different from rivers of milk and honey. Think of the country house in Sarah Scott's *Millennium Hall* (1762); or E. M. Broner's stone house in *A Weave of Women* (1978), the home to "wayward girls" of all sorts; Winterson's stone farmhouse in *The Stone Gods*. Or, as we will see in the Chapter 5, the "house in Karaj" outside Tehran in Shahrnush Parsipur's *Women without Men* (1989). These are all instances of homes that function as "islands" of safety, to which women make their way as if inevitably drawn, to find themselves incorporated as they are into a community that protects difference.

Like those stone houses, the Convent outside Ruby, Oklahoma is also located beyond the bounded and ordered, on the margin of "civilized" society, in the "middle of *nowhere*" (45, my emphasis). But the extraordinary nature of this "big stone house," also "in the middle of nothing" (169), is its explicit figuration of utopian desire at its *most* embodied, containing "in itself" both the phallic and the womb-anly. Its spectacular detailing – sculpted busts with jutting nipples, faucets with knobs like breasts and spouts like penises – are all "obvious echoes of [the owner's] delight" (71). The very layout of the place is heterogamous, with its "glowing tip" (72) visible from outside, and walls of its basement "womb" (229) found inside. The sexual body is rather obviously the metaphoric model for this communal body, as Siebers proposes. Not only does the image of sexual body/-ies animate the very form of the structure, but also, in its "emergence and symbolic character," the house symbolically catalyzes an opening up to, a widening embrace of, diverse outcasts and strangers.²⁷ The stone house's very history partakes of variable, heterogamous expressions of desire, first of a brotherhood of male embezzlers and party boys. They are succeeded by a religious sisterhood that supports and cares for Native American girls, outcasts of colonial intrusion. Finally, it stands as the "Convent," where still "[t]hey took people in – lost folk" (11).

This gradual incorporation into community figures the utopian trajectory of Morrison's appealing vision for America, a trajectory and a vision fueled by "questions about sexuality and gender [that] lie at [postmodernism's] heart."²⁸ As Patricia Storace brilliantly points out, the town of

Ruby itself, "named after a woman, is a kind of woman itself, a kind of ideal woman constructed by men for themselves and representing the ideals of the men. These women are, in a sense, where the Ruby men live" (66). The tension surrounding the eroticized structure of the Convent finds its way into figurations of erotic desire that proliferate throughout this novel. After the Convent house itself, the most spectacular of these tropes is the set of so-called fucking rocks. The search for these rocks is motivated by the character Grace in response to her now incarcerated boyfriend Mikey's description of this appealing monument to eternally fulfilled desire, located – where else? – in a town called "Wish":

A man and a woman fucking forever. When the light changes every four hours they do something new. At the desert's edge they fuck to the sky tide of Arizona. Nothing can stop them. Nothing wants to. Moonlight arches his back; sunlight warms her tongue. There is no way to miss or mistake them if you know where they are: right outside Tucson on I-3, in a town called Wish. Pass through it; take the first left. Where the road ends and the serious desert begins, keep going.... One hour, tops, you'll see loving to beat the sky. Sometimes tender. Sometimes rough. But they never stop. (63)

This is a monumental image of the postmodern heterotopia offered by Siebers – a living monument, in fact, because the polymorphous perversity of the rocks (or the persons looking at them) is such that descriptions of what the rock formation actually looks like are as varied as the individuals who observe them. The rocks "would have been a tourist attraction" Mikey tells Grace, but for the fact that so many regard the formation as obscene. In what way obscene, however, no one agrees for none can agree on *what* is being seen. Some local Methodists construe the rocks as "two women making love in the desert," while others "after an equally careful examination (close up and with binoculars) said, no, they were two males – bold as Gomorrah" (63). Mikey himself claims to have touched them and "knew for a fact" the rocks are man and woman. In any case, he observes, all these outraged critics, rocking between visions of graceful loving and enthusiastic fucking, "know they needed the couple … needed to know they were out there" (63). For this reason no one dares to destroy them. This implicit protection of the rocks stands in ironic contrast to the murderous mandate the men of Ruby will issue, frightened by their own, frankly obscene, projections upon another stone monument to love, the Convent itself.

This stone monument to desire is located nowhere anyone can find, for all the precision of Mikey's directions. His description inspires Grace to search for it, asking people along her aimless train route. Thinking perhaps the place is "too small for the map," she asks some state troopers, who mirthfully deny having seen fucking rocks – but have seen "'lizards do it.' … 'Cactus, mebbe?' 'Now there's a possibility.' They laughed themselves weak" at the idea. But for Grace, the reality or not of the rocks becomes less important than the idea of them, and what they monumentalize:

The eternal desert coupling, however, she held on to for dear and precious life. Underneath gripping dreams of social justice, of an honest people's guard – more powerful than her memory of the boy spitting blood into his hands – the desert lovers broke her heart. Mike did not invent them. He may have put them in the wrong place, but he had only summoned to the surface what she had known all her life existed … somewhere. Maybe Mexico, which is where she headed. (64)

This elusive vision of eternal, eternally evolving love animates and ulti-mately leads Gigi to an unexpected destination, where a fellow passenger has told her she will find not those rocks, but a second, nearer, figuration of desire: "a place where there was a lake in the middle of a wheat field. And … near this lake two trees grew in each other's arms. And if you squeezed in between them in just the right way, well, you would feel an ecstasy no human could invent or duplicate. 'They say after that nobody turns you down.'" This place, he says, is "Ruby. Ruby, Oklahoma. Way out in the middle of nowhere" (66). When she finds herself at a train sta-tion just there, she disembarks, seeing Ruby as a kind of way station to her ultimate destination: "I am not lost, she thought. Not lost at all.... She just wanted to see. Not just the thing in the wheat field, but whether there was anything at all the world had to say for itself (in rock, tree or water) that wasn't in body bags" (67). Between the Vietnam War, and the war at home on the streets, Grace has seen a lot of death, and not enough love.

It is no accident that both of these representations of an erotic utopia appear in the story of Grace, or Gigi as she more fetchingly calls herself. Although we never hear of Gigi actually visiting the embracing trees, we learn of others who did: Connie, the last survivor of the religious con-vent, and now the "new and revised Reverend mother" (265) of the new "coven"; and Deek, one half along with his twin brother of the "twinned leadership" of Ruby. Connie and Deek "competed with the fig trees for holding on to one another" (235), and the trees become, therefore, a vis-ible sign of unrestrained and unrestrainable desire. Given Ruby's proud self-image as an original all-black town, a racial utopia that has already lasted generations, the entangled trees also symbolize the town's great-est fear: the impurity of their line. As Ruby genealogist Pat Best realizes, *"everything that worries them must come from women"* (217) (italics in the original), in whose bodies the fruit of such corruption will grow.

The trees also stand as a prefiguration of the kind of utopian purity that the Convent women will exemplify: a generous love and hospitality so rare as to seem actually perverse and literally obscene in the eyes of Ruby's selfish and eventually menacing leading men. It is almost impossible in this context not to think of the mythic original of these trees entwined in each other's arms: Philemon and Baucis. The couple's unquestioning hospitality is so rare that they are rewarded by the disguised gods with stewardship of their temples, and with an eternal embrace in each other's woody arms at death. This couple signifies the longing for eternal love that the fucking rocks symbolize, but they point toward a model of generosity that acknowledges the divine in everyone. So keen is Morrison's attention to irony, however, that the replacement of the mythic linden and oak trees into which Philemon and Baucis are transformed, into two *infertile* fig trees cannot be overlooked. The revision draws this instantiation of pagan obedience and humility into a Christian, and markedly more negative, context. In the Scriptures (Matthew 21:18–19; 20–22, and Mark 11:12–14; 20–25) the fruitless fig tree is cursed by Christ, signaling condemnation of the Israelites. That tree was struck dead to the roots, with no hope, presumably, of generation in this or any future time (the death of old Israel). While this pair of fig trees lives on, it lives without issue, and without the gift of food for others' survival, as a fruited tree would have done.

By the time we are introduced to Ruby's proud population, the fruit of Ruby's embracing genealogical branches are dying right and left: Mavis's twins, Merle and Pearl; Soane's intentionally miscarried fetus ("a daughter perhaps?"); Arnette's baby boy, named Che by the Convent women, who survives a few days after being aborted, thanks to "the mop handle inserted with a rapist's skill ... [and with] the gusto and intention of a rabid male" (250) by its own "merciless" mother; the white baby who dies with his parents in a snowstorm the people of Ruby did not try hard enough to save them from; and finally, Save-Marie, the small daughter of a local couple, Sweetie and Jeff. The degradation and inhospitality of this town, "a backward noplace ruled by men whose power was out of control" (306) may already, it is suggested, be reaping its divine reward – no optimistic "reproduction futurism" here. And yet the Convent women worry about each and every baby, tending and speaking to them, even if, or when, the baby no longer lives, physically.

The theme of hospitality, then, is central to my reading of this novel's utopian sensibility. It is no accident that Ruby's Oven, at the center of the town's historical and hermeneutic controversy, no longer functions to feed anyone except, now, the "warming flesh" (104) of young lovers. In contrast, the center of the Convent community at the stone house is its kitchen, which feeds anyone who walks in, no matter what she is hungry for: "Left alone Mavis [a new arrival] expected the big kitchen to lose its comfort. It didn't. In fact she had an outer-rim sensation that the kitchen was crowded with children – laughing? Singing? – two of whom were Merle and Pearl [her dead children]" (41). Some time later, Gigi arrives at the stone house and is immediately "ravenous" (37, 69–70); a girl named Pallas arrives "starved," too (177). This hunger is, ironically, a mark of the threat these women present to the Ruby community. Each woman is a version of the original hungry woman, Connie, the "ravenous ground-fucking woman" who, after taking an erotic, blood-drawing bite of Deek's ear at the fig trees, is instantly shunned, no longer a play thing but a witch-like man-killer who would "eat" him "on a dinner plate" (280): "Who would chance pears and a wall of prisoner wine with a woman bent on eating him like a meal?" (239). When Pallas judges this place "free of hungers" thanks to its "blessed malelessness, like a protected domain" (177), she does not recognize her own hunger for safety from sexual exploitation – and for recovering her own integrity. She does sense the possibility that "she might meet herself here – an unbridled, authentic self ... in one of this house's many rooms" (177).

The fear of "unbridled" desire and genealogic contamination is the psychic ground in which Ruby's neurotic aggression against outsiders is cultivated. Thus, when the Convent, at the borders of a town as sexist as it is racist, is gradually reoccupied by a group of unrelated women, the men of Ruby can only read "female malice" (4) into every move that those "awful women" (10) make, with their "witch tracks" (11), with their animal desires ("like a shoat hunting teat" [276]), with their "liquids" of blood and liquor ("I hear they drink like fish too" [276]). These "loose women," every one of them an "easily had woman" (11), threaten to unravel Ruby's social fabric, "keep[ing] you from knowing who, what and where your children are" (278). The women's open display of hunger, desire, and hospitality draws people in, including Ruby's *own* women, who travel "out there," at the blue horizon, "minus invitation or reproach" (37), for food, medicinal potions, and the comfort that "[i]n this place every true thing is okay" (38). But the men's paranoid fantasies, fueled by the conviction that women tempt men to sin, lead them to the outright lusty attack that opens the novel.

Every road, muses Mavis in the opening chapters, "went somewhere didn't it?" (37). We learn that any woman with a desire to find that authentic self may appear to be "traveling resolutely nowhere" (138), but always ends up treading a pathway that is "narrow but sweetened with thyme" (225) – and with time, or rather a different sense of temporality. Late in the novel, Connie is described as "travelling in His time, not outside it. It was He who placed her there" (273). It is not just the Convent women, therefore, but also Ruby community women, who understand that "[t]he only way to change the order ... was not to do something differently but to do a different thing." One such woman, beaten down by the illness of her children and the intense claustrophobia of her life in Ruby, is Sweetie, who concludes that "[o]nly one possibility arose – to leave her house and step into a street she [Sweetie] had not entered in years" (125). A "walker going somewhere," Sweetie is accompanied by the latest of the Convent's new arrivals, Seneca, "the hitcher going anywhere." Both the familiar townswoman and the unfamiliar wanderer, "the wraith and her shadow" (126), are welcomed into the stone house, fed with whatever they need, and set to whatever work or task will teach them, as Lone says, "how to learn, to see for yourself."

This open attention to truth ("lies not allowed in this place" [38]) is at the heart of the Convent's hospitality, which "[n]ever saw a stranger inside" (43). Travelers there found "a swept world. Unjudgmental. Tidy. Ample. Forever" (48), supported by a vision of the "living God" in living men and women alike, and by the "endless work" of a Christian charity initiated by the Catholic sisters. Ruby's Convent has never locked a door against any person. Thus, the "flaunting parody" (279) of the novel is not the behavior of the women, "uncontrollable, gnawing" (279), but the behavior of the men, who exclude all difference, even among their own; as Morrison has famously said, "Our view of Paradise is so limited: ... it's really defined by who is not there as well as who is."[29] Thus the unintended parody of Ruby's annual Christmas performance of the story of Jesus, Joseph, and Mary, "no crib for his bed." In an ironical exercise of vanity, there is not just one Holy Family in the annual production, but *nine*, signifying the town's nine original founding families. By the time when this story is set, however, there are only seven on stage. Two of the families have been silently erased, for betrayal (local genealogist Pat Best surmises) of the community's insistence on the "purity" of its blood; that is, there were evil doings among the members of those families.

In the play, then, with seven sets of Holy Family on stage, Christ's parents inquire, "Is there room?" (209). In Ruby, the implicit answer to the god waiting at the door is, *not unless you are one of us, made in our image – not the image of who we are, but of Christian selves we fail to be.*

The admittance of "love" is entirely conditional, based on compliance to self-interested and mendacious narratives: "there was no pity ... they did not think to fix it [Ruby] by extending a hand in fellowship or love. They mapped defense instead and honed evidence of its need, till each piece fit an already polished groove" (274). Ruby's founding fathers had once sought freedom "Out There: space, once beckoning and free" (16), a space that offered "amplitude of soul and stature ... freedom without borders and without deep menacing woods where enemies could hide" (99). Now, *any* outsider is an enemy ("in this town those two words mean the same thing"), and the pasture from which this flock grazed could be only the one that "it had created ... grass from any other meadow was toxic" (212). The amplitude of vision they once had has narrowed to a single point, and the space offered for a "true home" is now "some fortress you bought and built up and have to keep everybody locked in or out" (213).

The utopian counterspace to this failed utopia is "out there" at the Convent, yet nearly every male citizen of Ruby sees not a place of amplitude and freedom, but a warning that "the entrance to hell is wide" (114). Over the course of the novel, there is nothing about the Convent that is untainted by the men's suspicions of it; even the Convent's signature barbeque sauce, craved by every man and woman in Ruby, is described as having a "heavenly reputation" from the "hell-fire peppers" that "grew nowhere outside the Convent's garden" (11). *Mustn't* there be something wrong with the urgent appetite for these women's "spice"? So runs the direction of guilty men's minds, as they construct the mental walls surrounding their community. By the novel's end, the narrator wonders, "when will they [the Convent women] reappear, with blazing eyes, war paint and huge hands to rip up and stomp down this prison calling itself a town" (308)?

But such vengeance is irrelevant to the desires of these women, and the trajectory of the Convent's history is moving another way. Once an embezzler's fortress against the law, the Convent has become a "real home" (213) to those who arrive with a desire to lower defenses and belong. The Convent's leader Connie, drunk and morbidly depressed for much of the novel, finally steps forward as "this ideal parent" who "locked no doors and accepted each as she was" (262). This stepping into God begins with her recollection of the aftermath of her affair with Deek, when she is shunned. The townspeople judge her association of the Living God with the body of "the living man" she met at the fig trees to be the work of the devil. Even Mary Magna, her Mother Superior at the Convent, meets her attempt to explain her love ("Sha sha sha, she wanted to say, meaning, he and I are the same," partners in the dance of love) with a silencing gesture that hardly assuages Connie's shame: "'Sh sh sh. Sh sh sh,' said Mary Magna. 'Never speak of him again.'" From the dance of Eros (*sha sha sha*) to *sha*me to the hu*sh* of her superior, Connie is reduced to the shell of the woman we meet early on. This reduction is confirmed, or so she thinks, when a "sunshot seared her right eye, announcing the beginning of her bat vision. Consolata had been spoken to" (241).

But Connie misinterprets. She has not been punished, but rewarded with a faculty of sight that allows her to see through people; literally, it seems, for she can see the unborn children of the women who come to her as well as the babies who have already passed from the physical world. Connie hears the women's thoughts, and can even enter their bodies – "stepping in" – and bring them back to life. A kind of "sixth sense," as with Tan-Tan's *eshu* and her gifted baby, connects Connie, reborn as a seer, with other-dimensional realities. Initially Connie resists this ability as sinful: "everything holy forbade its claims to knowingness and its practice" (244). Yet after years of serving a God who offers only a "refusing silence," Connie eventually comes to accept it as a gift from the God who embraces the holiness of all generous desires as virtuous rather than vicious. As her friend Lone convinces her, this "stepping in" or "seeing in" or "in sight" is a *gift* that "God made free to anyone who wanted to develop it.... The dimmer the visible world, the more dazzling [Connie's] 'in sight' became" (247). And Connie is rewarded again for her eventual acceptance of the gift. She is approached by one the novel's several mysterious traveling men – each of them a figure of physical or emotional desire. Whereas the man seems to know her, she does not recognize him. His words to Connie "licked her cheek," and she is charmed for the first time in years by "the way he had flitted over to her from the steps and how he was looking at her – flirtatious, full of secret fun ... [and how he] winked, a low seductive movement of a lid" (252). This man is the new image of the "living man," no longer impersonated by Deek, but transfigured into the one who speaks to Connie soundlessly, and whom she answers aloud, "as if anyone" could see him.

The hospitality theme is foregrounded just here. Connie, "*fully housed by the god* who sought her out in the garden" (283, emphasis added), enacts with her companions the "beginning" of a new world. Celebrating that other god and his welcoming voice she offers out to the women who have taken up there her own hospitable invitation: "'If you have a place ... that you should be in and somebody who loves you waiting there, then go. If not stay here and follow me.' ... No one left," as each of the women comes to realize "in no time at all ... that they could not leave the one place they were free to leave," with its "sweet, unthreatening old lady who seemed to love each one of them the best ... a perfect landlord who charged nothing and welcomed anybody" (262).

The Convent ceremony, in contrast to the Ruby version of the arrival of Joseph and Mary, offers room for everyone, in the "womb" of the house – not the attic, where madwomen live, but in the basement. As the women are asked to form a "template" by finding a position, naked, upon the floor, "[h]owever you feel" (263), Connie walks around each one and paints her body's silhouette. In this way begins a kind of rebirthing ritual during which each woman tells a story of the painful past that has brought her here. Connie invites each teller into a circle, symbolizing a love that does not "separate God from His elements" (244). This new dispensation celebrates a communal solidarity grounded not in the petrifying "8-rock" (or bedrock) of Ruby, but in a new, nourishing living rock from which springs the "bloodless food and water" that will "quench their thirst" and transfigure each one. This community acknowledges the virtue, rather than the vice, in difference. This ritual of so-called loud dreaming is frightening at first for these women whose presumed sins are always being (pre)judged. After the first session, "exhausted and enraged, they rise and go to their beds vowing never to submit to that again but knowing full well they will. And they do," eventually stepping in to each other in such a way as their individual tragedies are diffused among them all. Each one learns to "step easily into the dreamer's tale" (264), to share the dark memories of abuse and betrayal. Eventually, the women "[have] to be reminded of the moving bodies they wore, so seductive were the alive ones below," where the demons of the world "out there" are exorcised. Willing followers of Connie's generous god, they themselves are "revised" or transfigured in such a way the neighbors cannot help but notice a "sense of surfeit; the charged air of the house, its foreign feel and a markedly different look in the tenants' eyes – sociable and connecting when they spoke to you ... their adult manner; how calmly themselves they seemed.... [t]he Convent women were no longer haunted" (265–266). Their new dispensation has been achieved, the ritual transfigures "accusations directed to the dead" into forgiveness, old crimes "undone by murmurs of love" (264). This multiple birthing is another alternative to the reproductive futurism objected to by Edelman; these women seem to join Ruby's various spirit-babies on equal terms.

No wonder the chapter following the invention of the ritual is given to Lone, the town's one-time midwife (her skills now shunned by the "modern" young parents) and also a seer possessing the gift of insight. As noted earlier, no healthy babies are born during the "real-time" of the novel in the mid-1970s, as if the town's repudiation of her traditional ways cut the "family trees" off at the roots. Although she does not practice professionally, now, she does practice spiritually, to bring into the world the "words" of God, just as she has brought Connie into another, "gifted" world:

Playing blind was to avoid the language God spoke in. He did not thunder instructions or whisper messages into ears. Oh, no. He was a liberating God. A teacher who taught you how to learn, to see for yourself. His signs were clear, abundantly so, if you stopped steeping in vanity's sour juice and paid attention to His world. (273)

To the series of "empaths" whose paths we have followed – Lauren, Tan-Tan's *eshu*, perhaps the *douen* birds; Spike – we can now add Lone and Connie. These two also take on the responsibility of teaching others "how to learn, to see for yourself," to tease out and hone skills in perceiving *both* the physical and nonphysical worlds. *To pay attention.* Only a few may be truly gifted – but in every novel with such a seer or empath, it is made clear that everyone can possess this gift to some degree. Perception can be trained, just like any skill, but it is often easier not to see, not to attend to persons, worlds, ideas that do not conform to what we think we know.

This heightened attentiveness allows Lone, alone among the townspeople, to hear the men's vicious conspiracy against the women, to see the signs, and to warn others about the planned attack on the "Bitches. More like witches," and "worse, women who chose themselves for company, which is to say not a convent but a coven" (276). Fueled by paranoia and lust, the only truly communal decision made by these otherwise vain, divided, and duplicitous males is the one to invade the Convent and kill the women, a conviction that leaves them, ironically, "lighthearted and suddenly hungry" (282). While this near-erotic experience of violence takes place on July 4th, with its hopeful message of independence, no such liberation takes place. Neither shame nor guilt nor anger is assuaged, and the moderate preacher Richard Misner disbelieves most of the accounts he hears of what happened. Lone later "provided him with the livid details that several people were quick to discredit," firing back with stories that "[made] themselves look good … supported them, enhancing, recasting, inventing misinformation" (297).

The only defector from this monstrous hypocrisy is Deek, the one who so many years ago loved Connie, and then rejected her. He confesses to

Reverend Misner, in words that "came out like ingots pulled from the fire by an apprentice blacksmith" (301), that his life has become not simply inhospitable, but "uninhabitable" (302). He separates himself from his unrepentant twin brother, who had fired the shot that killed his former lover, Connie. Reverend Misner reminds him that it is the "Lack of forgiveness. Lack of love" (303) that has doomed Ruby's men, spurred on by their other religious leader, the fanatical Reverend Pulliam.

Like Connie, Reverend Misner is rewarded with his own vision, offered as well to his partner Anna:

> It was when he returned ... that they saw it. Or sensed it, rather, for there was nothing to see. A door, she said later. "No, a window," he said, laughing ... What did a door mean? what a window? focusing on the sign rather than the event; excited by the invitation rather than the party. They knew it was there. Knew it so well they were transfixed for a long moment before they backed away and ran to the car ... Whether through a door needing to be opened or a beckoning window already raised, what would happen if you entered? What would be on the other side? What on earth would it be? What on earth? (305)

Both petrified and jubilant at this vision, this "invitation" into some other dimension, Misner sees the window in the garden again, in the coffin lid of the only dead baby mourned openly in this novel. He is struck by the "beckoning" of this other dimension, "toward another place – neither life nor death – but there, just yonder, shaping the thoughts he did not know he had." Shaping, in other words, the next utopian horizon, "Out There," that will offer "the splendor" that is invisible to that congregation, but "lying in wait" (307). Morrison revives the images of doors and windows opening to the future[30] in her discussion of *Paradise* with Oprah Winfrey: "It's being open to all these paths and connections and ... [*unintelligible*] between."

The transcribed moment of "unintelligibility" elegantly tropes the "sense of perceptual uncertainty" that Timothy Aubrey, in an excellent piece on *Paradise*, correctly associates with the defamiliarizing narrative mode of the entire novel, which is at once "secretive but also in a sense excessively forthcoming."[31] However, the final chapter may not be actually "unintelligible." The aporia in the transcription of Morrison's comments is interesting: is the "unintelligible" thing there precisely the reader's own door or window to a new *rearticulation* of paradise, in each historical time? In preventing any stable interpretation, the novel leaves us looking through that imagined door/window, to another dimension in which the Convent women, presumed dead but mysteriously disappeared without a trace after the massacre, return to "visit" the living. Gigi appears before her long-incarcerated father; Pallas before her betraying mother; Mavis before the older daughter she abandoned; Seneca before the cousin who left her alone as a child. Connie's reappearance is more complicated, and significant. She is back as "Consolata," back in her original South American home whence she was adopted by the Christian nuns and brought to America. She is now in the company of Piedade, an indigenous female spirit who never speaks words but sings a song of "solace." In a signature example of Morrison's stealthy efforts to destabilize the reader's interpretive work and tease out new possibilities, this final scene in the novel links the attributes of the seductive "Living Man" who appeared before Connie in the garden, to the attributes of the "reborn" Consolata herself. The clues are precise: when Connie meets the traveler "he" knows her and reminds her that she knows him, but he has to inform Connie that he is not from town but "far country" (252). When he removes his hat "[f]resh, tea-colored hair came tumbling down"; he removes his "sunglasses – the mirror type that glitter" – to reveal eyes that are "as round and green as new apples." In the novel's final paragraphs, it is Consolata herself, resting in the lap of Piedade, who has "emerald eyes," no longer shaded by the sunglasses Connie characteristically wore in Oklahoma, once her eyes had gone dim; her hair is "tea brown." Returned, in essence, to love of herself, Consolata "enjoys the unambivalent bliss of going home to be at home – the ease of coming back to love begun" (318).

A PORTAL OF POSSIBILITY: "*SOMETHING TO DO WITH THE WAY WE LIVE NOW*"

Both Sontag and Morrison recall to us Wallace Stevens's lesson that "the imperfect is our paradise."[32] As Sontag concludes, paradise is always being lost, and she insists therefore on the ways in which the willful drive of exemplary American characters like Maryna must open out from individual desire: "Who would we be if we could not sympathize with those who are not us or ours? Who would we be if we could not forget ourselves, at least some of the time? Who would we be if we could not learn? Forgive? Become something other than we are?"[33] Certainly *In America* foregrounds a utopic sensibility that resists the fetishization of the individual so obvious in her earlier novel, and avows the centrality of a social space joined by the twin poles of action and imaginative feeling. Nevertheless, Maryna's reach toward her desire for America's future serves to solidify her "new nobility" as an American citizen. The elitism of her sensibilities and cultural affiliations does not suggest an embrace of the common man, but rather the endorsement of a privileged stage from which to mediate America's relationship to its own modern culture.

Morrison's vision, by contrast, invites us to a series of communal events that both solidify and, it turns out, undermine the community's moribund self-mythologizing: Ruby's explosive "Kentucky Derby" horse race; the town fathers' increasingly belligerent meetings; the dueling church sermons offered by Pulliam and Misner; the tainted KD/Arnette wedding; the idiosyncratic annual presentations of the story of Jesus, Joseph, and Mary. The lead actors' experiences of these events are, however, "textually subservient" compared to the care taken to report reactions and interpretations of each community member. The textual space of these competing narratives, the "multi-vocality" of this text, lies in distinct contrast to the domination of Sontag's novel by its heroine, Maryna. Furthermore, as previously suggested, Sontag is tone-deaf in *In America* to issues of race in particular. Class difference is acknowledged in the wealth and elitism of the group, who would never have considered traveling in steerage as so many of their compatriots did. But no African American or Native American makes a memorable appearance; Mexicans crop up only as "hands," or as objects of Bogdan's homosexual longing.

Although both novels explore the future in the present – those "seeds of prediction" – Sontag's celebrates the work of the will, consolidating a certain kind of driving American spirit that has served a certain version of this country – unnuanced and expansionist – very well. Toni Morrison's novel, on the other hand, spins out an alternative narrative that challenges more explicitly the effects of an anachronistic myth of exceptionalism and purity. But in doing so, *Paradise* offers a more sustaining and optimistic sense of hope and possibility. The fertility of Morrison's revised mythos springs from the heterogeneous forms of romantic love she explores. Morrison submits that for this very reason, the work of enacting the romance of love – whether between couples, families or communities – must include, as Tan-Tan learns from the *douen*, "all our senses" and faculties, physical and spiritual, rational and emotional.

Morrison's revision of America's original founding myths replaces corrupting arrogance and exceptionalism with consolation and pi(e)ty for acknowledged personal and national wounds. Morrison's attention to the excluded "migrants" – African Americans, Native Americans and now Mexicans – brings forth the complexity of what had been the "reverse side" of the American social fabric. Now, after this writer's subtle treatment, the reverse pattern surfaces as clearly as the front pattern – becomes, in fact, the front pattern.[34] The image of the slave ship sails into view once again, as in Butler and Hopkinson; but this new ship carries a crew and passengers who are "lost and saved, atremble, for they have been disconsolate for some time, shouldering the endless work they were created to do down here in paradise" (318).

The images of entangled lovers in *Paradise* – the fucking rocks and embracing trees – are most effectively animated in those utopian moments at the stone house, when the women dance, "[f]irst apart, imagining partners. Then partnered, imagining each other" (179), or when they "step into" each others' dreams, through the sympathy gained thanks to a willing coupling of minds as well as bodies. There is a faint glimpse of this sort of coupling in the relationship of Maryna Zalenska and Edwin Booth – but Maryna's pursuit of an audience is too self-centered to be openly hospitable. Sontag's novel ends with a fragile and ironical exhortation for care and compromise ("We have a long tour ahead of us") that is very different from Morrison's *un*ironical vision of the "endless work" of locating that "free place"[35] where a human(e) love is embodied. This utopian performative is very different from Maryna's, and it is offered out to anyone open to the "in-sight" that discerns a robust vision of community. This vision embraces and embodies what Aubrey calls "an open-minded negotiation with and between different kinds of otherness."[36]

Morrison's new mythos also springs from something more specific, and precisely located: "God's generosity," notes the narrator, "is nowhere better seen than in the gift of patience" (242). *This* love consists not simply in the humility of putting one's own will and self-centered desire aside, and certainly not in the Job-like suffering that Lauren rejects. It consists instead in the humanity of an enduring "wish for permanent happiness," however "thin the human imagination became trying to achieve it" (306). As others have observed, this "generosity" undergirds the novel's famous "effacement of race" in this novel. The author frustrates readers' efforts to identify racial difference among the women; and our ability in the last chapter to discriminate the quick from the dead.[37] Morrison's hope in and for her readership seems similar, at first, to Sontag's. As previously noted, Sontag considers the novel, and certainly *her* novels, to be romances (in the generic sense) leading to the "education of feeling" and the acquisition of a moral sensibility. For Morrison, the novel pursues something both more and less focused: first, the education of individual capacity for sympathy; second, the education of desire as itself a moral sensibility. The cultivation of an active moral sensibility engenders the kind of utopian sensibility that can reimagine and transform relationships between two people, reanimate ethical and political engagements, and make room for others on the transport carrying a community toward an aspirational horizon.

In this chapter I have traced erotic figurations of individual desire and intersubjective affiliations in two novels that represent utopian desire as erotic desire. Neither novel offers blueprints for new societies; neither author would regard that as a desirable task or even an ethical one. In this context, Morrison explicitly rejects, as Sontag would too, simple connections between her work and "any 'isms,'" particularly feminism, even though *Paradise* is celebrated for its envisioning of a "female reconstitution, both spiritual and communal."[38] Argues Morrison:

> In order to be as free as I possibly can, in my own imagination, I can't take positions that are closed. Everything I've done, in the writing world, has been to expand articulation, rather than to close it, to open doors, sometimes, not even closing the book – leaving the endings open for reinterpretation, revisitation, a little ambiguity. I detest and loathe [categories such as "feminist" or "any 'ist'"]. I think it's off-putting to some readers, who may feel that I'm involved in writing some kind of feminist tract. I don't subscribe to patriarchy, and I don't think it should be substituted with matriarchy. I think it's a question of equitable access, and opening doors to all sorts of things.[39]

Morrison constructs a model of utopia that envisions not simply the fulfillment of the individual, but the fulfillment of a community insofar (and only that far) as it embraces a model no longer defined by exclusion (the "necessary fall" [Flint, 607] of Ruby's African-American patriarchs). It is animated instead with a type of "utopian citizen" who speaks to the urgency of America's need to make of itself a home that is truly hospitable.

Morrison thus exceeds Sontag in her handling of fiction's own role in the staging of utopian desire and agency, and in her accomplishment of what others have called a "participatory reading and politics."[40] As Holly Flint's admirable essay proposes, we can learn from Gerard Delanty's recent work on new conceptions of cultural citizenship, which emerge from the "*learning* dimension of citizenship as a *constructivist* process" in the "informal context of everyday life."[41] Maryna's vision of her audience is still of a community set apart; but Connie's vision sees all "others," of any description whatever, who wander to her house. By the end, having been welcomed as they are, they are enacting their own rebirths, as described earlier, and reconstructing their identities. These transformations of identity call for an intersubjective in-seeing that Maryna, though an actress, seems to lack. Morrison's heroes are exceptional in a different way from Sontag's: in their attention to the ways in which stories – *their* stories, Ruby's stories, America's stories – interact. Morrison succeeds in offering what Aubrey describes as a "structure of empathy ... less individual-centered, less competitive, and more inclusive."[42] In an interview with Carolyn Denard, Morrison herself observes that the novel "suggest[s] something about negotiation that is applicable for the 90s ... something about the way we live now."[43]

Delanty argues that a new sense of citizenship "entail[s] both personal and cognitive dimensions that extend beyond the personal to the wider cultural level of society."[44] *Paradise* shows us that the life stories of the Convent women are the very stuff of her "hope" for America, not its detritus, no matter where each woman came from or what story she tells. The "endless work" of utopia in *Paradise* lies in the insistence on locating ways to interpret narratives that run against the grain, that are judged to be "nonsense," but that may tap a different source of wisdom. The work of interpretation can invent frameworks for thinking about individual and social identity, and for revaluating the central tenets of our American community. *Paradise*'s invention of the diverse communal space of the Convent, also a textual space of course, is the most hopeful turn of all. The active reader enacts the fluid, intersubjective affiliations where the education of desire, as well as of a new kind of feeling and sensibility, can take place. We are time- and space-travelers too, as we ask ourselves, *Is there room, in America?* If there is not, Morrison proposes, we need to open a different door, not just open wider the one we are standing at. Or perhaps we stop looking for doors at all, but seek "portals," neither doors nor windows but apertures, or bridges, indicating an "elsewhere," where desire, or "love," is shaped not by constructions of ego – self-love, in other words – but in the hospitality of the heart.

CHAPTER 5

Looking East for news from nowhere
Feminist mobility in Muslim women's speculative writing

One thing I discovered while scrutinizing my place in Paradise is that one ought to insist on the right to move freely in and out of it if one so desires. More important than Paradise is the freedom to move around without conditions; without qualifications; without permission. More important probably than the right to enter Paradise, is the right to leave it for no reason other than a totally arbitrary, whimsical desire to discover other horizons.

— Fatima Mernissi[1]

This final chapter's transition from well-known North American and British feminist writers to Arab feminist writers may be unexpected. Yet I hope it will be apt, after all, in a study that rejects exceptionalism and proposes an idea(l) of utopia as an embrace and performance of hospitality. For these narratives from the Middle East and Africa so clearly and robustly demand the "same impossibility": a worldly community reaching (for) a state of hospitality, a utopian commonwealth based on inclusion, not exclusion. If anything, this utopian imperative sounds the more urgently, emerging from Arab/Islamic traditions that regard hospitality as far more than a duty or some form of "mutual aid," but rather as a vital, moral virtue that lies at the heart of a just life and a just community. Furthermore, the following texts – particularly the narratives by Parsipur, Mernissi, and Alsanea – more directly address the nature of *the work left to do*, as individuals and as communities in search of a better world.

This study has persistently attended to what Jeanette Winterson calls "the strange that I am beginning to love." Recognizing otherness in oneself only prefigures the need to attend to the strangers that we are to one another – as partners, as family, as community, as nations. All the writers in this study seek paradigms for community *not* based in "disgust," fear, or war, but in something more than "mutual aid," tolerance, or even basic (obligatory) accommodation. Something closer to what Morrison imagines, "[f]irst apart, imagining partners. Then partnered, imagining each other" (*Paradise*, 179). The move, then, from individual transformation to communal transformation. But in tracking, once again, the journey toward "the strangeness within" that makes going forward – even what Morrison called "forward-dreaming" – possible, these feminist authors theorize political agency more coherently and urgently. "Imagining further" into possibility is one thing, but "spelling out" those dreams, "making wings," "giving birth to whole landscapes and worlds" is another. The image of birthing reappears, but what is born is not a person but a place and a time, a space, a world in other/outer space.

FIRST APART, IMAGINING PARTNERS . . .

In Nawal El Saadawi's remarkable short story, "She Has No Place in Paradise,"[2] a woman realizes that she has actually died and gone to Paradise. Thinking her (re)awakening is another iteration of a recurrent dream, she is unsure whether to believe or disbelieve: "The dream seemed impossible to her, for dying seemed impossible, waking after death even more impossible and going to paradise the fourth impossibility" (365). She wavers in her belief of its reality, even while observing the scene's identity to her dreamscape, with a bright and pure light illuminating into white her own dark skin. Her eyes, too, fill with light, looking "like those of a *houri*" (365). As a child, Zeinab imagines Paradise as a recreation of a childhood scene of simple desire, and of freedom from humiliation: "she pictured Paradise as a vast expanse of shade" where she would sit, holding the hand of Hassanein, the neighbor's son: "[H]er *imagination went no further* than holding hands and sitting in the shade of Paradise" (366–367, emphasis added). When she eventually marries, her image of Paradise is similar: "her imagination goes no further" than holding her husband's hand, an act of affection he never once offered to her during her lifetime. Now, ascending the stairs to her paradise house, her heart "beating wildly," she opens the bedroom door to find her husband, seated "like a bridegroom," accompanied in bed by two other radiant *houri*. While the text makes it clear that Zainab shares this spiritual radiance, her husband fails to see his wife arrive. She turns away from him and these strangers, closing the door to the house behind her: "She returned to the earth, saying to herself: 'There is no place in Paradise for a black woman.'"

Zeinab has found a fifth impossibility: demanding the impossible without imagining something more, without "going further," without an image of what a better world now, much less in the hereafter, might look like. In the story's refrain, "her imagination went no further," lies El Saadawi's warning. If, as Abdelwahab Bouhdiba proposes, "paradise is ... the reign of the imagination,"[3] where is the path to that realm when it is specifically closed off to women? And if a woman's speculations take her "somewhere" out of the "rigid ideological text" that not only Muslim or Arab women but women anywhere inhabit, where does she go? The answer, not surprisingly, is both backward and forward, like the uncanny footprints of the Abominable Snowman, and up as well as down. Footsteps on the air. These concurrent paths imagine possible, and potential, futures; a woman might travel into fantasy, in order to locate herself in reality.

In this final chapter, therefore, I explore three authors' interventions into the constrictions of ideological space – textual or otherwise. Through these interventions we are led not simply to feminist politics, but to a principle of potentiality that supports the reign of the imagination and desire, rather than the reign of reason or law alone. The primary texts I explore here include Shahrnush Parsipur's stunning speculative novel, *Women Without Men*, published originally in 1989 and appearing in English with The Feminist Press in 1998; the well-known 1994 literary memoir *Dreams of Trespass*, by Fatima Mernissi; and finally, the fictional "Internet memoir" of Rajaa Alsanea, the 2005 *Girls of Riyadh*, which appeared in English in 2007. Each author delineates an explicit investment in an Arab future that struggles against narratives of sameness, to embrace narratives of difference; as Amin Malak puts it, such narratives do not "deny conflicts or paradoxes, but ... accept, comprehend, and even, when possible fuse them" (131). Those paradoxes will include the tension between communal and individual identities, between entanglements of past and present in seeking the future, between tradition and modernity(-ies). Thus, although each author "foster[s] the explosion of abstract space and production of a space that is other" into a space of ambiguity,[4] she nevertheless challenges the status of this unreality. Among these writers, as among those previously studied, there is a variable faith in what Judith Butler, in a rather different context, calls the force of fantasy.

This tentativeness, worked in and through each imaginary arena for dialogue and debate, is a distinctive feature of these texts, as they engender resistance to traditionally regulated spaces that define the particularities of their cultures. As these authors pull ideological spaces into ambiguity, this tentativeness must not be characterized as weakness but as the strength of a conviction that a more perfect society approaches through a process of critique and self-critique of the "terminology and categories of dissent, change, and appropriation … already within the traditional or indigenous social, culture, and political forms of Islam."[5] Each pushes beyond any blueprint model, therefore, and instead illuminates the footprints and handholds marking the transit toward such spaces – "island-hopping" is one way Mernissi tropes this progress. As before, the role of the reader is finally critical. The generation of art's spaces is inevitably thematized, with particular attention to the entangling of desires brought to that space by ones who, like ourselves, are reading, looking, listening, and feeling. The texts educate us not into a "common sense," certainly not into "the comfort of civilization" or even into any simple form of "solidarity." They lead us into a commitment whose source is *imaginative sympathy*, and whose currents of potentiality run deeper than those of simple "common interests," or transient coalitions.

IMAGINING FURTHER IN THE "MIDDLE OF NOWHERE": SHAHRNUSH PARSIPUR'S *WOMEN WITHOUT MEN*

Iranian writer Shahrnush Parsipur composed *Women Without Men* over a long period of time, first as separate stories, which she then joined together. It took much less time, after the novel's publication in 1989, for this text and others of her writings to be banned in Iran, where it remains officially unavailable.[6] Like El Saadawi, Parsipur was incarcerated for two months in 1990 for writing a story exploring themes of sexuality and gender deemed unacceptable, or "anti-Islamic, unethical and contrary to this, that, or other things"[7]: rape, domestic violence, honor killing, prostitution, and the ways in which "women have been captive of a situation of their own inferiority."[8] Parsipur's relationship to feminism at times seems less robust than her Egyptian colleague's: she has said that she is not a feminist, and endorses marriage as a kind of "nest for children. For this you need a man and a woman … The woman needs a man to elevate the children."[9] Furthermore, she does not see herself, despite her writing and incarcerations, as an activist: "I'm just an observer." Parsipur acknowledges that "I was the second woman to write a novel in Iran, and I have written most of the novels about Iranian women. In this way, maybe I have a good place in Iranian literature."[10] That "good place" is the difficult textual space in which Parsipur follows her conviction, also described in interviews, that women must talk about sexual matters as much as possible, openly and honestly, in order to "make it possible for women to get to know their own bodies. So she knows who she is and where she stands. Don't get me wrong, I don't believe in sexual anarchy, not at all. But I completely endorse sexual freedom. This must come to pass so that women can become somebody."[11]

Parsipur insists on the need to understand sexuality and "hav[ing] sexual experiences" in order to "enter the domain of public work" and to resist the manipulations of "those in power," who keep women in ignorance and thus "transform women to sexual objects" who "repress and denigrate women – then they direct them to put a wedding gown on and go to their husband's home and come out wearing a shroud."[12] She has suggested that a historical need to protect women from outside aggression ironically evolves itself into another form of violence, from within: "Middle Eastern people have always been under attack and in wars and conflict, and this has made them take on a role of guardians of sex and sexuality of women … But they've become such guardians that they've become oppressors."[13]

This is the backdrop to *Women Without Men*, which conveys how damaging – psychologically and often physically – modern forms of systematized oppression can be. The humiliation of women by the Iranian government, Parsipur observes, goaded women like herself into writing: "these same women understood their condition like never before. For them, the only opportunity to rise up was with their words." Both the particularity of her interests, and her belief that women writers have "found a way to become political through writing," reinforce the transnational appeal of Parsipur's work. Finding "a way" toward social justice and gender equality *means writing*, mobilizing against misogyny and the betrayal of women and women's sexuality.[14]

As the linguistic polyvalence of the word suggests, the "way" that is found is both a method, and a path or journey. Like many of the texts treated in this study, this novel is at heart a travel narrative, a speculative journey away from what is known and into a zone of uncomfortable experiences. The new knowledge gained on that trip eventually reorients and recenters the traveler's perspective, and brings her to a new place. In the case of this novel, that place is a house that sits in a garden in Karaj, outside Tehran. As in El Saadawi's parable, this house is a version of the one each of Parsipur's characters has left. In contrast to that tale, however, each of the five women who come to its doorstep is not ignored but taken in, "accepted as she is." This hospitality is in stark contrast to the inhospitable nature of the houses of the fathers, husbands, brothers, and pimps who have aggressively, even violently, defined and/or defiled these women. The women include: Farroklaqa, who buys the garden in Karaj; Faizeh, an unpleasant and manipulative woman who betrays her friend, Munis, in order to get at her handsome and eligible brother; Munis herself, who is killed by that brother for "disgracing" him – and brought back to life to travel to the garden with her betrayer; Zarrinkolah, a young prostitute who tires of her exploitation and seeks the purity of the garden; and Mahdokht, a woman of Karaj who "plants herself" in the garden that will become, "with a little touching up, … a paradise" (85).

Whereas reviews and commentaries on this novel do refer to the "utopic space" of the house and garden in which it sits, it would be a mistake to think that Parsipur presents this as simply a pocket utopia in which women live without men. This misrepresents, in fact, the movement and certainly the conclusion of the novel. One critical lesson of the novel is the imperative to *keep moving forward*, not to settle in any space. This is something that Munis recognizes, invested as she is in traveling to find truth after a thirty-eight-year lifetime of being lied to:

Unfortunately, this is not a good time for a woman to travel alone. She has to be invisible to travel, or just stay at home. I can't stay home any longer, but because I am a woman, I must stay home somewhere. I can make a little progress, then get stuck in a house, then go a little further, and get stuck in another house. At this rate I might be able to go around the world at a snail's pace. (99)

Traveling itself, in other words, is a contradictory state/status for a traditional woman: either she must be "invisible" as she travels, or else not travel at all. She cannot be "at home" *in* traveling; rather, home is identified only as "stasis" – tradition, and the rigidity of the patriarchy. The immobility of the women is clearly a sign of their subservience; as Munis's brother observes, "'It doesn't make sense for a woman to go out in the first place. Home is for women, the outside world for men'" (28). The woman who does travel enters the world of "non-sense," in more ways than one in this novel.

Indeed, one form of this nonsense is the very mode of the novel: the uniqueness of *Women Without Men* is characteristically attributed to its "magical realism" alongside a conventional realist description. This "dislocation of representational modes"[15] is played up visually by Shirin Neshat, the director of the remarkable film version of this novel, because in her words this dislocation allows you to "imagine it [the novel] has one foot in reality while the other is in the imaginary."[16] The narrative is tethered to modern Iranian history by the clear reference to the coup against Mohammad Mossadegh in August 1953. It also refers to very real conditions and consequences of contemporary Iranian women's (and men's) resistance to deeply ingrained sexism. Interwoven with that social realism is also a fundamental mysticism to which Parsipur herself refers in interviews. This mysticism propels unlikely events in sometimes humorous ways: Munis's resurrection after death; the appearance of headless men as clients before the prostitute, Zarrinkolah; the transparency of Zarrinkolah during pregnancy, and the lily-flower child born to her and the gentle gardener; and, most spectacularly and mysteriously, the flowering of a human tree, the woman formerly named Mahdokht, whose pathological commitment to virginity leads her to "plant herself." This darkly comic mode, according to Karim, is a "narrative tool to express some of the irrational and expressible aspects of women's existence." Perhaps more significantly it also blurs the boundaries of reality and unreality, and "bothers" the limits of the known and unknown, as each character "navigat[es] the space in between" those categories.[17]

The navigations of these women are not only geographical, but also spiritual, mirroring the allegorical nature of Islamic narratives in which "the soul [of a male or female person], represented as and personified by a woman, wanders along the narrow difficult path that leads to the beloved,"[18] or to a heavenly paradise. In such texts, what is important is the *journey*, that "pursuit of knowledge as cognizance of God,"[19] for which the garden in Karaj is, for most of the women, in fact nothing more than a temporary dwelling. Thus, although it is easy enough to understand the garden simply as a "female utopia" in which the women find refuge from a brutally patriarchal social structure, to leave it at that risks missing the rich ambiguities at play. This garden aligns with traditional images of garden paradises and the legendary stories around them, on the one hand; and actual gardening practices on the other, representing "the rather extravagant hope of inventing paradise on earth," on the other. Gerard Grandval observes that whereas Western gardens generally seek to "battle with surrounding nature," Persian landscape architects "invented islands of vegetation, a succession of cool moments in a hostile desert land."[20] The applicability of this to the gathering of these women in Karaj is evident as each finds protection from the hostility (real and imagined) of men, in the cool peacefulness of Farroklaqa's garden, with its widespread shade, its stream running through, and its careful tending by the single loving (and nameless) male in the novel, the gardener.

The garden also recalls many a paradise garden from Qur'anic and other traditional sources. Not the least of these are the medieval Islamic garden paradises cited by Fedwa Malti-Douglas: highly erotic, male utopias in which one reads of "hybrid" sexual couplings of, for example, men and fish; or of the appearance of beings who are a "cross between a plant and animal" (86); and, finally, of stands of trees "that bring forth women" who hang down like fruit. The flowering tree-woman, Mahdokht, seems akin to these extraordinary figures, although she has achieved a sexless reproduction presumably antithetical to the male fantasy expressed in these medieval visions. Also relevant is the rather more abstract conception, by some Qur'anic interpretations, of the garden paradise *not* as a physical place at all, but as a metaphoric garden where souls can grow, a fertile place, in other words, for the cultivation of self-awareness. The garden or *jannah*, then, is a place that both is, and is not, real, with a kind of "simultaneous perplexity" of movement and stasis characteristic of Persian gardens and central to their symbolic content as "one of the main fields or loci of a Muslim's referen[t]ial journey in life."[21]

This conception of the garden as a metaphorical space, rather than (simply) a literal one, means that while each woman comes to dwell there, the willing inhabiting of and movement within this space contrasts with certain kinds of immobility – psychological, social, and (especially) psycho-sexual – experienced by the women in the urban center, Tehran. This is most evident in the story of Farroklaqa herself, who, whenever her husband was near, "would lose her ability to move, and she would hide in a corner. She had a thirty-two-year-old habit of not moving. She had gotten used to immobility. She only knew this, and she knew it instinctively, that when Golchehreh [her husband] went out, mobility and happiness would come to her" (56). When her husband "went out" for good, killed accidentally by herself when she (mistakenly) thinks he is going to attack her, Farroklaqa's mobility and happiness do indeed come. She takes the money she has inherited, buys the house and garden in Karaj, and pursues her own interests (artistic) and ambitions (political) as she pleases, "in the middle of nowhere" (95).

Before her transformation into a tree, Mahdokht's culturally induced phobia of sex and desire is so severe that she is described by her first (rejected) suitor as being "like ice" (7), in sharp contrast to the "something burning and hot" that she sees in the yearnings of others. Musing that she is "not like ice" but that she "[is] a tree" – "My virginity is like a tree" (10) – her leap to rhetorical figuration is matched by a physical reconfiguration into a hybrid creature who is both human and not, who is immobile, and not: "She would stay and plant herself. Perhaps she would turn into a tree.... Mahdokht would grow. She would become thousands and thousands of branches. She would cover the entire world" (11). Rooting herself in the earth of Karaj at her family's country house, her family abandons her out of "shame" of the unnatural form Mahdohkt has taken.

But she becomes the centerpiece of the garden purchased by Farroklaqa, the garden that becomes an alternative space for women. The tree is built into the restorations of the house and garden that Farroklaqa commissions – a tender acknowledgment by the new owner of the tree-woman's inability to move, an immobility she herself has so long experienced in marriage. There the tree-woman is tended to by the several women who travel there, fed with human milk (Zarrinkolah's) by Munis and the gardener. Mahdokht does achieve the possibility of reproduction without sex altogether, flowering and dispersing herself across the globe, her seeds carried with the winds to Africa. This achievement fulfills a desire to travel there "so that she could grow … a tree in a warm climate" (12), and not, presumably, in a climate that is "cold, like ice."

Critics tend to celebrate Mahdokht's achievement of reproducing without sex – but this does not strike me as a positive form of feminist mobility, much less identity. Indeed, at the end of the novel's opening chapter – the centrality of Mahdokht must be indicated by pride of place – we learn also that she is descending into a kind of madness, "[banging] her head on the wall again and again" as she considers her global proliferation through asexual reproduction. She would go to Africa, she decides, because "[s]he wanted to, and it is always desire that drives one to madness" (12). The real estate agent confirms that "The poor woman lost her mind and planted herself in the earth" (87). She has lost her voice as well – as mute, ultimately, as a statue, and "perfected" by her adherence to a compulsory virginity. The wise gardener will remind Munis, near the novel's conclusion, that Mahdokht's transformation was only "one-way" (127); in other words, it is a kind of escapism that only immortalizes the woman's damaging compliance to an enforced association of moral purity and/as sexual virginity.

A somewhat more positive figuration of the movement away from sexual oppression and repression is found in the character of the "moon-faced" Munis, whose story may be a version of the traditional story of Sassi, "the Moon-like One." Both stories are of women who "desire" nothing other than to wander about eternally in search of love.[22] Like Mahdokht, Munis is a sexual innocent, still a virgin at age thirty-eight, and with a child's view of virginity as "a curtain," without knowing that this refers to the physical marker of virginity, the hymen. When her manipulative friend Faizeh (also, at age twenty-eight, a virgin) informs her (with equal naiveté) that virginity is "not a curtain" but "a hole," Munis, a "pleasant companion" as indicated by her name, is filled with a "cold rage" (30) at this new knowledge. In a phrase that suggests the loss of sexual innocence

Munis feels, in her anger, that "[s]omething inside of her had broken" (30). Innocent no more, she is determined to "settl[e] all the scores" for enduring lifelong ignorance and self-denial. As a child Munis refrained from climbing trees as a child, although she "used to gaze longingly" at them; she feared "for her virginity" and for that fragile "curtain." In contrast to the pathological "planting" of Mahdokht and her vision of innocent travel, Munis does the opposite: she begins traveling in order to see *everything.*

She leaves home for weeks, becoming both an observer, particularly of the political unrest taking place in 1953 Tehran; and a voyeur, peering into people's windows and surreptitiously scanning the shelves of bookstores seeking, as it turns out, the following: *The Secret of Sexual Satisfaction or How to Know Our Bodies* (32). After twelve days of staring at this title, she finally summons the courage to purchase the text, and reads it continuously for three days. At the end of the third day, knowledge has transformed her world: "The trees and sunshine and streets all had new meanings for her. She had grown up" (33). She had also earned the utter contempt of her brother, who regards her as a "shameless woman" (34), and stabs her for her disobedience. Munis is buried, but like El Saadawi's Zeinab, returns to life, with the power now to move about as she likes, unhampered by any sense of restriction or obligation, and armed with the disarming ability, after a lifetime of deception, to read the true thoughts in people's minds and to tell truths without repercussion. To her old acquaintance Faizeh, who betrayed her in a bid for the affections of her brother, Munis is now feared as a kind of "daemon," which in fact she is: "I've decided to live with you and leave this house" (48) Munis announces, and then compels Faizeh to travel with her "to Karaj," away from the city and "the prison of family life" (95), away from the ideal of innocence that has damaged them both.

On the road they will eventually find a real loss of innocence; both are raped on the road to Karaj. Munis no longer cares, realizing, like Carter's Marianne, that this rape is "the first step toward discovering some logical order" and is therefore "the first bitter experience of travelling" (97). When they arrive at Karaj, Munis is clear that this is just a step along the path of her journey. While "I must be at home somewhere," she also explains her ongoing commitment to mobility: "I was thinking of going to India and China to see the world. I want to comprehend everything, and not just sit around and let other people tell me what's what ... I've decided to take a risk and seek knowledge. Of course it's dangerous to walk along the road" (96). Because her progress might be therefore "at a snail's pace," "[t]hat's why I accept your invitation [to stay] with pleasure" (99). Like a nomadic gypsy, Munis becomes mobile, free, and unfailingly, bluntly truthful. What Milani says of gypsy figures who appear in Iranian literature is true of Munis: she represents both "the ideal and the counterideal. She combines many intense and contradictory feelings about womanhood." Her very mobility makes her suspect, "unmindful of rules of modesty,"[23] as when she dismisses Faizeh's mortification at having been raped as an irrelevancy.

The last of the five women is no stranger to sex and the female body. Zarrinkolah is a twenty-six-year-old prostitute in Tehran, with up to thirty clients a day, and with a feisty spirit that leads to frequent beatings from her pimp. "Tired of working," she is startled one day to see every one of her clients suddenly appear, to her eyes only, as "headless." Fearing madness, she is determined to purify herself of "sexual pollution" (75) through repeated bathing rituals, and fervent prayers performed stark naked in the bath house to seek Allah's forgiveness. So stringent are her ablutions, physical and psychological, that "her body felt like a piece of straw" (76), and she asks the *hammam* attendant where one might, at this time of summer, get a drink of "cool water." "With pity," he advises her to go to Karaj: "There was nothing in her face to show that she had once been a prostitute. She had become a small woman of 26 with a heart as big as the sea. She went to Karaj" (77).

By the time all five women convene in Karaj, Parsipur's intertwined themes are clear: the ignorance in which women are kept regarding sexuality and desire; the policing of women's bodies (especially virginal bodies); women's complicity with this kind of policing; the ideology of the "ideal Iranian woman" and images of masculinity; the inability to love in a healthy way, when relationships are so deformed by ignorance, fear, and lack of respect; the unregulated violence of men against women; the limits and limitations of women's lives; their immobility within the conventional social spaces and conventional gender ideologies; and the risk of madness in pushing against those limits. As Farrokhlaqa gazes upon the curious, "shameful" and unnatural human tree growing in the garden she is about to purchase, she indicates her willingness to reject convention with these simple words: "I accept it as it is" (90). With this declaration, the garden becomes a safe zone in which the development of each woman takes place, at her own pace and only to the degree to which each is willing to explore and change. The affiliation of the women is loose – they do not necessarily even like each other – but it resides in their recognition of their dislocation in conventional society, and the need to travel to a new one in order to find grounds more fertile for their own identity development.

This kind of tentativeness colors the novel's ambiguous conclusion. The garden is not, as reviewer Asghar Massombagi correctly notes, "a kind of all-woman Eden" or feminist utopia, for the women stay divided by their prejudices. But the conclusion is hardly as incoherent as Massombagi suggests, arguing that "no sooner has the writer brought her characters to the garden [than] she sets out to tear down its foundation."[24] Rather, the conclusion – as in so many feminist narratives – is open-ended. The garden remains at the end: what has changed, to greater and lesser degrees, are the women. Of them all, Zarrinkolah is the one who achieves most happiness: she gains a loving partner (the unnamed gardener) and becomes pregnant. Her pregnancy also initiates the gradual transformation of her body – not in the usual way, but thus: she becomes "crystal clear, was one with the light" (116). This transformation unmistakably and ironically (given her previous employment as a sex worker) recalls the transparent radiance of traditional *houri* in Paradise, as we have seen in the aforementioned El Saadawi story. The child to whom Zarrinkolah gives birth is "actually" a lily flower, a child of the garden as much as of its human parents, who themselves, at the novel's end, transform into smoke and "[rise] into the sky" to a place where "we don't need clothes" (111) or any material things. Ironically, Zarrinkolah alone of the women achieves this mystic goal of becoming "totally transformed into love itself," and "know[ing] no separation between lover and beloved"[25] – in fact, this is a dissolution of identity that opposes the formation of the individual ego.

Brave Munis, by contrast, is envious of the prostitute, for she understands herself to be, in truth, "rotten inside ... rotten from waiting. She knew that it was love that led to the feeling of light" and her continued fear of "real experience" came; she knew the still deeply ingrained "fear of disgrace" (118). She is envious of Mahdokht, whom she helps to feed "with Zarrinkolah's milk," to go literally to seed, and to release herself to the world. The gardener advises her that the way of Zarrinkolah or of Mahdokht need not be here own: "Look at your friend ... Unfortunately she did not become human, she became a tree. Now she can start over so that she can become somewhat human ... Seek darkness, see in the darkness, in the beginning, in the depths, in the depths of the depths where you will find light at the zenith, in yourself, by yourself. That is becoming human, go and become human!" (128). Munis, who had once said that "if I had wings I would fly" (100), turns around, "flew off into the sky" (128), and traveled, alone, for seven years through seven years, and returns "filled with experience" but with little else. Like Sassi of the fable, Munis ends up "tired and thin, and had lost hope" (128). Perhaps she is reminded, as Sassi is, that "To die along the path is supreme happiness."²⁶ Returning to the city, Munis "became a simple schoolteacher" (128), continuing her own self-education as well as that of others.

Farroklaqa's own mobility has also not taken her to where she wants to go, although her world is wider now than in the days when she was immobilized by the fear and hatred of her husband, and by his contempt for her. Socially ambitious, she marries a man who could help her "do some social climbing.... Their relationship is satisfactory, neither warm nor cold" (130). Faizeh changes little, still resentful of other women, and still desirous of Munis's brother Amir. Although he has married another he is unsatisfied; eventually, Faizeh finds him again, gradually reels him in, and eventually marries him, secretly, as his co-wife. Amir installs her in a second home. "Their life is neither good nor bad. It just goes on" (126). Like Farroklaqa, Faizeh has squandered her opportunity at transformative mobility, neither abandoning the expectations of a patriarchal organization nor entertaining the imagination of a new vision of the world.

Massombagi suggests that the importance of this novel is that it is more than just "about what it means to be a woman in Iran"; it is also concerned with "how to *write* about" what it means to be a woman in Iran. Furthermore, "the fact that the garden fails to live up to its utopian promise is not a measure of the writer's pessimism but her sobriety."²⁷ It may be clearer now why Parsipur might resist any easy notion of the term "feminist": none of these women can be said to achieve any triumphantly "real" power in the world; most do not achieve "happiness." But I would argue that nevertheless they are all changed, some fundamentally and some not, by their time in the garden. It is a time, an interval, during which the tension between immobility and mobility – terms that mean something a little different for each one – can be safely explored. All become gypsies of a sort, traveling to this island of safety, this walled garden, a counterspace in "no danger of intruders" (86). Through the ability to travel into, out of, beneath and above this hospitable safety-zone emerges the possibility of understanding how "women" themselves become "intruders" in a patriarchal Iranian society, and how difficult it is in fact to travel both within it and outside it. This is feminist writing in a radical register; as Milani argues in her study of contemporary Iranian women poets, such writing is critical in mobilizing against the patriarchy of contemporary Iran, and in motivating the "transcendence of three central cultural fears: woman's visibility, woman's mobility, and woman's voice."²⁸ For all her characteristic demurring, Parsipur is exemplary in her commitment to imagining a more vital identity for Iranian women.

FATIMA MERNISSI: ISLAND HOPPING IN *DREAMS OF TRESPASS*

Fatima Mernissi's splendid memoir, *Dreams of Trespass*, is not strictly a novel, but it is no more "realistic" an autobiography than Jeanette Winterson's *Oranges are not the only fruit*. Because there is so much in it of the speculative, and certainly of the utopian, I include it here. It is a text constantly preoccupied with walls – physical, mental and ideological – with barriers and with frontiers. It is also preoccupied with *islands*, and with traveling to them. Mernissi's picture of the familial harem is nothing if not insular, its borders clearly demarcated by tradition, although the tides of modern culture, national politics, and world war are eroding its shores. What interests Mernissi is just that activity at the harem's insular borders, the ways in which her restless relatives begin imagining how things might be different. Acknowledging the comforts of their insular stability, the women obsessively observe the porousness of harem borders, and yearn for the challenges of navigating the spaces in-between, seeking an oppositional logic of identity that eventually, as I will argue, highlights the tension between law and desire, reality and fantasy.

Mernissi explores the limitations of the island metaphor and the ways in which the boundedness of the island image does, and does *not,* offer a spatial image of a *feminist* utopian identity. In a 2008 article in *Hypatia*, María Martínez González explores the figure of the *island* as "close, metaphorically" to a "modern notion" of collective identity: the island is a *figuration* of a "unitary *fiction of identity*" that underlies "the logic of identity and clearly shows a main dualism of modernity: between the inside and the outside."²⁹ Nowhere does she mention the strong affiliation of this figure with the concept of utopia – but she might usefully have done so because recent theorizing about utopia follow similar lines of argumentation. Lucy Sargisson opens her study of contemporary feminist utopianism with a discussion of the "mythical character of these understandings of utopianism."³⁰ So in the González piece, which points out that "[i]dentity just *appears* to be unity, but it contains the difference in itself."³¹ Bothering the logic of an insular, stable identity, González asks this question: "But what about the social space that appears in the *in-between*? What happens in the space between two islands?"

González argues that the in-between offers new metaphors of identity, exceeding the limitations of the image of the island, and leading us to now familiar metaphors of journeying or becoming (Braidotti); border-lands (Anzaldúa), and the hybrid or cyborg (Haraway). From those new metaphors of individual identity, she hopes, we might develop "metaphors of collective identity in order to build cartographies that bring together the complexities of contemporary feminist mobilization."[32] The island, she suggests, now seems an inadequate metaphor – but perhaps only because we look at "islands" from a two-dimensional perspective. Sargisson, herself following Ruth Levitas, anticipates González in suggesting that "form" does not represent the best approach to utopianism if we can hope to believe that "Utopia" could actually change "real life." A more appropriate approach to feminist utopianism to her mind is precisely the notion of "approach," itself – not a destination, but a traveling toward: an active and ongoing "striving for open-ended definitions, or, to borrow [Lyman] Sargent's phrase, to seek definitions with 'porous boundaries.'"[33]

These theorists provide particular theoretical contexts within which to consider Fatima Mernissi's account of a harem childhood in Morocco. *Dreams of Trespass* is an autobiographical bildungsroman of sorts, revealing the sociologist/feminist/activist's coming into a decidedly feminist identity, although marooned as it were within the confines of her family's Moroccan *harem*.[34] The account is shot through with the yearnings and feminist ambitions of herself and many of her female family members – ambitions that are based on their belief that Islam actually requires the equality of the sexes ("Allah said so ['everyone is equal']. His Prophet preached the same" [26]). The memoir is carefully shaped by structural motifs common to utopian texts, most notably that *ur*-image of the island. González's questioning of the island/identity figure urges us to consider how social movement theory also relates to this text – not only its imagining of individual identity, but also of a collective identity so strongly, yet so problematically, associated with the harem. All the more reason to reconsider the island metaphor, because its literary source in Mernissi's text is likely not Sir Thomas More at all, but the much older tales of Scheherazade in *A Thousand and One Arabian Nights*.[35]

In that difference is a shift of perspective both from West to East, and from male to female. Mernissi's explores the ways in which the bounded-ness of the island image offers a spatial image of a feminist identity close to what Gonzalez proposes. What Mernissi's text demands is not only an image of the creative individual identity, but an image of utopian political praxis as well that prefigures her own career, later, as a feminist scholar and activist. Specifically, I wish to argue that metaphors of Scheherazade's "island"[36] and especially of "island hopping" tie in directly with Mernissi's own feminist utopian aspirations. She does not seek some kind of feminist commonwealth, for all the joys of the female community and solidarity she does in fact experience in the harem. She searches for a dynamic and ongoing movement motivated by a commitment to voicing women's desire. In addition, she seeks a vision of harmonious society that contrasts with the dual threats that pervade her childhood: local male dominance, on the one hand; and Western domination – the colonization of Morocco by France and Spain, the specter of World War II, and a feared invasion of Morocco – on the other.

Mernissi's fascination with breaking down barriers of public and private space, the required and desired, Logos and Eros, is evident even in an apparently innocent childhood game. Warned to stay out of her older cousins' early-morning games, she "would put my little cushion down" and engage in a game of her own she calls "the seated promenade," which "consists in contemplating familiar grounds as if they were alien to you" (4). She proceeds to "read" the spatial architecture of her own family harem, from the "square and rigid courtyard," where even the central fountain "seemed controlled and tamed" (4); to the little square of sky framed at the top of that courtyard, which looked tame at first – "because of the man-made square frame" – but whose movement of stars during the early morning "became so intense that it could make you dizzy." This juxtaposition of the man-made and the natural, the structures of human homes and institutions, against the movement of time, is characteristic of Mernissi's reflections on "inside" and "outside," and *between* "the moment" and history – and a remarkable autodidactic technique for the "social scientist" this young girl would become.

This paradigm of observation and critique characterizes many of her relatives, as they create between-spaces where conventional boundaries of time and space are suspended. These were the "out-of-the-way spaces, top floors, and terraces" – that is, spaces not assigned strictly to domestic activity – where the rich and varied forms of the harem women's entertainments thrived. And these counterspaces are where the women's own "islands" are seen and explored. In fact, "the island" in *Dreams of Trespass* is itself a fantasy space. Speaking in early pages of her Aunt Habiba's near-"magical" storytelling skills, she recalls how, "[w]ith words alone, she could put us onto a large ship sailing from Aden to the Maldives, or take us to an island where the birds spoke like human beings. Riding on her words, we traveled past Sind and Hind (India), leaving Muslim territories behind, living dangerously, and making friends with Christians and Jews" (19). Already, in a text obsessed with boundaries and frontiers – the *hudud* – Fatima is being taught a kind of critical method, like Scheherazade's kingly auditor who learns from Scheherazade's stories to "get close to the strangeness within himself, ... his prison" (15). Malak is right in detecting "an aching need [in *Dreams of Trespass*] to open up space to discuss gender politics away from the rigid boundaries and taboos erected by patriarchy and reified notions perpetrated by some Western feminists."[37]

Thus, Mernissi connects the experience of mental travel to "alienation" – the strangeness within oneself. In describing the rich forms of harem women's entertainments in those private spaces, young Fatima revels in her mental traveling: "with my legs crossed, I journeyed all over the world, hopping from one island to the next on boats that were always being wrecked and then miraculously set afloat again by resourceful princesses" (113). Her aunt's tales seem explicitly escapist: "when you happen to be trapped powerless behind a wall," she would say, "stuck in a dead-end harem ... you dream of escape. And magic flourishes when you *spell out* the dream and make the frontiers vanish. Dreams can change your life, and eventually the world" (114, emphasis added). Whereas Fatima recalls her aunt "hammering at us about this magic within" (114), what she brings away in retrospect is a utopic sensibility, a sense that "there were no limits to hope." She takes away, too, the more critical notion that the "magic" only takes effect when it is "spelled out," voiced aloud, or expressed in some way – in stories and even in embroidered images of island-hopping.[38]

Fatima's mother and her cousin, Chama, express their frustration with harem life by producing the embroidered figure of a peacock, that image itself regarded by the conservative matriarch of the family, Fatima's grandmother, as a "criminal violation of our sacred tradition" (207). This peacock is not simply "a strange bird, instead of ... the same old desperately repetitive Fez design." The peacock image is taken directly from a particular *Arabian Nights* tale, Scheherazade's "The Tale of the Birds and the Beasts." Mernissi records that Chama loves this story because "it combined two things she adored, birds and uninhabited islands" (208). In this tale, a peacock and his wife – the "talking birds" Fatima refers to in her first reference to islands – flee their land in fear of wild beasts that threaten them. The birds travel from place to place until they reach a paradise island, "abounding in streams and trees." According to the memoirist, what thrilled Chama about this story was the fact that when the couple did not like the first island, they went looking for a better one. The idea of flying around to find something which would make you happy when you were discontented with what you had, entranced Chama, and she made Aunt Habiba repeat the beginning of the story over and over again, never seeming to have enough of it ... Everyone was so anxious to know what happened to the birds, for they identified strongly with those fragile yet adventurous creatures undertaking dangerous trips to strange islands. (208)

Chama interpreted for those women too stubborn to understand her own fascination with the image of island exploration: "'This story is not about the birds. It is about us. To be alive is to move around, to search for better places, to scavenge the planet looking for more hospitable islands. I am going to marry a man with whom I can look for islands!' Aunt Habiba would then beg her not to use poor Scheherazade's tale as her own propaganda, and disunite the group again" (209).

The association of the embroidered bird with utopian yearning for individual freedom and the pursuit of personal desires is clear enough. But this moment also points toward an important lesson about collective identity. The memoir is filled with stories of strong communality, even solidarity on some points; but on *this* point – the insistence on freedom – differences in generational and personal circumstances quickly emerge. The women are continuously bumping up against each other, and "deep down there was no cohesion at all ... although Aunt Habiba had referred to the women as a group.... The split between the women was unbridgeable, with the conflict over the embroidery design emblematic of much deeper, antagonistic world views" (209). For all the coherence of this proudly female community, the *agon* to which Mernissi refers is between a traditional "male-centered" ideology of femininity and women's social roles, and a progressive, "woman-centered" image of expansive female possibility(-ies). Despite her reluctance to promote corporate disunity, Habiba would continue with the tale behind that controversial bird image – in part, surmises Mernissi, because "she needed help to revive the fragile flame within" (210) as a counter-response to her aunt's resignation to a delimited existence.

The remainder of the tale also indicates the level to which the women acknowledge the degree of danger – physical and psychological – from any challenge to sanctioned gender ideology. The island at which the birds alight is like paradise not just because of its lush vegetation and plentiful water, according to Mernissi's summary, but also because it was "blessedly out of the reach of man, that dangerous creature who destroyed nature"

(210–211). From "the son of Adam," Scheherazade's narration tells us, "none is safe ... and neither bird nor beast escapeth him." Thus the birds seek a safe haven "located far away in the middle of the sea, out of the reach of the humans' boats and their trade routes" (211). Chama reportedly became very agitated at this part of the story, relating it directly to her brothers' sport of killing sparrows from the terrace. Watching her brothers lure and kill the birds, she would mutter that "something must be terribly wrong with a place where even harmless sparrows, just like women, were treated as dangerous predators" (212). Chama's interpretation of the island and the birds brings together the realms of metaphor and reality. Her reading clarifies her recognition that women's identities, individually and corporately, are limited by the boundaries set by the male tradition of protection through the harem. The violence of "Adam's sons" relates also, the narrative makes clear, to the freedom of the nation of Morocco, already colonized by Western powers who separate themselves into their *own* form of harem, the French *ville nouvelle*. Indeed, as Malak has pointed out, the memoir proposes a parallel between the women who are subject to the traditional protection of male family members and the nation of Morocco, which is under threat of invasion from the European soldiers at war among themselves to their north: "This sundering of the country [between the colonial powers of France and Spain] is replicated in the partition of the Mernissi household between men's quarters and women's: the harem. The suggestion here is that the women were doubly colonized."[39] Both threatened parties – the women and the Moroccan nation – are under siege in a general way from the same thing – modernity – and the struggle between tradition and modernity is at the heart of this memoir.

One of the ironies of the embroidered bird episode is the fact that in order to produce this controversial image – indeed, in order to express in color and silk any embroidered fantasy – the insulated women are forced to gain access to materials through a service of a man. Unable to step outside and shop, the harem women

had to explain what they wanted to Sidi Allal [a third cousin to Fatima's grandmother] ... the less gifted among the women begged the more eloquent ones to describe their dreams for them. Women's wishes had to be spelled out patiently to Sidi Allal, because without his collaboration, one could not get very far. So each woman described her dream embroidery – the kind of flowers she wanted and their colors, the hues of the buds, and sometimes whole trees with intricate branches. Others described entire islands surrounded with boats. Paralyzed by the frontier, women gave birth to whole landscapes and worlds. (213)

And because Aunt Habiba is divorced, and thus an even lower dependent among the family, her own nontraditional embroidery pattern is of little interest to Sidi Allal, so that she "had to keep her birds buried deep down in her imagination. 'The main thing for the powerless to have is a dream,' she often told me ... 'True, a dream alone, without the bargaining power to go with it, does not transform the world or make the walls vanish, but it does help you keep ahold [*sic*] of dignity'" (214).

Habiba adds, furthermore, that dreams "give a sense of direction" (214–215), although she acknowledges this is hardly enough. A woman needs also to develop wings, like those birds. Indeed, early in the memoir Habiba tells another tale, called "The Woman with Wings," about one who "could fly away from the courtyard whenever she wanted to. Every time Aunt Habiba told that story, the women in the courtyard would tuck their caftans into their belts, and dance away with their arms spread wide as if they were about to fly" (22). Chama convinces young Fatima that "all women had invisible wings, and that mine [Fatima's] would develop too, when I was older," something the girl-author believed literally for a while. Literal or metaphorical, it is a powerful self-image also endorsed by Fatima's mother and even one of her father's co-wives: "Life is looking good for women now, she said, 'with the nationalists asking for their education, and the end of seclusion. For you know, the problem with women today is that they are powerless ... Just concentrate on that little circle of sky hanging above the well ... don't look down, look up, up, and off we go! Making wings!'" (170). So many of the women in this memoir had their eyes fixed, as Mernissi puts it, "on an invisible horizon" (216). The entire memoir is structured as a journey of "island-hopping" in search of that "paradise" – and of the wings to get there.[40]

There is one further application of the island trope to women's spaces: the *hammam*, or baths, where the women complete their weekly beauty treatments, rinsing off the layers of henna, creams, and oils. Mernissi describes the *hammam*, "[t]hat combination of ivory light, mist, and nude adults and children running all around" as "like a steamy-hot, exotic island that had somehow become adrift in the middle of the disciplined Medina. Indeed, the *hammam* would have been paradise, if it had not been for its third chamber [where alternately scalding hot and ice-cold water were doused on them]" (235). This allusion to an island-paradise has two registers: the *hammam* is described on the one hand as a kind of perfected space of female collectivity that the women and girls of the harem treasure and defend. On the other hand, the *hammam* is read explicitly as revealing the "porous borders" between the women's private enclosure and political, public spaces beyond them. As she explains, Islamic culture regards the skin as a critical connective membrane between individual and universe: "A human being was connected to the world through his or her skin, I said, and how could someone with clogged pores feel the environment or be sensitive to its vibrations? Aunt Habiba was convinced that if men wore beauty masks instead of battle masks, the world would be a much better place" (220). As this passage suggests, this "politics of the female body," centered in the Mernissi text in the *hammam* scene, goes beyond the politics of the body; there is an implication here that the "right perception" of reality outside the self is influenced directly by the care of the integumentary borderland separating the flesh of the human body from the nourishments and corruptions alike of the "real" space (environmental, social, political, cultural) in which it navigates.[41]

Mernissi appreciates retrospectively how the very boundaries and boundedness of the harem gifted her with a desire not only for individual freedom, but for collective identity as well, and that appreciation gives the memoir its characteristic warmth. Deprived of movement outside, this insular female space[42] challenges the women to find ways, continually, of breaking down the borders defining inside and outside, private and public. I have detailed some of the artful ways – through storytelling, theatrical productions, embroidery, even cosmetology – by which they do so, at least for a time: "From the harem, the possibilities to make life enjoyable seemed infinite – walls were going to disappear, and houses with glass ceilings were going to replace them. Imprisoned behind walls, women walked around dreaming of "frontierless horizons" (179); "paralyzed by the frontier, women gave birth to whole landscapes and worlds" (213).

But the limitations of these expressions of desire are also acknowledged. The women develop furtive ways of letting themselves out (by jumping out of windows and off roofs, risking sprained ankles) and, to the extent they can, letting the outside in (by stealing room keys to gain access to the single household radio, with its updates on Moroccan nationalism, and its ominous news of the world war beyond).[43] What Mernissi takes away from men's unwillingness to allow women to fly is that there exists a profoundly deep a lack of trust. Fear emerges wherever trust is missing, as the author clarifies in one of the several interpolated, italicized "musings" of forward-dreaming:

Oh, yes, I would tell them about the impossible, about a new Arab world, in which men and women could hug each other and dance away, with no frontiers between them, and no fears.

Oh, yes, I would enchant my audience, and re-create, through magic words and calculated gestures, just like Asmahan and Chama [two singers much admired by the Mernissi women] before me, a serene planet on which houses had no gates, and windows opened wide onto safe streets.

I would help them walk in a world where the difference needed no veil, and where women's bodies moved naturally, and their desires created no anguish.

I would create for and with the audience, long poems about the absence of fear. Trust would be the new game we could explore, and I would humbly confess that I knew nothing of it either. (111)

The "absence of fear" and consequent cultivation of trust among men and women, most immediately, and among Arabs and Christians, only slightly more distantly, is a critical catalyst to the kind of social transformation Mernissi proposes, not only in this text but in her other scholarly works, as a "possible" way toward a vision of an open, modern Arab world.

The image of the "serene planet"[44] is important here. It is more than a distant version of the paradise island trope we have followed from the tradition of Scheherazade and More into the inner and outer spaces of science fiction. It is also a figuration of a shift from the two-dimensional "inside-outside" logic of unitary identity, and toward a complex multi-dimensional structuring of both space and time. It is also a version of her own war-torn planet. Co-wife Mina tells Fatima on the memoir's last page that the world is split by "a cosmic frontier" that "indicates the line of power because wherever there is a frontier, there are two kinds of creatures walking on Allah's earth, the powerful on one side, and the powerless on the other." Asks Mernissi, "how I would know on which side I stood. [Mina's] answer was quick, short, and very clear: 'If you can't get out, you are on the powerless side'" (242).

These power plays are the stuff of this memoir. In the opening pages, Fatima's mother warns her that it is unwise to play even the most apparently innocent childhood game unless she knew how to defend herself. "Even playing is a kind of war," her mother grimly asserts. But in the long interpolated passage just cited, Mernissi imagines a new game characterized by porous boundaries and unstable rules. To borrow her metaphor, "new rules of the game" are being organized around trust rather than fear, and centered around goals of cooperation and sharing, rather than competitive acquisitiveness and domination. What I have been calling a *speculative standpoint* imagines such a field of play.

We return here to the theme of hospitality. Mernissi encourages an *approach* to another, rather than hostility. The approach need not necessarily be neutral, but as "humble" as possible, like that of, say, a good anthropologist or sociologist, as Mernissi came to be.[45] It also marks the approach of a feminist who would unveil difference and approach the threats of Adam's sons in the here and now rather than fleeing from one imagined island to the next in search of an "impossible" safety in a new Arab world. From reading this memoir we know that little Fatima was able to escape the bounded space of the harem she called home as a child. Her relatives, who taught her how to "fly," also told her how to approach danger, real and perceived, head-on. Her family taught her how to "humbly" acknowledge history, to see the effects – positive and negative – of boundaries and the communities they delimit. And they taught her to explore responsibly not only the cartographies of those islands but also to map out *approaches,* however tentative and slow, toward better islands, way-stations in the transit to a distant "serene planet."

Importantly, the Mernissi women's fantasy spaces fail to register as a political space with their male relatives who overlook the manner in which abstract, imaginary spaces become real against and despite the patriarchal and traditional power geography. The women, meanwhile, stage their performances of escape and freedom in harem spaces vertically superior to their living spaces, close to the open sky and wheeling stars. In other words, their own geography recognizes the significance of the moving sky as a sign of temporality or change, and thus resists the reduction of imaginary space to "mere abstraction." Lefebvre argues that it is "time" that resists the reduction of space to mere abstraction: "Within time, the investment of affect, of energy, of 'creativity' opposed a mere passive apprehension of signs and signifiers. Such an investment, the desire to do something, and hence to 'create,' can only occur in a space – and through the production of a space."[46] These performance spaces highlight the "disjointed unity" of the harem and a certain potentiality that is certainly political, if not yet politicized. Mernissi signals the need for a "real" appropriation of space – a kind of dimensional shift, in her attention to the moving sky framed by the harem's courtyard – in her vision of a "serene planet." The so-called magic within finds its outlet in private entertainments, in the ensuing arguments and debates, and in actual efforts to escape out of windows; or to steal the keys that offer *access* to the outside. Those keys also give access to the precious radio, "precious" because it offers glimpses of the global and political space, the theater of World War II, in which Morocco plays its own role.

This fierce hunger for "news" is indicative of and motivates the memoir's ultimate act of solidarity: the delegation of women who insist – to their husbands, uncles, and brothers – on allowing young Fatima Mernissi entrance into the new, non-Qur'anic school. The women are too insulated to understand the contemporary military movements of World War II that impinge on their country. Nevertheless, they are far too intelligent and astute to underestimate the ramifications of these movements to the future of Morocco, the Arab world generally, and the women, men, and children within it. Their "investment in time" is their investment in the future of their girl children, and particularly, in the common recognition that young Fatima could "change the world" if she is allowed into it.[47]

THEN PARTNERED, IMAGINING EACH OTHER . . .

The 2005 first novel by Rajaa Alsanea's *Girls of Riyadh*[48] is also a fictional memoir, structured by its own utopian conceit: cyberspace. This novel, published originally in Arabic, surprised its author with its success, which allowed an English translation (by the author and Marilyn Booth) to appear in 2007. Like Mernissi, Alsanea attempts to locate interstices of space in which debates over conflicting notions of gender and identity can freely occur. By forming a subscription-only Internet discussion group, Alsanea's anonymous listserv master follows the lives of herself and her closest friends, taking on contemporary Saudi mores associated, both explicitly and implicitly, with Saudi Arabia's conventionally conservative gender ideologies.

As in the Mernissi text, there are two particular foci: (1) the intersection of Logos and Eros, narrowly translated at one level into scenes of romantic desire running afoul of rules of social and religious decorum; and (2) the intersection of Logos and Eros translated as a clash between tradition and modernity. Thus, the expressed purpose of this text is to expose what Mernissi called "the strangeness within ourselves," and what Alsanea's heroine calls "contradictions within myself" (137). These contradictions are explicitly connected with the clash between "our *spiritual* sides as well as our *not-so-spiritual* sides" (137) (emphasis in the original) and with the "changing times" in the Muslim world. These changing times demand not only, as one of Alsanea's characters opines, the enlightenment of Saudi men who are "slaves to reactionary customs and ancient traditions even when their enlightened minds pretend to reject such things, ... pawns their families move around the chessboard" (270), but also demand the enlightenment of Saudi women in "a crooked society that raises children on contradictions and double standards" (270).

This declaration is the ongoing justification of this novel's exposure of the private and (pre)professional lives of this group of well-heeled young women and men, an educated and techno-savvy younger generation in a city far more cosmopolitan, at the turn of the century, than Mernissi's 1940s Fez. Alsanea's fictional cyber-memoirist takes advantage of sexual and political geographies that are both familiar as well as novel, *through* the use of technology. Although the Mernissi women understood instinctively the importance of the entrance of new technologies in their lives, and new forms of modernity with those technologies, the particular ambiguities of gendered space and spatial dynamics in Muslim culture is rehearsed at yet another level in the digital age, as new communication networks and expanded public access to those networks alter the very frames of reference by which such spaces are regulated.[49] Both the Mernissi women and the young Saudis are attracted to technology as a way of satisfying a hunger for discovery and debate – and as a way of inventing social and political spaces where they can live more freely, and in which critique of society and self can flourish.

In considering what Muslim feminist spaces "look like," the more interesting story is the one that emerges through the first-person frames of each posting, addressed directly to the "you" of the listserv audience, under the protected screen name of *seerehwenfadha7et*. Without freedom of speech or movement in the public space, which is so highly regulated (not least by the older women related to the group of young women portrayed here), *seerehwenfadha7et* retreats, as it were, to this unregulated dimension of public space, where she feels "at home." The space she creates, however, is an intentionally uncomfortable one, not a nostalgic turn to inward safety. The text recreates a call-and-response debate, as the narrator opens up the lives of her friends for comment, seeking critique and clarification of the contradictions and pressures molding their lives. A new community is born around this blog as *seerehwenfadha7et* responds with postings that are variously challenging, defensive, playful, aggressive, or hortatory. *Seerehwenfadha7et* is not seeking the fantasy of heterogeneous community overturning the patriarchal ideals of female inequality and submission, nor a world of women without men. Rather, the community she seeks is one comprised of resisting readers who will mobilize each other to debate. Alsanea's narrator acknowledges and welcomes this resistance early on, as response to her website grows. Nearly all of her initial respondents, we learn, are men, who alternately encourage her, flirt with her, seek names and phone numbers of her friends – and also challenge her. After only several postings, in which her own voice is friendly, even flirtatious (she mentions several times her "signature bright red lipstick" – and refuses to reveal the brand), her tone changes after she receives her first disapproving responses: "Men have written to me saying: Who authorized you to speak for the girls of Najd?! You are nothing but a malevolent and rancorous woman deliberately attempting to sully the image of women in Saudi society" (28). Later, she notes that men and women alike are responding in a tone as often "threatening and scolding" (110) as supportive: "Everyone is blaming me for the fury I have stirred up around 'taboo' topics ... But isn't there a starting point for every drastic social change?" (97). In the meantime, she begs for King Abd Al-Aziz City (the major Internet provider in Saudi Arabia) to refrain from "trying to block my site to dam up the channels of communication" and "ward off ... all causes of corruption or evil": "I only ask for a small space on the World Wide Web to tell my stories through. Is that too much to ask?" (82). Several weeks later, she realizes it might be, as she has been warned she is "too close to the red line" (114).

By interjecting appeals to allow her blog to remain active, we are reminded that this little bit of web space is indeed an increasingly political, politicized, space. This space enables a "multiplication of agency" and, potentially at least, erodes the power of "authorized" voices concerning religious and cultural decorum.[50] *Seerehwenfadha7et*'s project – which is to say, Alsanea's novel – is an instance of what Eickelman and Anderson call the "cultural entrepreneurship" associated with the rise of new media and shifting communications practices. As "debates about Islamic requirements" and related cultural practices become more public through the use of the Internet and other social media, Alsanea's blogger still appeals to familiar tropes from popular romance novels. What makes this novel interesting is watching these young Saudis, and especially *Seerehwenfadha7et*, seek ways of revising the past and present for envisioning a future that will belong to them. They effect this by translating "existing cultural practices to new communicative environments."[51] Given, once again, the ambiguous status of authority and voice in these new environments, it is not surprising to read *seerehwenfadha7et*'s defense of her own writing in terms of Qur'anic scripture and the *hadith*:

May God consider my writings as good deeds, as I have only good intentions.... I work hard to correct my errors and to cultivate myself. If only those who find fault with me would turn around and straighten themselves out before they start agitating to straighten me out ... The true and shameful wrong, the way I see things, would be for any of us to stand in each other's way, disparaging each other, even though we all admit the unity of our goal, which is reforming our society and making every one of us a better person. (57)

This appeal to ongoing debate about ideological contradictions is consistent throughout the text, as the narrator insists that for all the furor the postings have created, the "fertile material for exchange and debate" will remain "for a long time to come" (102). The "fault," she suggests, may not lie with her publicity of the numerous cultural tensions she writes of, but with the very fact of the society's willingness to turn away debate and "respectful dialogue" (147).

The emphasis on debate and its relationship to feminist transformation is critical to all the texts explicated in this chapter. In this novel, we see Alsanea exploring, in an often light-hearted way, a serious sociological and political shift. Although according to Eickelman and Anderson, "public dialogue has long held a special place in the Muslim world," the nature of that public arena is dramatically changing: "This combination of new media and new contributors to religious and political debates fosters an awareness on the part of all actors of diverse ways in which Islam and Islamic values can be created ... [This combination] feeds into a new sense of a public space that is discursive, performative, and participative."[52] Yet the relationship of traditional authorities or state governments to these new media (in the Western and non-Western worlds alike) can make that space risky, rather than safe, as political and religious authorities alike become expert in manipulating new media and social networking in their own interests. In a nation like Alsanea's Saudi Arabia, which is deeply invested in cutting-edge communication technologies, to limit access in order to control criticism or unwanted media messages is to risk disrupting business interactions and creating both economic pressure and political pressure.

Of the many consequences of the engagement with new media identified by Eickelman, Anderson and other scholars of "new political geography of communications" in the Muslim world, perhaps most relevant to my reading of *Girls of Riyadh* will be, as I have suggested, the "emergence of a public sphere."[53] In that sphere, former distinctions between private and public communications are blurring, with chat rooms and blogs enabling "a public of anonymous senders and recipients" and thus "a rhetoric of norms that transform the social imaginary and the idea of the public."[54] The creation of an unregulated "participative" space is precisely what the narrator proposes, a place to examine the clash of tradition and modernity with regard to Saudi ideologies of romance, courtship, and marriage. As Mernissi points out, "[a]part from the ritualized trespasses of women into public spaces (which are, by definition, male spaces), there are no accepted patterns for interactions among unrelated men and women,"⁵⁵ and no rules governing it. Yet "improvisation" in those spaces where sexual desegregation is occurring is nevertheless illicit.

This fictional account of a young woman's exploration of cyberspace also corresponds to accounts by Fereshteh Nouraie-Simone and others about the critical role that the Internet has come to play in the lives of Islamic youth. For Islamic women cyberspace offers a kind of mobility, including mobile identities that are otherwise denied in public spaces, where the "regulated uniformity" of men's and women's bodies includes a "disappearance of privacy and the right to anonymity in public space."⁵⁶ The retreat to cyberspace represented in this novel mirrors the "retreat to private space" as a "refuge from the watchful eyes of disciplinary control" that Nouraie-Simone describes among the Arab youth who "improvise" their own way "around restrictions of the social sphere." Their "improvisations" include such activities as "car cruising, exchange of telephone numbers in the middle of a traffic jam, and meetings in religious gatherings, coffee shops, and Internet chat rooms."⁵⁷ These activities are the stuff of *seerehwenfadha7et*'s text.

For this reason, anonymity is critical as "a tactic that transforms the notion of the public toward participation, as might illicit leaflets."⁵⁸ These developments erode conventionally established boundaries between public and private spaces. The bloggers create new arenas, or what Eickelman and Anderson refer to as "intermediate, connective spaces"⁵⁹ for active participation in open public debate. Ironically, however, the disguise of the memoirist's "real" identity and those of her friends is deemed necessary. Only as *seerehwenfadha7et*, her protected screen name, can the narrator promise to approach "a new world, a world closer than you might imagine. We all live in this world but do not really experience it, seeing only what we can tolerate and ignoring the rest" (1). Paradoxically, the memoirist suggests here that the world represented in this virtual medium is in some ways *more real* than the one in which many actually live. But because of her anonymity, she can make visible, rather than "ignore," the ways in which double standards and taboos damage women and men alike.

The narrator and her elite "velvet class" friends may not be living in harems, but as Mernissi teaches us the walls "in our heads" can be as strong as any physical constructs. The narrator addresses "all of you *out there,* those huddled in the shadow of a man, or a wall, or a man who is a wall, or simply stays put in the darkness" (2). In the same posting she quotes verse from modern poet Nizar Qabbani (b. 1923–d. 1998) concerning the way women live as "inmates," behind "doors that fail to open," their desires "slain in their cradles ... buried in pillows, in silence" (3). *Seerehwenfadha7et* seeks the electronic nowhere of a listserv to create a virtual arena without walls and doors, for the exposure – even publicity – of the clash of traditional gender expectations with the modern aspirations of contemporary women (primarily) and men. Although private communications in web chat rooms, over phones, and PDAs appear practically unmonitored, the "publication" of these communications, gathered for *seerehwenfadha7het*'s online memoir, places those private engagements in a new kind of public space.

The nature of that space itself changes over the course of the novel. *Seerehwenfadha7het*'s original intention is to represent the emotional economy of romantic and professional desire in the new Saudi Arabia, but the author is gradually invited into a broader economic and communication system. She discovers reviews and editorial pieces about herself appearing in "eminent national newspapers," with speculations about her identity. These commentaries focus on the "uproar" caused both by those who support "this young woman" and from those "who boil with rage at the revelation of what they consider to be the excesses that are going on around them in our conservative society" (102). Reader responses inform the blogger that many readers are entirely immersed in this virtual world of hers and *seerehwenfadha7et*'s own responses record either her appreciation or dismissal of narrative judgments and options. Yet eventually the limits of her society's own psychic economy emerge. Part of the story becomes, thereafter, *seerehwenfadhe7et*'s own reaction to the "discussions swirling like a sandstorm around *me*" on Saudi Internet forums; she coyly notes that it feels like "watching a bullfight – that is, two bulls fighting. Can any of you out there believe that someone would call for my blood?" (66). In the feminist project *seerehwenfadha7et* is working through, she herself is one of the "two bulls," pitted against patriarchal adversaries in this public arena.

The reader of *Girls of Riyadh* follows not one, but two narratives. First, there is the sometimes soap-opera-ish stories of the narrator's friends; and second, the linked "frames" of each weekly email chain of postings tracing the larger story. The latter narrative is more interesting, as the novel cleverly interweaves threads of narrative and interpretation spun by the yearnings of *seerehwenfadha7et*'s approving and disapproving readers, who alternately clamor for more details and revelations (including "real" names) or who clamor to shut down this discussion.

Returning full circle to chapter one of the novel, we realize that the novel traces the development of *seerehwenfadha7et* herself as a character rather than simply the muse or medium through which the stories of these others flow. This text, too, is a bildungsroman, whereby *seerehwen-fadha7et* is acculturated into the world of social entrepreneurship through technology. She entertains suggestions "to create a Web site for myself ... where I will publish my e-mails.... This will protect them from literary theft or loss, and I can increase the number of visitors with some advertisements and I can make money if I agree to put links to other Web sites on my Web page" (162). Although professing to be uninterested in making money, she does acknowledge the ego payback: "everyone, everywhere, seems to be talking about ME" (150). And after all, she decides, she will wait "for a more tempting offer," maybe even a "TV program all to myself" (162). Her increasingly entrepreneurial manipulation of media plays off of her initial, more narrowly intellectual (and naïve), intention to enlighten herself, her readers, and contemporary society.

In a reach toward metafiction, the author-narrator leads us to surmise that the appearance of this very novel we are reading, *Girls of Riyadh*, may have emerged as an idea proposed by "one of the guys reading my e-mails." He has proposed organizing all the postings into chapters for a book so that anyone and everyone could read them:

Ya salam! That's really something. For me to have a novel all my own! A book that would be displayed in bookstores and hidden in bedrooms. A book that some people would beg others to bring from oversees [*sic*]. (That's assuming that it would be banned here in Saudi.) And would I see my charming photo gracing its back covers – or defacing it – just like other writers? I was astonished but also frightened at the suggestion (188–189).

The author has also been working "diligent[ly]" herself to widen the reach of her work, "using addresses of subscribers to Yahoo and Hotmail" to involve literally thousands more readers. She continues, therefore, to entertain "enticing offers'" for television series and other modes of publication and publicity, imagining her story spilling over Saudi borders, into "neighboring Gulf states" and even onto the international scene.

The gradual dispersal of her message over cyberspace and the widening of her audience recall the general movement of the previous two novels examined in this chapter: the symbolic seeding of Mahdohkt around the world and the no-place of Mernissi women's creative elaborations, which promise freedom from the strictly gendered spaces of the harem and the city beyond its walls. Alsanea ends her novel with a chapter entitled "Between You and Me," addressed not only to the narrator's friends, but also to the fictional respondents, the public who both supported and challenged her effort to create this space of debate. The address is also to yet another audience: the readers, the public outside the text who, Alsanea hopes, might actualize this "new Arab world" in response to the debate that has taken place. And there is yet another distinct public who is addressed in some editions of this novel. Alsanea wrote an "Author's Note" for the 2007 printing of her novel in English. There, the author expresses satisfaction at being able to challenge Western clichés and misperceptions, and to show that some Arab women are, as she says, "beginning to carve out their own way – not the Western way, but one that keeps what is good about the values of their religion and culture" while allowing for reform (x).

Alsanea's epigraph from the Qur'an – placed between the "Author's Note" and the opening of the novel – indicates the critical catalyst for change: "*Verily, Allah does not change a people's condition until they change what is in themselves*" (The Chapter of Thunder, verse 11). These readings extend inevitably into contemporary debates about the relationship of Muslim or Islamic feminisms to Western feminisms, and the presence in both cultures of an ongoing "textualization of misogyny."[60] After explaining the various editorial enhancements designed for publication in the West, the author concludes by acknowledging women in Islamic society may indeed "live under male dominance." However, many are "full of hopes and plans and determinations and dreams" (x).

The possibility of revising traditional social identities and social contracts is not only "on the horizon" but, as such, always in the here and now. The global scaling of this vision (the dispersal of seeds, the "serene planet," cyberspace) confirms that these investments of desire are more than a momentary fantasy, but entanglements of reality and imagination expressed through gesture and language, animating desires in their cradle, birthing them into a widening political dimension.

Being at home somewhere

The function of the imagination is not to make strange things settled, so much as to make settled things strange.

– G. K. Chesterton

I prefer to think of imagination as a transitive act.

– Sonallah Ibrahim[1]

THE WORK AND PLAY OF POSSIBILITY

In the contemporary speculative fictions investigated in *Postmodern Utopias and Feminist Fictions*, the search for utopia has not meant the pursuit of impossible desires. It has meant the pursuit of ways in which desire remains possible. This is what I take to be the real work of utopia, and the ongoing goal of the work of the imagination. Louis Marin's concise and, to my mind, unmatched definition of utopia points at just the notion of utopian work and/as imaginative work that underlies the position laid out in the introduction to this book, as well as in its readings:

Utopia is the infinite work of the imagination's power of figuration. Utopia is the infinite *potential* of historical figures: it is this infinite, this 'work,' this *potential* that the Greek negation *ou* allows to be understood as a prefix to the name *topos*. Utopia is the plural figure of the infinite work of the limit or frontier or difference in history. *Totality and infinity: Utopia at the horizon of a voyage (travel).*[2]

As I have argued, that essential plurality is expressed in various tropes of generation: new bodies, new beings (human and not-quite), new narratives, new worlds and dimensions. But the sense of achievement in any single text is enjoyed only when the sense of an ending becomes its opposite: the sense of ongoing creativity or inventiveness, the realization of a reflexively creative logic. Call it speculation or *transitive imagining* – Sonallah Ibrahim suggests (in the second epigraph) that what I am calling speculation is thus an *action*, by which we "arrive at the process of imagination, or rather [at] the process of creating through the act of imaging." This is a succinct articulation of this study's effort to describe a speculative standpoint *as* a utopian positioning.

In the context of working through a speculative standpoint, however, this inventiveness of transitional tropes and figures is effective only as it reflects (on) the partiality of its contexts. The invention must be an *inter-vention*, a coming toward or across that comes between, and creates a new oppositionality – more like an apposition. Its figuration is not a field of war, but a field of play. It is not a singular place, nor even a certain time, but a particular situation that opens up both space and time. A tangential dimension. A landing place that is also a launch pad, or a portal. Octavia Butler, Nalo Hopkinson, Ursula LeGuin, Doris Lessing, Jeanette Winterson, Toni Morrison, Fatima Mernissi, Shahrnush Parsipur, Rajaa Alsanea: each gestures toward such a discovery. The purpose of locating such portals is not to achieve the state of being at home nowhere and everywhere, living in a culture of no culture. It is not the work of imposing will, particularly when that will stems from certain knowledge. Rather, the work of speculative standpoint becomes being at home *somewhere*, to recall Munis's striking formulation, but only temporarily, until one is urged on. "We only know that movement is the key," confirms Winterson, and the convention of utopian literature as travel romance underscores the imperative of movement. But the in(ter)vention of these novels is the joining of the archaeologies of the past *and* of the future with the present,[3] a triple-helix, to generate an endless work of vision and revision. The evolution of these connections is the plot of each of these novels; any one of them could be titled *Transit*, with a nod to Lessing's Roman historian.

The figure of the self-generated, embodied perfect knower with whom I began this study is thus countered, from one novel to the next, by the figure of another "generation" of human being: a baby with or without "that extra limb"; a Robo *sapiens*, or some other figuration of emergent subjectivity. This is true whether the text is more concerned with intercourse between two individuals or with the social intercourse that makes up a community. As we have seen, Tobin Siebers would propose conflating these two possibilities in terms of what he insightfully identifies as a tropological touchstone for utopia in the postmodern period: the couple, and the coupling,[4] of persons, of ideas, of one community to another, one country to another, one historical moment to another, backward or forward. The sensibility cultivated through speculative standpoint, however, makes possible a re(con)figuration of history that is neither "simply" linear nor cyclical. Rather, it is the inventiveness of a weaving and reweaving of threads, connecting "parallel Lines of Memories" as well as parallel lines of anticipation or hopeful imagining. This is the work of speculative fiction, to invent ways to intervene that are not always just a disruption but an evolution. Either way, the critical element of this work is the alienation or strangeness from ordinary consciousness that these novels have consistently attended to, in the figure I am calling a feminist speculative observer. This work opens up a space of momentary "objectivity," if not neutrality, that approaches the "space of critical no-whereness"[5] privileged in contemporary feminist standpoint thought.

More than that, these texts show us the ways in which the view from and of "nowhere," and the ways of *being* nowhere, teach us the fictions of truth, and the truths of fiction. There are many ways of being nowhere for a woman, from the abjection of Offred's submission in *Handmaid's Tale*, to the kind of partially developed, speculative standpoint in which one is "at home" nowhere, like Munis. The most successfully figured instances of that standpoint, at home nowhere and everywhere, are characters such as Lauren Olamina, the heroine of Octavia Butler's *Parable of the Sower,* or Hopkinson's Tan-Tan, or the representation of the young Fatima, or the robot, Spike. "Space could be our future," says Lauren Olamina early in *Parable of the Sower* (20), and Lauren's childhood, like Fatima's, is full of dreams of flying. In Lauren's first recorded dream, she reports that "I'm learning to fly, to levitate myself. No one is teaching me. I'm just learning on my own, little by little, dream lesson by dream lesson" (4). In one version of this recurrent dream, there is a wall burning before her that she struggles to avoid, sometimes unable to. These dreams foreshadow the incendiary reality Lauren will inhabit, but also prefigure the risks all these traveling protagonists invite when they challenge a reality that no longer makes sense. They model the multiple narratives, disjoined temporally yet connected via the time-bridges that are constructed, deconstructed, and reconstructed, continually. The dreams catalyze shifts in consciousness, personal and social, and in the personal and social "dimensions" of speculative narrative. Such is the nuanced sensibility of Octavia Butler's work that it is able to build on the narratological advances of Joanna Russ, for instance, in order to fully engage us in imagining a more hospitable elsewhere than any of the future options offered in *The Female Man.*

The most complex and groundbreaking of the novels studied here reveal the alterity not only of the "elsewhere" to which we are transported, but the alterity(-ies) of the world in which we live, as well as the strangeness and contradictions "in ourselves." The implications of that confrontation, a face-to-face speculation on "the other" inside and outside each individual, can be extensive, as Susan Buck-Morss has so eloquently shown us in her *Thinking Past Terror*.[6] Inhabiting "the strange we are" is a method of reorienting our perspective, contextualizing reality anew such that we are more able to *see* the risks of any speculation. As Winterson and Atwood alike are fond of reminding us, it is a gamble – and nothing so simple as a numbers game or a word game either. It is more like playing against the rules of the game, while simultaneously figuring out what the rules are. And while Fatima Mernissi's mother warns that even playing is a kind of war, our English word "game" also suggests an alternative metaphor: a communion, a "people together" (P.Gmc. **ga*-collective prefix+**mann* "person"). Such a community is also (this same etymological history tells us) an experience of "joy, fun," even "merriment" and "glee."[7] Even here, the metaphors strain toward community and modes of shared connectivity, toward a feminist hospitality rather than opposition or hostility.

Ultimately this book claims the need for effective speculative work as invention and as intervention. This could be said of all utopian, speculative, and science fictions of course. But the distinction of these texts, authored by some of our great contemporary women writers, is a change in the writer's "economy of purpose." In *The Stone Gods*, this phrase refers to the fine-tuning of an ideological system that rationalizes every aspect of its global (even extraterrestrial) operation. In that same novel, however, the word "purpose" begins to shift away from a masculinist sense of "willful purpose" leading to mastery and efficiency. In that economy of purpose, the work of an artist is inefficient, and thus of little use or value socially or politically. An "economy of the human body" proposes a different model altogether, depending on other forms of exchange, other currencies. Its purpose is not maximum efficiency for maximum profit. Rather, it proposes a purposeful approach toward a progressive, generous relationality, toward an erotics of community as well as of art: a "beginning to love," say both Morrison and Winterson. That "love" is not taken (only) in the narrow sense of emotional attachment or even erotic passion, but more in a broader sense of *hospitality* toward another or others, a welcoming of another into one's home and self, hoping, if not expecting, to be welcomed by others.

A feminist "economy of the human body" means turning away from the so-called dismal science of economics, and away from a vision of the future that creates "a new generation of humans made out of the hatred of others," as Jeanette Winterson so grimly puts it. It means, to recall Jill Dolan, performances of gestures that "clarify" if only for a "utopian moment" a robust relationality revealing, as Molz and Gibson observe, "its complex nature in a range of places, moments, objects and fantasies, from the material gestures of a warm smile, laden table or cozy bed, to the moral tales of Philemon or the Good Samaritan, to the iconic symbols of an open door or of the Statue of Liberty."[8] Furthermore, we can extend the purview of this relationality to include ecological gestures such as beach cleanups, an animal rescue, a reforestation project. This economy would value decisions to refuse single-use plastics, to buy local and organic, to avoid using one's car, to boycott irresponsible corporations who dissociate their products and methods of production from the damage it does to the environment, and to human and nonhuman creatures alike. It values any clear gesture of an *ecological*, as opposed to traditionally *economical*, good purpose. Only in the performance of these gestures – small and large, individual or national or international – do we even *think* of making productive "a human society that wasn't just disgust,"[9] thus tending toward exclusion of others; instead, we might make productive a human society that assumes equal measures of strength *and* fragility, and tends toward inclusion.

At the same time, we are urged to remember that the concept of hospitality – like the concept of utopia – embodies "its own impossibility," and thus brings into view all the images of exclusion and violence (walls, gated communities, arson, orgies, racism, sexism, etc.) that mark the landscapes and cityscapes of these novels. Although Toni Morrison and Fatima Mernissi remind us that "all paradises, all utopias," are designed by the people who "can't get in," each author will realize that an ideal home is *not only* the "one place" where each is truly welcome and free to stay; it is also the only place they are free to leave. Recall Mernissi's challenge that "[m]ore important probably than the right to enter Paradise, is the right to leave it for no reason other than a totally arbitrary, whimsical desire to discover other horizons."[10] Consolata, in Morrison's text, would concur. But both learn that when such a "perfect intimacy" is rejected as a goal, the most likely counterforce is intimidation.

Only by attending to such contradictions inevitably in play and in place can we remain aware that there is always more than the personal at stake. I think of Buck-Morss's call for a global public, to be cultivated through a commitment to a contemporary notion of a cosmopolitanism that requires not just face-to-face confrontation, but self-reflexive confrontation as well. One of overarching themes of this study, therefore, has been the necessary evolution of a tradition of hospitality that has long embodied a suspicion of feminine alterity. In such a context, a woman is never at home in a man's house. These feminist speculative novels shift the metaphors of hospitality away from gates, doors, and windows – figures that connote discrete borders, such as the slash marks between mine/ not mine, male/female, us/them, Squirts/ Clefts, even human/nonhuman signifies. Derrida's analysis of the fundamental impossibility of hospitality, Karima Laachir notes, resists a definition that is

marked by the paternal and the phallogocentric, or by the logic of the master/host, nation, the door or the threshold. His critique calls into question the limitations of this specifically "European" history of hospitality and suggests a future beyond this history, and thus a hospitality beyond the logic of "paternity" (and its extension to the nation) or the *logos*.[11]

Such a logic, the novels in this study suggest, come from beyond the *Logos*; rather, it is the logic of the coming-together-of-bodies. *Eros*. For all their differences, these novels share the goal of exploring the dimensions of hospitality. The hospitable space would not exclude but include by creating an aesthetic community, one that Siebers describes as "[rivaling] any worldly republic and that can be realized on the strength of the desire for community inspired by its very imagination. It is not a pure community – one purified of conflicting interests – but a community with many different stories."[12]

What an apt description of the narrative task of these novels, particularly as we move from Chapters 1, 2, and 3 of the study, which focus more on individual heroes, and into Chapters 4 and 5, which shift our attention more deliberately toward community. The "endless work" (Morrison) is the infinite task of dwelling among the network of affiliations, extending hospitality elsewhere, such that one imagines community as itself a kind of living, desiring entity, a loving communion where everybody comes. This is an economy of purpose related not to mastery and the production of sameness, but to the play of difference, diversity, and heterogeneity. This economy values the "contextuality" of a moral maturity that attends to empathy and sympathy,[13] and its currency is in the generous gesture. Such a moral economy embraces a new vision of citizenship in the heterotopic communities of which Siebers speaks.[14]

REGARDING THE WAY WE LIVE NOW:
"WHAT ARE OUR SAVING GRACES?"

How many sailors have been wrecked in pursuit of islands that were merely a shimmering? – Margaret Atwood[15]

Every one of the writers treated in *Postmodern Utopias and Feminist Fictions* acknowledges the riskiness of this "utopia work." The question just cited in the epigraph would suggest proceeding with caution, but Atwood's recent novels show as well as anyone's that the greater risk is to fold up the treasure map to Utopia. Every novel begins with the question "What if?" as Atwood claims in an interview on *Oryx and Crake*. Her sense of her own speculative, what-if project is to confront what she regards as an oncoming "perfect storm"[16] in human history: the triumph of an "economy of purpose" in the confusion of rationality and passion, of egoism and morality, of technology and art, of all gendered oppositions. "The *what if* of *Oryx and Crake* is simply, *What if we continue down the road we're already on? How slippery is the slope? What are our saving graces? Who's got the will to stop us?* … It's not a question of our inventions – all human inventions are merely tools – but of what might be done with them."[17] Not just inventions, as I have been arguing, but interventions. This is as true of the work of art as it is the work of technology.

The novels therefore focus increasingly on the nature of responsibility, and on our own education into an ethical future both in terms of individual and "corporate" (whether as national or global citizens) well-being. To recall my discussion of irony in the introduction, these texts are also Janus-faced, looking backward and forward, attending to both the obscure motives and even obscurer consequences of what has happened already in history. The invisibility of risk rises to the surface of these narratives, particularly those of Chapters 4 and 5, although the theme is clearly visible in the very earliest examples of feminist speculation. We see it in Mary Shelley's *Frankenstein; or, The Modern Prometheus*; we see it also in the much earlier *Blazing World* of Margaret Cavendish, in which a sea voyage begins for a wealthy young Lady when an enraptured merchant "forced her away" from her father's home. What else? – a rape. It seems worth pointing out that in both of these early speculative narratives, a violation of hospitality incites journeys for places were such violations are unimaginable.

As noted in the Preface, Atwood has for decades now warned against hardening ourselves against the other. Thus, the "blinders" of Offred's uniform and the Wall that becomes the backdrop of Gilead's reprisal against dissent. Thus, Crake's bubble-dome compound, Paradice; its walls and gates insulating and isolating this center of power from the roles of public inspection.[18] Like the handmaid Offred before him, Jimmy/ Snowman now sees, too late, what he looked at for years and *didn't* see: the unwitting – or was it witting? – complicity to a "perfect system" – a utopia – that gradually undercut individual free will and social freedoms.

In her own speculative trilogy, Atwood's narrative examines the duplicitous ethics and politics of modern risk *un*consciousness. The novels in *Postmodern Utopias and Feminist Fictions* nearly all speak to the ways in which open speculation is stamped out by those who understand and manipulate the relationships of power to knowledge. Scientific myths of progress – bolstered by promises of financial, technological, and thus social progress – can undermine the objectivity of science, blinding experts and laypersons alike to the perception of possible, or even likely, negative consequences. Regarding contemporary risks in our own world – climate change, for instance, or genetic enhancement technologies – we are consistently warned against being "doomed by hope," as Atwood's Crake puts it (120). That is, doomed by an unexamined desire for "more and better" that may "eventually overwhelm" (295) our own future, as it did Jimmy's and Crake's. If that happens, Atwood grimly proposes, the fault will be our own. The privilege of ignorance betrays us by offering false images of reality and of what the future could, and should, look like. Atwood and the other authors of apocalyptic threat urge a "reflexive modernity," as sociologist Ulrich Beck would call it.[19] Such a stance, Adam and Van Loon remind us, "requires us to be meditative, that is, looking back upon that which allows us to reflect in the first place."[20]

Beck reminds us that the temporal not-yet of risk can blur the very perception of that risk. The non-yet of the most unlikely, yet riskiest scenarios allows them to be characterized as fictions to be dismissed as too improbable to be true or "realistic." Unwanted criticism of, or interference with, risky ventures is therefore often dismissed as "mere speculation." But that speculation is, of course, precisely what is needed to identify the hidden risks in the first place. Social theory such as Beck's helps us "transform 'the language of risk' from the ethos of calculation (and binary logic) to the ethos of mediation."[21] So do art-works that help us discern what Winterson calls the "economy of purpose," as opposed to the "economy of the human body." Artists such as Carter, Butler, and Hopkinson; Winterson and Atwood; Sontag and Morrison; LeGuin and Lessing; El Saadawi, Parsipur, Mernissi, Alsanea – all ask a question similar to Atwood's "What if?": What if it were not the best, but the worst possible world? What then? What *are* our saving graces?

The possibilities of the imaginative arts counteract epistemologies of ignorance by foregrounding (in the stories and scenarios they construct) the political nature of social constructions of risk. These texts show us again and again that to gain a critical understanding of the situatedness of our own knowledge, art is as rigorous a pedagogical tool as science.

Art and literature are the indispensable products of *social* rationality, as defined by Beck: not the logic of so-called pure intellect, but the logic of the heart, which comes to know things in a different way. The calculations of a social rationality are based on emotional and ethical "data," information provided by subjective experience, rather than on unchallenged myths that organize the definitions of objectivity, truth, and "what counts" as knowledge.

Atwood, in particular, will not countenance the demeaning of the imagination's unique accounting of the relationships between desire and reality. She rarely allows her readers to forget that art's critical role of mirroring back to us who we "really are" is itself only realized when society is free. Free enough to permit artists a stab at getting to the truth, as they see it; free enough to let readers or spectators be guided on an artist's journey through heaven or hell. Both kinds of freedoms are grounded by a moral responsibility each human being has, to be mindful of how far we are from heaven, and how close we are to "Hell, monsters, angels and all." Atwood's insistence on art's affiliation with "some kind of standard of humanity" (Sontag would call it sympathy) requires "freedom," not just to live but also to love. These are freedoms, notes Atwood, "which any such regime is going to violate. They will violate it saying that it's for the good of all, or the good of the many, or the better this or better that. And the artists will always protest and they'll always get shot. Or go into exile."[22] Take Shahrnush Parsipur, for example.

Every writer treated in *Postmodern Utopias and Feminist Fictions* remains staunch in her defense of humanity's imaginative capacity to express "something that is true to itself" and to offer thereby

a revelation of the full range of our human response to the world – that is, what it means to be human, on earth. That seems to be what "hope" is about in relation to art. Nothing so simple as "happy endings" … An approach to perfection, if you like. Hope comes from the fact that people create, that they find it worthwhile to create. Not just from the nature of what is created.[23]

That is to say, the sterile environment of traditional epistemology and its self-generating knowledge *must* be contaminated, "touched together" with alternative ways of knowing. As we think about the "contamination" of so-called knowledge with alternative epistemologies, therefore, we must think beyond yet again – to the community beyond the human, and our responsibilities to the nonhuman. As we have seen in the work of Octavia Butler and Margaret Atwood in particular, the constructedness of Nature, framed by scientific narratives and exploitative economic practices, is an aspect of human experience we must continue to deconstruct. Our footprints in the sand mark the heavy, heedless tread of humanity's wasteful exploitation of natural resources, another "nauseous" story[24] belonging to the ethical crises of our historical moment. Most of the texts studied here explore a different relationship with the nonhuman other, with animals and with nature, proposing (sometimes explicitly) the emergence of a new environmentalism that, thankfully, we are beginning to see. This movement pushes back against an "economics of purpose" motivated by the twin desires of profit and control. While this study primarily explores speculative fiction's transitive imagining of bridges among individuals and communities, it foregrounds, too, these authors' interest in exploring the border between humanity and nature. It proposes that we reconsider the aptness of the border metaphor in that context, at all.

Where this study of feminist speculative fiction has led me is to another growing body of speculative literature: climate-change fiction. The politics of knowledge and the purveyance of doubt are likely to remain at the center of literary and filmic narratives regarding climate change and the assault on environmental health. This project grows naturally out of *Postmodern Utopias and Feminist Fictions*, as the relationships between humanity, technology, and nature have haunted many of the novels examined here. The body of fiction focusing on climate change remains small, and as a subgenre it is underdeveloped. But environmental degradation provides a backdrop for an increasing number of narratives. Although he was not the first to register the effects and threats of climate change in fiction (J. G. Ballard's *The Drowned World* [1962] and *The Drought* [1965] as well as Le Guin's *The Lathe of Heaven* [1971] are personal favorites), science fiction writer Kim Stanley Robinson kickstarted interest in climate-change fiction "as such" just as the twenty-first century opened. Robinson's *Science in the Capital* trilogy (2004–2007) imagines the costs of the kind of willed ignorance Atwood is interested in, and speculates on what it would take to prompt both science-makers and policy-makers to allow, or even welcome, the contamination of their own (self-)interested ways of knowing and thinking, and to collaborate on imaginative and responsible actions.

As the realities of global warming continue to fuel specious (non) debates about the very existence of "climate change," there is no question that the politics of knowledge production is a conundrum to be reckoned with. This reckoning becomes the very plot of the novels themselves, as in Robinson's trilogy, or, among those included in this book, *Oryx and Crake*, *The Stone Gods*, and also more recent novels: Liz Jensen's *The Rapture*

(2010); the deeply ironical *Solar*, by Ian McEwen; Paolo Bacigalupi's *The Wind-Up Girl* (2009); James Jaros's *Burn Down the Sky* (2011); Tobias S. Buckell's *Arctic Rising* (2012); and more. As we consider alternative models of generating knowledge, I cannot think it to be an accident that the cultural meme appearing most consistently is *the virus*. This is not a new trope, but it has established itself in our cultural imaginations – and my suspicion is that it has something to do with the self-generating genius that every virus represents.

However, I want to suggest here another kind of story that might get told. I have been promoting a notion of hospitality based in imaginative sympathy (love) rather than suspicion and hostility, collaboration rather than contamination or conspiracy. If at the bottom of the philosophical debate about hospitality is a battle of the sexes (from the time of Clefts and Squirts, by Lessing's account), that battle may be troped in contemporary literature of climate catastrophe by an *agon* between gendered political economies. *Oryx and Crake* certainly argues this.[25] Winterson's presentation of a contrast between a clearly masculinist "economy of purpose" and an ungendered "economy of the human body" is important and useful. But to extend our thinking about the relationship between humankind and nature in terms of climate change and environmental impact, I propose a different contrast, between an economy of purpose, and an economy of *regard*.

"Regard" is a word describing a type of "looking" that is intensive (from *re-*, intensive prefix, + O.Fr. *garder* "look, heed"). The word evolved to connote "consideration, appearance, kindly feeling," and a kind of "esteem, affection."[26] Behind this shift is a valuation that becomes clear when we remember that the words *regard, guard,* and *guardian* are closely related. One guards only what is regarded as valuable. In the peculiar way etymologies have of surprising one, all those words are related to the word "ward," the O.Fr. *garder* corresponding to Frankish **wardon*, which refers to a "collective sense of 'a keeping, a custody.'" It gives give us our word, "ward." "Regard" would be therefore a form of attention, a "taking notice of" that suggests an ongoing effort, a valuation. Thinking about environmental degradation, those connections between looking, attending to, responding to and being responsible for become critical. Once again, it becomes a matter of "accounting." How then are we to "regard" Nature? What is the basis for being a guardian of Nature? Is it possible to feel at home in Nature? Is it possible, I would like to know, to have "no regard" for nature, and have a high regard for humankind at the same time? No wonder, in *The Stone Gods*, that Billie struggles to keep intact the tract of verdant, English farm acreage, which comes to symbolize her original home. She has the deepest regard for nature.

The warning that "the day of reckoning is upon us" is hard to take seriously when it has come and gone so many times. Yet the ways and means of "reckoning" or "accounting for" the interconnections of gender and climate are suggestive. The textual analyses in this study lead consistently to the nature of relationships between knowledge and ignorance, risk and reward, inattention and fear response. In future work I hope to extend these investigations into the literature of climate change, be they scientific narratives, poetical or fictional ones, be they works of visual art (the "Avant-Guardians," for example) or movement arts, or music. We will need art to clarify how and why we are inattentive to, even wilfully ignorant of, the risks we are taking with future, encouraged by the false economies of purpose and of profit[27] – that is, of economic "futures," and not ecological ones.

Ignorance and inattention (not the same thing) hide from us the desires, psychological and ideological, driving the science and the story that society tells about itself and its objects of study. That story – where it comes from, how it gets structured, who gets to tell it and who has to listen, who sees it as a "gospel truth" and who recognizes it as a fiction, truthful or not, who or what is at risk in the telling and living of the story, and who is not – is the one that interests Atwood in her recent novels. The riskiest business we engage in today is not the business of science, but of looking elsewhere while we become entangled[28] in the threads of a (his)story that gets written for us. The nature of our journey is a commitment to yet one more Atwood injunction; in fact, these sentences close the aforementioned defense of art:

Understanding the imagination is no longer a pastime or even a duty, but a necessity; because increasingly if we can imagine it, we'll be able to do it.

Therefore, not farewell, dear reader/voyager, but fare forward.[29]

Our saving grace, then, is yet another story.

Notes

PREFACE

1 Toni Morrison, interview with Elizabeth Farnsworth. Retrieved at: www.pbs. org/newshour/bb/entertainment/jan-june98/morrison_3–9.html
2 Donna Haraway, "Situated Knowledges: The Science Question in Feminism and the Privilege of Partial Perspective," *Feminist Studies* 14.3 (Autumn, 1988), 584.
3 Susan Sontag, "Against Postmodernism, etcetera." Retrieved at: http://www. iath.virginia.edu/pmc/text-only/issue.901/12.1chan.txt.
4 Susan Sontag, quotation retrieved at http://www.susansontag.com.
5 William Godwin, "Of Love and Friendship (Essay XV)," retrieved at: http://www.readbookonline.net/readOnLine/60096/.
6 Jeanette Winterson, *The Stone Gods* (New York: Mariner Books, 2007), 88.

INTRODUCTION

1 Rachel DuPlessis, *Writing Beyond the Ending: Narrative Strategies of Twentieth-Century Women Writers* (Bloomington: Indiana University Press, 1985), 142 and 161.
2 DuPlessis, *Writing Beyond the Ending*, 178.
3 Mary Anne Doane, "Post-Utopian Difference," in *Coming to Terms: Feminism, Theory, Politics*, ed. Elizabeth Weed (New York: Routledge, 1989), 177.
4 See Marleen Barr, *Future Females, The Next Generation: New Voices and Velocities in Feminist Science Fiction Criticism* (New York: Rowman & Littlefield Publishers, 2000), xxix. Also see: Lucie Armitt, *Contemporary Women's Fiction and the Fantastic* (New York: St Martin's Press, 2000); Nina Auerbach, *Communities of Women: An Idea in Fiction* (Cambridge, MA: Harvard University Press, 1978); Angelika Bammer, *Partial Visions: Feminism and Utopianism in the 1970s* (New York: Routledge, 1991); Marleen Barr, *Feminist Fabulations: Space/Postmodern Fiction* (Des Moines: University of Iowa Press, 1992); Frances Bartkowski, *Feminist Utopias* (Lincoln: University of Nebraska Press, 1989); Jennifer Burwell, *Notes on Nowhere: Feminism, Utopian Logic and Social Transformation* (Minneapolis: University of Minneapolis Press, 1997); Nancy Miller, "Changing the Subject," in *Coming to Terms*,

173–204, and also Nancy Miller's *Subject to Change: Reading Feminist Writing* (New York: Columbia University Press, 1988); Jenny Wolmark, *Aliens and Others: Science Fiction, Feminism and Postmodernism* (Iowa City: University of Iowa Press, 1994).

5 Bammer, *Partial Visions*, 16–17.

6 Louis Marin, "Frontiers of Utopia Past and Present," *Critical Inquiry* 19 (1993): 397–420.

7 See: Ernst Bloch, *The Utopian Function of Art and Literature, Selected Essays*. Trans. Jack Zipes and Frank Mecklenburg (Cambridge, MA: MIT Press, 1988); David Harvey, *Spaces of Hope* (Berkeley and Los Angeles: University of California Press, 2000); Fredric Jameson, *Archaeologies of the Future: The Desire Called Utopia and Other Science Fictions* (London and New York: Verso, 2005); Louis Marin; Erin McKenna, *The Task of Utopia: A Pragmatist and Feminist Perspective* (New York: Rowman & Littlefield Publishers, 2001); Ruth Levitas, *The Concept of Utopia* (1990. Oxford and Bern: Peter Lang, 2010); Tom Moylan, *Demand the Impossible* (New York and London: Methuen, 1986), and *Scraps of the Untainted Sky: Science Fiction, Utopia, Dystopia* (Boulder, CO and Oxford: Westview Press, 2000); Lucy Sargisson, *Contemporary Feminist Utopianism* (New York: Routledge, 1996). Sargisson's newest book is entitled *Fool's Gold? Utopianism in the Twenty-First Century* (London: Palgrave-Macmillan, 2012). As the book was not yet released as I wrote this, I was unfortunately not able to incorporate her always provocative arguments and models for thinking about utopia.

8 Martha Meskimmon discusses "transitivity" and the "transitive affects" of imagination through artwork in *Contemporary Art and the Cosmopolitan Imagination* (New York: Routledge, 2011). See esp. ch. 3, "Passage – transitive affects" (53–73). This is only one of several projects engaged with recuperating a "strong sense" of the imagination and the critical connection of imagination with sympathy and hospitality.

9 See Phillip E. Wegner, *Life between Two Deaths, 1989–2001: U.S. Culture in the Long Nineties* (Durham, NC: Duke University Press, 2009), 15. This wonderfully rich and carefully argued study affirms the role of imagination and the visionary in inventing "new imaginaries of radical political agency" (15). Also see John Su's equally valuable *Imagination and Contemporary Culture* (New York: Cambridge University Press, 2011). Both speak to and enhance my own arguments, from different approaches and angles.

10 This theme of work relates of course to the Marxian roots of standpoint theory. See Nancy Hartsock, *The Feminist Standpoint Revisited and Other Essays* (Boulder, CO: Westview Press, 1998), esp. ch. 6 (105–132). Also see Sandra G. Harding, *The Feminist Standpoint Theory Reader: Intellectual and Political Controversies* (New York: Routledge, 2003). The kind of creative work that art might do is not something she takes up here; rather, it is picked up by theorists such as Donna Haraway and Rosi Braidotti.

11 Margaret Atwood, in *Waltzing Again: New and Selected Conversations with Margaret Atwood*, ed. Earl G. Ingersoll, (Princeton, NJ: Ontario Review, 2006), 220.

12 Fredric Jameson, *The Cultural Turn* (New York: Verso, 1998), 92. The entire chapter, "'End of Art' or 'End of History,'" gives important background to this introduction, and the questions addressed by this study.

13 Richard Kearney, *The Wake of Imagination: Toward a Postmodern Culture* (Minneapolis: University of Minnesota Press, 1988), 392.

14 Kearney suspects the ability of irony and parody to reduce an image to a "floating signifier without reference or reason"; the imagination "ceases to function as a creative centre of meaning" (*Wake of Imagination*, 13). Nor is it necessary to insist on a "certain *narrative identity*" that is unified, as Kearney's form of critique of postmodernism implies. Understanding the multiplicity of identities in social contexts is itself an ethical task. It is just here that a feminist intervention can be made (see n. 19).

15 See Sarah Lefanu, *Feminism and Science Fiction* (Bloomington: Indiana University Press, 1989): "engagement with the here and now [fuels] the desire for something else, for something 'elsewhere'" (53). Also see Bammer, *Partial Visions*, esp. 48–66 and 119–53.

16 Donna Haraway, *Modest_Witness@Second_Millenium.FemaleMan©_Meets_ OncoMouse™: Feminism and Technoscience* (New York: Routledge, 1997), 35.

17 Franco Moretti, *The Way of the World: The Bildungsroman in European Culture* (New York: Verso, 2000), 121.

18 Fredric Jameson, *The Ideologies of Theory: Essays 1971–1986, vol. 2: The Syntax of History* (London: Routledge, 1988), 87–88.

19 Linda Hutcheon, *Irony's Edge: The Theory and Politics of Irony* (New York: Routledge, 1995), 105.

20 Iris Marion Young observes that dismissal of irony and other figurative types of language presupposes a unity of the subject, whereas feminist models of communication acknowledge "the multiple meaning that any movement of signification expresses" (71). See Young, "Impartiality and the Civic Public: Some Implications of Feminist Critiques of Moral and Political Theory," in *Feminism as Critique*, ed. Sayla Benhabib and Drucilla Cornell (Minneapolis: University of Minnesota Press, 1987), 57–76.

21 On the concept of horizon, see Hans-Georg Gadamer, *Truth and Method*, 2nd rev. edn., trans. Joel Weinsheimer and Donald G. Marshall. (New York: Crossroads, 1990), 302–307.

22 Miller, *Subject to Change,* 15–16.

23 Rosi Braidotti, "The Subject in Feminism," *Hypatia* 6.2 (Summer 1991): 162.

24 Mary Ann Doane, "Commentary: Post-Utopian Difference," in *Coming to Terms*, ed. Weed, 78.

25 Su, *Imagination and the Contemporary Novel*, 4.

26 Haraway, *Modest_Witness*, 199.

27 Haraway, *Modest_Witness*, 23.

28 Hartsock, "Postmodernism and Political Change," *Cultural Critique* 14 (1989–1990): 20.

29 Lorraine Code, "Taking Subjectivity into Account," in *Women, Knowledge and Reality, Explorations in Feminist Philosophy*, ed. Ann Garry and Marilyn Pearsall (New York: Routledge, 1996), 206.

30 Haraway, *Modest_Witness*, 23.

31 Haraway, *Modest_Witness*, 24.

32 Haraway, *Modest_Witness*, 36.

33 The word *virtue* derives from the Latin *vir*, "man," and acquired the meaning, "hero." Attributes of virtue are coded masculine; "female virtues" are named as such, referring to virginity, submissiveness and agreeableness, piety, and so forth.

34 Haraway, *Modest_Witness*, 147.

35 Haraway, *Modest_Witness*, 148.

36 Haraway, *Modest_Witness*, 30. See 30–36 for full discussion.

37 Rosi Braidotti, *Nomadic Subjects: Embodiment and Sexual Difference in Contemporary Feminist Theory* (New York: Columbia University Press, 1994), 72.

38 See Marilyn Frye: "[I]t is in the structures of men's stories of the world that women don't make sense – that our own experience, collectively and jointly appreciated, can generate a picture of ourselves and the world within which we are intelligible.... Assuming our perceptual authority, we have undertaken, as we must, to re-write the world." See "The Possibility of Feminist Theory," in *Women, Knowledge, and Reality*, ed. Ann Garry and Marilyn Pearsall (1996). The theme of "common sense" and nonsense is an important marker of ideology in the English novel; see Su, *Imagination and the Contemporary Novel* on the Kantian background of this term (192, n. 34).

39 Donna Haraway, "Situated Knowledges: The Science Question in Feminism and the Privilege of Partial Perspective," in *The Feminist Standpoint Theory Reader: Intellectual and Political Controversies*, ed. Sandra Harding (New York: Routledge, 2004), 94.

40 Haraway, "Situated Knowledges," 96.

41 Braidotti, *Nomadic Subjects*, 22.

42 Haraway, *Modest_Witness*, 198–199.

43 Haraway, *Modest_Witness*, 127.

44 Haraway, *Modest_Witness*, 39.

45 See Joseph Rouse's "Feminism and the Social Construction of Scientific Knowledge," in *Feminist Standpoint Theory Reader*, ed. Harding, 353–374. Rouse's efforts to work together feminist standpoint theory and philosophy of science in order to read a "social understanding of science" (354) has been fundamental to my thinking about standpoint and utopia.

46 Haraway, *Modest_Witness*, 199.

47 I allude both to Haraway's use of the word in describing Joanna Russ's "Female Man" and the feminist witness generally as "a generic scandal" (*Modest_Witness*, 71), one who does not conform to "categories of culture," her "boundaries ... messed up from the start" (71). The scandal of being a woman is also discussed in the co-authored introduction to *The Scandal of Susan Sontag*, ed. Barbara Ching and Jennifer Wagner-Lawlor (New York: Columbia University Press, 2009), 1–19.

48 See Darko Suvin, *Metamorphoses of Science Fiction: On the Poetics and History of a Literary Genre* (New Haven: Yale University Press, 1971).

49 The term comes from Whitehead's *Process and Reality*, corrected edn., ed. David Ray Griffin (New York: The Free Press, 1978), and is explicated in Part I, chapter II, esp. section IV (19–30).

50 Nancy Hartsock, *Feminist Standpoint Revisited*, 245.

51 Haraway, "Situated Knowledges," 89. See Braidotti's discussion of this critical essay in *Nomadic Subjects*, ch. 7, "Images Without Imagination" (189–212).

52 Haraway, "Situated Knowledges," 96.

53 Haraway, *Modest_Witness*, 26.

54 See Lennard J. Davis, *Factual Fictions: The Origins of the English Novel* (New York: Columbia University Press, 1983); Margaret Anne Doody, *The True Story of the Novel* (New Brunswick, NJ: Rutgers University Press, 1998); Terry Eagleton, "What is a Novel?" in *The English Novel: An Introduction* (Oxford: Blackwell Publishing, 2005), 1–21; Fredric Jameson, *The Political Unconscious* (Ithaca, NY: Cornell University Press, 1981); Richard W. F. Kroll, ed., *The English Novel, vol. I: 1700 – Fielding* (Longman Publishing Group, 1998); Michael McKeon, *The Origins of the English Novel, 1600–1740* (Baltimore: The John Hopkins University Press, 1987); Patrick Parrinder, *Nation & Novel: The English Novel from its Origins to the Present Day* (New York: Oxford University Press, 2006).

55 Haraway, *Modest_Witness*, 35.

56 Haraway, *Modest_Witness*, 75.

57 See Julie Giese, "Comic Disruption in the World of Maxine Hong Kingston," in *Performing Gender and Comedy: Theories, Texts and Contexts*, ed. Shannon Hengen (Amsterdam: Gordon and Breach, 1998), 111 (emphasis added). Also see Braidotti, *Nomadic Subjects*: "Implicit in [the choice of this figuration] is the belief in the potency and relevance of the imagination, of myth-making, as a way to step out of the political and intellectual stasis of these post-modern times. Political fictions may be more effective, here and now, than theoretical systems" (4).

58 Lucy Sargisson, *Contemporary Feminist Utopianism* (New York: Routledge, 1996), 168.

59 On the importance of postmodern "play" (of "heterogeneity, dissonance, worldviews") to feminist theorizing, see the conclusion (249–252) to *Feminist Standpoint Revisited*, ed. Hartsock. The work and play of feminism directs itself toward "open possibilities for both resistance and transformation" (252).These manipulations also relate to what David Hayman, in *Re-Forming the Narrative* (Ithaca: Cornell University Press, 1987), describes as the "impossible objectivity" of narratives that are looking for ways to "revitalize and revise the baroque tradition of magic space, a convention that insists upon its power to generate illusions rather than upon the validity of the illusions per se" (68).

60 See *Speculations on Speculation: Theories of Science Fiction*, ed. James Gunn and Matthew Candelaria (New York: Scarecrow Press, 2005), esp. the two essays by Darko Suvin himself (23–40 and 29–78). Tom Moylan is a second longtime scholar of cognitive estrangement, alienation and utopian narrative. See esp. Moylan's *Scraps of the Untainted Sky: Science Fiction, Utopia, Dystopia* (Boulder: Westview, 2000). Fredric Jameson's work on this is extensive; *Archaeologies of the Future: The Desire Called Utopia and Other Science Fictions* (New York: Verso, 2007) represents his most recent and sophisticated set of positions. Phillip Wegner outlines the relationships between estrangement and the role that narrative utopia plays "in teaching its readers how to become modern subjects"; see *Utopia, the Nation, and the Spatial Histories of Modernity* (Los Angeles: University of California Press, 2002), 24.

61 See Jeanette Winterson, *The Stone Gods* (New York: Mariner Books 2009), 88. This emphasis on "strangeness" also coincides with Wegner's insight that narrative utopia, beyond being "designed to fail," as Fredric Jameson has argued, is also *designed to succeed precisely in* "*its failures to 'transcend' its present moment....* That is, by not becoming an unknowable trace [of any given "present" moment] ... the utopian representation enables its readers to think of their shared present in a new way, teaching them to imagine and conceive of it as in continuous process, in formation, and subject to the disrupting, dissolving energies of modernity." It is in this sense that the narrative utopia, as Wegner argues, "transforms the closed circle of ideology or belief into an open spiral.... [T]he narrative utopia ... provides a concrete symbolization of this historical *process*" (23–24).

62 Kearney, *Wake of Imagination*, 395.

63 Peter Melville, *Romantic Hospitality and the Resistance to Accommodation* (Waterloo, ON: Wilfrid Laurier University Press).

64 Melville, *Romantic Hospitality*, 8.

65 See Phillip Wegner, *Utopia, the Nation, and the Spatial Histories*, 21.

66 The term "locational feminism" is Susan Stanford Friedman's, from *Mappings: Feminism and Cultural Geographies of Encounter* (Princeton: Princeton University Press, 1998).

67 Siebers, *Heterotopia*, 3.

68 Shahrnush Parsipur, *Women Without Men: A Novel of Modern Iran [Zanan bedun mardan]* (1989), trans. Kamran Talatoff and Jocelyn Sharlet (New York: The Feminist Press, 2004), 99.

69 Tobin Siebers, *The Subject and Other Subjects: On Ethical, Aesthetic, and Political Identity* (Ann Arbor: The University of Michigan Press, 1998), 14 (emphasis added).

70 Rajaa Alsanea, *Girls of Riyadh*, 2005, trans. Rajaa Alsanea and Marilyn Booth (New York: Penguin Books, 2007), 281.

71 Haraway, *Modest_Witness*, 199.

72 Jeanette Winterson's *Oranges Are Not the Only Fruit* (New York: Grove Press, 1985), 166.

CHAPTER I

1 Smith's proposal for a feminist "re-organization" of "matters and methods" in the field of sociology seems remarkably apt as a model for a feminist bildungsroman narrative. See: "Women's Perspective as a Radical Critique of Sociology," *Sociological Inquiry* 44.1 (January 1974), 11.

2 Angela Carter, *Heroes and Villains* (1969. New York: Penguin Books, 1993); Octavia Butler, *Parable of the Sower* (1993. New York: Grand Central Publishing, 2000) and *The Parable of the Talents* (1998. New York: Grand Central Publishing, 2000); Nalo Hopkinson, *Midnight Robber* (New York: Grand Central Publishing, 2000). Subsequent page references are given in the text.

3 Donna Spalding Andréolle anticipates me in describing Butler's *Parable of the Sower* as "fall[ing] into the category of the female *bildungsroman*, or female novel of self-awakening and self-fulfillment"; see "Utopias of Old, Solutions for the New Millennium: A Comparative Study of Christian Fundamentalism in M. K. Wren's *A Gift Upon the Shore* and Octavia Butler's *Parable of the Sower*," *Utopian Studies* 12 (2001): 119.

4 See Esther Kleinbord Labovitz, *The Myth of the Heroine: The Female Bildungsroman in the Twentieth Century* (New York: Peter Lang, 1986), 246.

5 See M. M. Bakhtin, "The *Bildungsroman* and its Significance in the History of Realism (Toward a Historical Typology of the Novel)," in *Speech Genres and Other Late Essays*, eds. Emerson and Holquist, trans. Vern W. McGee (Austin: University of Texas Press, 1986), 23.

6 Franco Moretti, *The Way of the World: The Bildungsroman in European Culture* (New York: Verso, 2000), xii (emphasis added).

7 Susan Sontag, *At the Same Time: Essays and Speeches*, eds. Paolo Dilonardo and Anne Jump (New York: Farrar, Straus, and Giroux, 2007), 89 (emphasis added).

8 Moretti, *Way of the World*, xiii, ix–x.

9 Georg Lukács, *The Theory of the Novel*, trans. Anna Bostock (Cambridge, MA: MIT Press, 1971), 41.

10 The studies began with a 1984 article in *Women's Studies* on the nineteenth-century American female bildungsroman by Beverly R. Voloshin ("The Limits of Domesticity: The Female *Bildungsroman* in America, 1820–1870," *Women's Studies* 10 (1984): 283–302. Also see Esther Kleinbord Labovitz's full-length study, *The Myth of the Heroine* (1986), followed by Susan Fraiman's important monograph, *Unbecoming Women: British Women Writers and the Novel of Development* (New York: Columbia University Press, 1993).

11 Todd Kontje, "Socialization and Alienation," 226. Todd Kontje describes the bildungsroman in similar terms, as "the meta-discourse in which we witness the birth of man…. But evidently *not* the birth of women" ("Socialization and Alienation in the Female Bildungsroman," in W. Daniel Wilson and Robert C. Holub, eds., *Impure Reason: Dialectic of Enlightenment in Germany*

(Detroit: Wayne State University Press, 1993), 222. Also see John Smith on the bildungsroman and the construction of male identity: "The strict gender codification at the basis of *Bildung* ... makes female *Bildung* a contradiction in terms" ("Sexual Difference, *Bildung*, and the *Bildungsroman*," in *Michigan Germanic Studies* 13 (1987): 216, 220).

12 See Susan Gubar, "The Birth of the Artist as Heroine: (Re)production, The Kunstlerroman Tradition, and the Fiction of Katherine Mansfield," in *The Representation of Women in Fiction*, ed. Carolyn Heilbrun (Baltimore: The Johns Hopkins University Press, 1983). Also see Aránzazu Usandizaga, "The Female Bildungsroman at the Fin de Siècle: The 'Utopian Imperative' in Anita Brookner's *A Closed Eye* and *Fraud*," *Critique* 39:4 (Summer 1998): 325–340. Usandizaga offers a useful survey of criticism of the female bildungsroman, following Susan Gubar's notion, in a 1983 study of Katherine Mansfield's fiction, of a modern "utopian imperative."

13 Moretti, *Way of the World*, 7.

14 Moretti associates the "comfort of civilization" with the symbolic logic of the bildungsroman's bourgeois underpinning. The "exchange" in which "comfort" is gained also means freedom is lost (see especially 52–56 and 65–67).

15 Moretti, *Way of the World*, 46.

16 Moretti, *Way of the World*, 19.

17 Rosi Braidotti, *Nomadic Subjects: Embodiment and Sexual Difference in Contemporary Feminist Theory* (New York: Columbia University Press, 1994), 73.

18 Moretti, *Way of the World*, 53–54. For Goethe's Wilhelm, "There is the warning of the Society of the Tower that accompanies him constantly – it almost torments him: 'Remember to live! ... What is important is to be able to dispose of one's energies *at every moment* and to employ them for the countless occasions or opportunities that life, little by little, takes upon itself" (45).

19 See Lewis Mumford, *The City In History: Its Origins, Its Transformations, and Its Prospects* (New York: Harvest Books, 1968), 3.

20 Moretti, *Way of the World*, 141.

21 Moretti observes that the protagonists of post-ideal bildungsroman narratives "act" in order to "be": they are "basically 'dynamic' and 'theatrical,' but that also means ... that they incline to 'unnaturalness' and 'parody'" (*Way of the World*, 106). Thus, Marianne's urges to escape and to masquerade as a boy; thus too Tan-Tan's masquerade as the Robber Queen in Nalo Hopkinson's *Midnight Robber*, discussed later in this chapter.

22 See Sarah Lefanu, *Feminism and Science Fiction* (Bloomington: Indiana University Press, 1989), on this novel's "obsession with time," and the presence of clocks at its beginning and ending (79–83).

23 Moretti, *Way of the World*, 44.

24 Moretti, *Way of the World*, 45.

25 Moretti, *Way of the World*, 62.

26 Lefanu, *Feminism and Science Fiction*, 80.

27 This important image has its source in *Robinson Crusoe*, and recurs in Winterson's *The Stone Gods*, and Atwood's *Oryx and Crake*. I will take up its significance in later chapters.

28 Moretti, *Way of the World*, 55.

29 Carter's deft handling of fairy-tale narratives and tropes is well documented. A terminological coincidence has Moretti describing posthumous (per)versions of "classical *Bildungsroman*" dismissing beliefs of individual autonomy and socialization as "so many fairy-tale illusions" (*Way of the World*, 75) – an accurate enough summary of *Heroes and Villains*.

30 Moretti, *Way of the World*, 55.

31 For the "real of the bare life," see Tobias Boes, "Beyond the Bildungsroman: Character Development and Communal Legitimation in the Early Fiction of Joseph Conrad," *Conradiana* 39:2 (2007): 122.

32 I am thinking of Erin McKenna's use of the term in her *The Task of Utopia: A Pragmatist and Feminist Perspective* (New York: Rowman & Littlefield, 2001), 164. *Utopian Studies*' 2008 special issue (volume 19.3) on the work of Octavia Butler contains many useful articles on this and many other aspects of the novel. For this chapter, I especially recommend Sarah Outterson's "Diversity, Change, Violence: Octavia Butler's Pedagogical Philosophy," 433–456. I concur with many of her observations and conclusions, although my focus is on the interaction of literary utopian form with the separate subgenre of bildungsroman. See Tom Moylan's important reading of the first *Parable* book, in *Scraps of the Untainted Sky* (Boulder, CO: Westview Press, 2000): "Butler's willingness to explore the empowering force of a spiritually motivated but materially transcendent vision that is rooted in difficulty and difference allows her to posit a politicizing process that produces a vulnerable but viable utopian alternative" (237). Also see Ruth Levitas, *The Concept of Utopia* (Syracuse: Syracuse University Press, 1990): "Anti-utopianism involves the active denial of the merits of imagining alternative ways of living, particularly if they constitute serious attempts to argue that the world might or should be otherwise" (30). Finally, see Angela Warfield's useful "Reassessing the Utopian Novel: Octavia Butler, Jacques Derrida, and the Impossible Future of Utopia," *Obsidian III* 6.2 (2005): 61–71.

33 Moretti, *Way of the World*, 11.

34 Bakhtin, "*Bildungsroman* and its Significance," 58. The following series of quotations from this article are on pages 50 and 49.

35 Ruth Levitas, "For Utopia: The (Limits of the) Utopian Function in Late Capitalist Society," in *The Philosophy of Utopia*, ed. Barbara Goodwin (London: Routledge, 2001), 37.

36 These remarks come from "A Conversation with Octavia E. Butler" in the *Reading Group Guide* at the end of the 2007 reprinting of *Parable of the Talents* (410).

37 Moretti, *Way of the World*, 7.

38 Bakhtin, "*Bildungsroman* and its Significance," 52.

39 Rev. Kenneth M. Kafoed, "Eshu" (entry), *Encyclopedia Mythica*. Retrieved at: www.pantheon.org/articles/e/eshu.html.

40 The name, from Caribbean legend, describes the evil spirits of unbaptised children who supposedly trap and carry off or kill other children.

41 See Pin-Chia Feng, *The Female Bildungsroman by Toni Morrison and Maxine Hong Kingston: A Postmodern Reading* (New York: Peter Lang, 1997), on the politics of "rememory" in ethnic bildungsroman texts.

42 See Lucy Armitt, *Contemporary Women's Fiction and the Fantastic* (New York: St Martin's Press, 2000), on contemporary SF's "computer networks" (181) as protagonist – interfaces that make the insistence on "the split between human and machine" increasingly less plausible.

43 Donna Haraway, *Modest_Witness@Second_Millennium. FemaleMan_Meets_ OncoMouse: Feminism and Technoscience* (New York: Routledge, 1997), 12.

44 Haraway, *Modest_Witness*, 130.

45 Haraway, *Modest_Witness*, 38 ("innocence and transparency are not available to feminist modest witnesses").

46 Bakhtin, "*Bildungsroman* and its Significance," 23.

47 Bakhtin, "*Bildungsroman* and its Significance," 36.

48 Haraway, *Modest_Witness*, 3.

49 See John Harvey, "Movement in Fiction," in *An Introduction to Contemporary Fiction*, ed. Rod Mengham, (Cambridge, UK: Polity Press, 1999). Harvey suggests that "the work that novels do is to translate value into movement. To take the most patent example, in the old novel a certain sort of marriage – of man with woman, but also of property with charity, and of morality with fertility and beauty – is not explicitly preached and exhorted: rather, it is made the destination of a journey" (70).

50 See Lee Edelman, *No Future: Queer Theory and the Death Drive* (Durham: Duke University Press, 2004), 12.

51 Edelman, *No Future*, 9.

52 Edelman does not consider implications of conception by rape, such as what "obligation to the future" the mothers of such so-called "monster children" possess and what children typically experience in terms of self- and social identity. I point here to the ambiguous position of children born of the Gilead commanders to the Handmaids, or even more disturbingly, the offspring of Octavia Butler's other works: the T'Gatoi grubs born of both male and female human hosts, for instance; or the children peopling her *Bloodchild* short stories; or the genetically-altered, hybrid vampire Shori in *Fledgling* (2005), who walks the earth in the *form* of a child but who betokens a much more entangled temporality than words like "past" and "future" would suggest. Yet, as Ali Brox and others have argued, *Fledgling* can be read and should be read as a continuation of Butler's exploration of utopian and speculative scenarios – and of conceptions of utopia that reject "the illusion of purity" (399) but rather embrace diversity and the need to change. See Ali Brox, "'Every age has the vampire it needs': Octavia Butler's Vampiric Vision in *Fledgling*," *Utopian*

Studies 19.3 (2008): 391–409. Sarah Outterson provides a powerful proposal regarding the "necessity" of violence in Butler's work, challenging her vision of a utopian communal consciousness that is challenged by the apparent inevitability of humans to become violent; see esp. 440–445.

Finally, Phillip Wegman has a critical discussion of the child image in his *Life between Two Deaths*; see chapter eight, entitled "We're Family," 195–217. This includes a discussion of Butler's *Talents*, including his conclusion, anticipating my own, that this novel "reverses the conventional hierarchy of blood and consensual affiliation that serves as the foundation for our dominant notions of kinship" (209).

53 See Lorna Ellis, *Appearing to Diminish: Female Development and the British Bildungsroman, 1750–1850* (Lewisburg: Bucknell University Press, 1999), 29. Ellis stresses the early female bildungsroman commitment to a coherent sense of subject and social ideal, even while mounting a "pointed critique" (10). The modest goal of creating "a model for female development … while encouraging them to manipulate societal expectation" (23) is radicalized by the deconstructions of twentieth- and now twenty-first-century women writers.

54 See Annis Pratt, *Archetypal Patterns in Women's Fiction* (Bloomington: Indiana University Press, 1981), 29.

55 See Lucy Sargisson, *Contemporary Feminist Utopianism* (London: Routledge, 1996), 41.

CHAPTER 2

1 Jeanette Winterson, *Art & Lies* (New York: Vintage Books, 1994), 137.

2 Jeanette Winterson, *Oranges Are Not the Only Fruit* (New York: Grove Press, 1985). Subsequent references are given in the text.

3 On the gender, identity, and the cyberspace metaphor, see *Cyberspace Textuality: Computer Technology and Literary Theory*, ed. Marie-Laure Ryan (Bloomington: Indiana University Press, 1999); and Susanna Paasonen, *Figures of Fantasy: Internet, Women, & Cyberdiscourse* (New York: Peter Lang Publishing, 2005).

4 Jeanette Winterson, *Sexing the Cherry* (New York: Grove Press, 1989), 150. All references, to be given in the text, are to these editions: Jeanette Winterson, *The Passion* (New York: Grove Press, 1987); *The PowerBook* (New York: Vintage Books, 2000).

5 See Anne Balsamo, *Technologies of the Gendered Body: Reading Cyborg Women* (Durham: Duke University Press, 1996), 116.

6 Jeanette Winterson, *The World and Other Places* (New York: Vintage Books, 1998), 10.

7 See Gregory J. Rubinson's valuable article, "Body Languages: Scientific and Aesthetic Discourses in Jeanette Winterson's *Written on the Body*," *Critique* 42.2 (Winter 2001): 218–232.

8 Pauline Palmer, "The Passion: Storytelling, Fantasy, Desire" in *'I'm telling you stories': Jeanette Winterson and the Politics of Reading*, ed. Helena Grice and Tim Woods (Amsterdam and Atlanta: Rodopi, 1998), 106.

9 Balsamo, *Technologies of the Gendered Body*, 127.

10 Winterson, *Art Objects*, 59.

11 Julia Kristeva, *Tales of Love*, trans. Leon S. Roudiez (New York: Columbia University Press, 1987), 5.

12 Kristeva, *Tales of Love*, 5.

13 Jeanette Winterson, *Art Objects: Essays on Ecstasy and Effrontery (New York: Vintage International,* 1997), 175–176.

14 John Su, *Imagination and the Contemporary Novel* (New York: Cambridge University Press, 2011), 23.

15 See Rubinson, "Body Languages," for a discussion of Winterson's "espousal" of a "traditional Romantic (i.e., anti-Enlightenment) ideal of art as salvation" (227); also see Christy L. Burns, "'Fantastic Language': Jeanette Winterson's Recovery of the Postmodern Word," *Contemporary Literature* 37 (1996): 278–306.

16 Winterson, *Art Objects*, 60.

17 Winterson, *Art Objects,* 58.

18 See Josh Cohen, *Interrupting Auschwitz: Art, Religion, Philosophy* (London: Continuum, 2003), 53. Christy Burns is right in her analysis of Jeanette Winterson's "evolving subject" when she states that there is in her work an "incommensurate relation between the imaginary and the real to some degree. Winterson's apparent priority is to reinvigorate passion "Fantastic Language: Jeanette Winterson's Recovery of the Postmodern World," *Contemporary Literature* 37 (1996): 278–306."

19 Winterson, *Art Objects*, 59–60.

20 Margaret Atwood, *Curious Pursuits: Occasional Writing 1970–2005* (London: Virago Press, 2005), 88–89. Subsequent quotations in this paragraph are from these pages.

21 Margaret Atwood, *Writing with Intent: Essay, Reviews, Personal Prose, 1983–2005* (New York: Carroll & Graf Publishers, 2005), 95.

22 Margaret Atwood, "My Life in Science Fiction," *Cycnos* 22 (2006). Retrieved at:www.revel.unice.fr

23 Atwood, *Curious Pursuits*, 339.

24 Margaret Atwood, *The Handmaid's Tale* (New York: Random House, 1985). Subsequent references are given in the text.

25 See Jennifer A. Wagner-Lawlor, "The Play of Irony: Theatricality and Utopian Transformation in Contemporary Women's Speculative Fiction," *Utopian Studies* 13.2 (2002): 114–134.

26 See Lois Feuer, "The Calculus of Love and Nightmare: *The Handmaid's Tale* and the Dystopian Tradition," *Critique* 38 (1997), 90. Lee Briscoe Thompson is an exception, allowing for the important role verbal irony plays in the novel's peculiar and grim humor; see *Scarlet Letters: The Handmaid's Tale* (Toronto: ECW Press, 1997).

27 Atwood, *Curious Pursuits*, 182.

28 See Madonne Miner's "'Trust Me': Reading the Romance Plot in Margaret Atwood's *The Handmaid's Tale*," in *Twentieth-Century Literature* 7 (1991), 148–168.

29 Margaret Atwood, *Oryx and Crake* (Nan A. Talese/Doubleday, 2003). Subsequent references are given in the text.

30 Atwood, *Curious Pursuits*, 339. Elsewhere I discuss Atwood's interest in the risk of genotech industries; see my "'Doomed by Hope': Environmental Catastrophe and the Structured Ignorance of Risk in Margaret Atwood's *Oryx and Crake*," in *Changing the Climate: Utopia, Dystopia and Catastrophe*, ed. Andrew Milner and Simon Sellars (Melbourne: *Arena Journal* 35/36, 2011), 173–195. Ulrich Beck's work is central, particularly his *Ecological Politics in an Age of Risk* (1988), trans. Amos Weisz (Cambridge, UK: Polity Press, 1995).

31 Beck, *Ecological Politics*, 180.

32 For a provocative account of "animals and/as technology," see chapter 8 in Sherryl Vint's *Animal Alterity: Science Fiction and the Question of the Animal* (Liverpool: Liverpool University Press, 2010), 182–206. Of course, there is extensive literature on this area, with Donna Haraway clearing a feminist path.

33 In an interview, Atwood notes that "[the setting] had to be a place with fairly low-lying coastal areas, which could be flooded by the melting of glacial ice and by a tidal wave" (interview with Mel Gussow, *New York Times*, June 24, 2003, B5). Massachusetts (or parts just north) is a likely setting, as Snowman dons a Boston Red Sox cap.

34 On the role of Jimmy's mother to the ethical debates of this novel, see Danette DiMarco, "Paradice Lost, Paradise Retained: Homo Faber and the Makings of a New Beginning in *Oryx and Crake*," *Papers on Language and Literature* 41.2 (Spring 2005): 170–195. Also see J. Brooks Bouson's valuable essay on *Oryx and Crake*'s "satiric vision of a bioengineered posthuman future" ("'It's Game Over Forever': Atwood's Satiric Vision of a Bioengineered Posthuman Future in *Oryx and Crake*," *Journal of Commonwealth Literature* 39 [2004]: 139–156).

35 On the "paired opposition" of Jimmy and Crake, see Bouson, "'It's Game Over Forever,'" 140–142; and Danette DiMarco, "Paradice Lost, Paradise Retained," 179–181.

36 On Atwood's longtime interest in the fate of art, see Earl G. Ingersoll, "Survival in Margaret Atwood's Novel *Oryx and Crake*," *Extrapolation* 45 (2004): 162–175.

37 See Shuli Barzilai's provocative essay, "'Tell My Story': Remembrance and Revenge in Atwood's *Oryx and Crake* and Shakespeare's *Hamlet*," *Critique* 50.1 (Fall 2008): 87–110. Barzilai sees the "multiple genre affiliations" of this novel as a strategy offering an "illusion of synthesis, of making sense, serv[ing] as a defense in facing the profoundly disordered world" (see esp. 87–90).

38 Rosi Braidotti, *Nomadic Subjects: Embodiment and Sexual Difference in Contemporary Feminist Theory* (New York: Columbia University Press, 1994), 72.

39 See *The End of the World*, ed. Eric Rabkin, Martin Greenberg, and Joseph Olander (Carbondale: Southern Illinois University Press, 1983), esp. those by Robert Plank (20–52), Brian Stableford (97–138), and W. Warren Wagar (139–172).

40 Winterson, *Oranges*, 166.

41 Margaret Atwood, *The Blind Assassin* (New York: Anchor Books, 2001), 518.

42 Ingersoll describes her as "a variety of Mother Goddess, bringing together the only two versions of the female in the economy of [Crake's] desire – mother or whore," whom Crake, as male deity, "supplants and dominates as his consort" ("Survival in *Oryx and Crake*," 169).

43 Atwood, *Curious Pursuits*, 391. In the same essay, Atwood describes Wells' Eloi in terms applicable to the Crakers, as "pretty as butterflies, but useless" (385).

44 See Atwood on Angela Carter's work: "Perhaps *play* is the operative word – not as in *trivial activity*, but as in word-play, play of thought, or play of light. [...] She was born subversive. [...] She had an instinctive feeling for the other side, which included also the underside, and for the other hand, the sinister one" (*Curious Pursuits*, 156).

45 Burns, "'Fantastic Language,'" 302.

46 Margaret Atwood, *The Year of the Flood* (New York: Nan A. Talese/ Doubleday, 2009), 201. Subsequent references are given in the text.

47 Atwood, *Curious Pursuits*, 388.

48 Atwood, *Curious Pursuits*, 389.

49 Atwood, *Curious Pursuits*, 323. Emphasis in the original.

50 See Ulrich Beck, *Risk Society: Towards a New Modernity* (London: SAGE Publications, 2004), esp. 51–52.

51 See Amanda Cole, *"In Retrospect*: Writing and Reading *Oryx and Crake*," *Philament* 6 (2005), who explores what I am calling the "Janus-like" glance of this narrative, as the novel "recalls a present which is, as yet, the reader's future" (1). Cole contrasts the method of "imaginary retrospect" with that of Larkin Olamina (see 2–3). Retrieved at: www.arts.usyd.edu.au/publications/ philament.

52 From interviews with Martin Halliwell, "Awaiting the Perfect Storm," in *Waltzing Again*, ed. Ingersoll, 261–262; and with Brian Bethune, "Atwood Apocalyptic," *Maclean's* 116 (2003): 49.

53 DiMarco, "Paradice Lost, Paradise Retained," 172. The footprint image appears in Carter's *Heroes and Villains* as noted in chapter one. It reappears in chapter three's discussion of Winterson's *The Stone Gods*.

54 Barzilai argues Snowman's culpability lies in his acquiescence to being "caught in a web of language ... Simply put, the numbers man did a word-number on the humanist" ("'Tell My Story,'" 91).

55 Siebers, *Heterotopia: Postmodern Utopia and the Body Politic* (Ann Arbor: University of Michigan Press, 1995), 19.

56 Atwood, "My Life in Science Fiction," n.p.

57 Atwood, "My Life in Science Fiction," n.p.

58 Atwood, in *Conversations,* ed. Earl Ingersoll, 220.

CHAPTER 3

1 Jeanette Winterson, *The Passion* (New York: Grove Press, 1987), 62. Atwood compares her novel's conclusion to Orwell's *1984*. Her "Notes," like his essay on Newspeak "mean that the regime has fallen, and that language and individuality have survived." The parallels "should be evident." See "George Orwell: Some Personal Connections," in *Curious Pursuits: Occasional Writing 1970–2005* (London: Virago Press, 2005), 338.

2 Lessing, *The Cleft* (New York: Harper Perennial, 2007). Subsequent references are given in the text.

3 Winterson, *Art Objects: Essays on Ecstasy and Effrontery.* (New York: Vintage International, 1997), 59–60.

4 For an important consideration of "truth, temporality and theorizing resistance," see Susan McManus, "Truth, Temporality, and Theorizing Resistance," in *Exploring the Utopian Impulse: Essays on Utopian Thought and Practice,* ed. Michael J. Griffin and Tom Moylan (Bern: Peter Lang, 2007), 57–81.

5 Quoted in *The Cambridge Guide to Women's Writing in English* (Cambridge: Cambridge University Press, 1999), 388.

6 "The Nobel Prize in Literature 2007," May 1, 2011, retrieved from http://www.nobelprize.org/nobel_prizes/literature/laureates/2007/

7 Julie Phillips, "Eden Undone" (review of *The Cleft*), *Ms. Magazine*, November 4, 2007, n.p., retrieved from www.powells.com/review/2007_11_04.html

8 Jeanette Winterson, "What Planet is Doris On?" *The Guardian*, August 14, 2001, n.p., retrieved from www.guardian.co.uk/books/2001/aug/15/edinburghfestival2001.edinburghfestival

9 This series of quotations come from: Olivia Glazebrook, "Nags versus cads," *Spectator*, January 20, 2007, retrieved from www.images.spectator.co.uk/books/27469/nags-versus-cads.thtml; Julie Phillips, "Eden Undone," 74; John Leonard, untitled (review of *The Cleft*), Harper's Magazine (August 2007), 82. Retrieved from http://harpers.org/media/free/2008/JohnLeonard/HarpersMagazine-2007–08–0081651.pdf. For other reviews, see: Nancy Kline, "Of Fish and Bicycles," *New York Times*, Sept 2, 2007. Retrieved from www.nytimes.com/2007/09/02/books/review/Kline-t-1.html. Jeremy Treglown, "Myths and Memories," *Financial Times* (London), January 20, 2007, 32; Philip Hensher, "The golden writer," *Spectator*, October 17, 2007. Retrieved from http://www.images.spectator.co.uk/books/268666/the-golden-writer.thtml.

10 Roberta Rubenstein, *The Novelistic Vision of Doris Lessing: Breaking the Forms of Consciousness* (Urbana: University of Illinois Press, 1979), 8. On the estranging effects of Lessing's interest in fragmentation and/as generic strategy, see Radha Chakravarty, *Feminism and Contemporary Women Writers* (2008), 47–65, and Rachel DuPlessis, *Writing Beyond the Ending: Narrative Strategies of Twentieth-Century Women Writers* (Bloomington: Indiana University Press, 1985).

11 On this trope, see Fredric Jameson, *The Political Unconscious: Narrative as a Socially Symbolic Act* (Ithaca: Cornell University Press, 1981), 220.

12 See Alison Stone, "On the Genealogy of Women: A Defense of Anti-Essentialism" in *Third Wave Feminism: A Critical Exploration*, eds. Stacy Gillis, Gillian Howe, and Rebecca Munford (expanded 2nd edn. New York: Palgrave Macmillan, 2007), 16–29.

13 For a more sympathetic reading of the Roman's methodological responsibility, see Phyllis Sternberg Perrakis, "The Porous Border Between Fact and Fiction, Empathy and Identification in Doris Lessing's *The Cleft*," in *Doris Lessing: Border Crossings*, ed. Ridout and Watkins (New York: Continuum, 2009), 143–159.

14 See Tom Wilhelmus, "Time and Distance," *The Hudson Review* 46.1 (Spring 1993): 247–255, on Lessing's lifelong interest in historiography and in the "elaborate superstructure of history and myth" required to "create perspective and distance" (249).

15 One can only speculate that Lessing knows of Brigid Brophy's playful *In Transit* (Chicago: Center for Book Culture, Dalkey Archive edn., 2002), in which gender "indecisiveness" leads the protagonist to all manner of postmodern slippages, in terms of gender expectations, narrative expectations, and readerly expectations.

16 Even here the Roman is sensitive: the Clefts would have said "female and male"; later historians assume a reverse order, reflecting the presumption that "we males were first in the story and in some remarkable way brought forth the females. *We* are the senior, *they* our creation" (25–26).

17 Cp. The Roman goddess, Rumor (or *Fama*), typically depicted with multiple eyes, many tongues, and delivering messages not completely true, but not untrue either.

18 Jeanette Winterson, *The Stone Gods*. (New York: Mariner Books, 2009). Subsequent references are given in the text.

19 See Philip Tew on nostalgia in contemporary British novels, esp. "The Past and the Present," in *The Contemporary British Novel* (New York: Continuum, 2004), 118–149, which surveys narrative traditions and strategies that authors (including Winterson [120–121]) use to represent interpenetrating temporal dimensions. See also Ursula K. Heise's *Chronoschisms: Time, Narrative, and Postmodernism* (Cambridge: Cambridge University Press, 1997), esp. 11–74; and David Hayman, *Re-Forming the Narrative* (Ithaca: Cornell University Press, 1987), 147–211, for a comprehensive look at the motivations and implications of *parataxis*, which connects spatial-to-temporal shifts to narrative disruption and even farce.

20 See Tobin Siebers's discussion of repetition and/as interpretation as the characteristic trope of postmodernism in *The Subject and Other Subjects: On Ethical, Aesthetic, and Political Identity* (Ann Arbor: The University of Michigan Press, 1998). Siebers mentions Judith Butler and Donna Haraway as theorists seeking resistance to "the bad effects of repetition," including violence and ethical humiliation (6).

21 See Klaus Mainzer, "Science, Technology and Utopia: Perspectives of a Computer-Assisted Evolution of Humankind," in *Thinking Utopia*, ed. Jörn Rüsen, Michael Fehr, and Thomas W. Rieger (New York: Berghahn Books, 2005), 104–119.

22 Mainzer cautions that this utopian fantasy is just that – yet even chaos and nonlinearity can open "a cosmic window to an island 'utopia' where freedom, creativity and fantasy are temporarily possible" ("Science, Technology and Utopia," 118).

23 See chapter four (105–146) in David Hayman's *Re-Forming the Narrative* (Ithaca: Cornell University Press, 1987).

CHAPTER 4

1 "Against Postmodernism, etcetera," retrieved fromwww.iath.virginia.edu/pmc/text-only/issue.901/12.1chan.txt.

2 Susan Sontag, *At the Same Time: Essays and Speeches*, ed. Paolo Dilonardo and Anne Jump (New York: Farrar, Straus and Giroux, 2007), 89. Subsequent references in this paragraph are from the same page.

3 Sontag, *At the Same Time*, 90.

4 Fredric Jameson, *Archaeologies of the Future* (New York: Verso, 2005), 211.

5 Toni Morrison, "Rootedness: The Ancestor as Foundation," in *Black Women Writers (1950–1980): A Critical Evaluation*, ed. Mari Evans (New York: Anchor Press, 1984), 341. Also see: Heike Raphael-Hernandez, *The Utopian Aesthetics of Three African American Women (Toni Morrison, Gloria Naylor, Julie Dash): The Principle of Hope* (Lewiston: The Edwin Mellen Press, 2008); Patrick Bryce Bjork, *The Novels of Toni Morrison* (New York: Peter Lang, 1992) on Morrison's invention of "site[s] of renewal" (164); and Holly Flint argues that the reader is offered "some hope … despite its fallen body politic.… Ruby's future is 'here and now, a community to be created.' This future is the paradise that Morrison offers" ("Toni Morrison's *Paradise*: Black Cultural Citizenship in the American Empire," *American Literature* 78.3 [September 2006]: 607–608).

6 February 2, 2001 conversation between Elizabeth Farnsworth and Susan Sontag. Retrieved from www.pbs.org/newshour/conversation/jan-june01/sontag_02–02.html.

7 David Morris, "Postmodern Pain," in *Heterotopia: On Ethical, Aesthetic, and Political Identity* (Ann Arbor: The University of Michigan Press, 1998), 151.

8 Susan Sontag, *In America: A Romance* (New York: Farrar, Straus Giroux, 2000). Subsequent references are given in the text.

9   See Sontag's 2003 essay on Anna Banti's *Artemesia*, which describes Banti's way of "prowling" around her own text. Sontag continues to be interested in the character – whether fictional or authorial – who functions as "a time-traveler, a visitor" (*At the Same Time*, 43).

10 Sontag is aware of this: "Utopists cannot hide; they set the ground rules for their utopias. Therefore, they consciously or unconsciously reveal their deepest desires and fears as they describe the worlds they have created with their imaginations" (*In America*, 5).

11 Judith N. Sklar surveys major American utopian experiments, including Fourierist efforts such as Maryna's; see "What Is the Use of Utopia?" in *Heterotopia*, ed. Tobin Siebers, 40–57.

12 See Susan Sontag with Edwin Newman, "Speaking Freely" (1969 interview) in *Conversations with Susan Sontag*, ed. Leland Poague (Jackson: University Press of Mississippi, 1995), 16–17.

13 Susan Sontag, "On Style" (1965) in *A Susan Sontag Reader* (New York: Vintage Books, 1982), 151, 152.

14 Isabella's lines are quoted in the text (353):
    But man, proud man,
    Dress'd in a little brief authority,
    Most ignorant of what he's most assur'd, …

15 Carol Iannone, "At Play with Susan Sontag," *Commentary* (February 2001). Retrieved from www.commentarymagazine.com/article/at-play-with-susan-sontag/.

16 February 2, 2001 conversation on NPR between Elizabeth Farnsworth and Susan Sontag. Retrieved fromwww.pbs.org/newshour/-conversation/jan-june01/sontag_02–02.html.

17 Susan Sontag, *The Volcano Lover: A Romance* (New York: Anchor/Doubleday, 1992), 330.

18 Jill Dolan describes "gestic moments of clarity" in performance, of which this rapprochement between Maryna and Booth is one: "Perhaps in these moments of communal, almost loving rest, when the flesh stops and the soul pauses, we come together, at attention and relieved, to feel utopia" ("Performance, Utopia, and the 'Utopian Performative,'" *Theatre Journal* 53 [2001], 477). Dolan importantly connects such moments to a practice of reception, "when those crystallized, moving pictures of social relations become not only intellectually clear but felt and lived by spectators as well as actors" ("Introduction," *Modern Drama* 47 [2004], 172).

19 Michael Wood reads the novel more darkly, suggesting that Sontag longs for "a historical time when wishing was an option, and for the fantasy time when wishing was enough" ("Susan Sontag and the American Will," *Raritan* 21.1 [Summer 2001]: 147). My reading disagrees. The frame, and the novel's plot itself, say to me that there is *no* historical moment when wishing has been and would ever be "enough."

20 Louis Marin, "Frontiers of Utopia: Past and Present," *Critical Inquiry* 19 (1993), 413.

21 Peter Brooks describes Sontag as "ethically noble but utopian" in her argument in *Illness as Metaphor* (443). Also see Erica Munk on Sontag's "ethical idea" of the theater ("Only the Possible: An Interview with Susan Sontag," *Theater* 24 [1993]), 31.

22 Sontag, *Where the Stress Falls*, 271.

23 Susan Sontag, retrieved from http://www.susansontag.com

24 Toni Morrison, from an interview with Elizabeth Farnsworth, March 9, 1998. Retrieved from http://www.pbs.org/newshour/bb/entertainment/jan-june98/morrison_3–9.html

25 See Patricia Storace's very brilliant review, "The Scripture of Utopia," *New York Review of Books*, xlv.10 (June 11, 1998): 64–69.

26 Toni Morrison, from an interview with Elizabeth Farnsworth. Retrieved from http://www.pbs.org/newshour/bb/entertainment/jan-june98/morrison_3–9.html

27 See Roberta Rubenstein, *Home Matters: Longing and Belonging, Nostalgia and Mourning in Women's Fiction* (New York: Palgrave, 2001), emphasizing the linkage of home, nostalgia and community, and Morrison's long-standing interest in "inclusion and exclusion, insiders and outsiders" (145). My understanding of hospitality and its relationship to feminism is based heavily on the important book by Tracy McNulty, *The Hostess: Hospitality, Femininity, and the Expropriation of Identity* (Minneapolis: University of Minnesota Press, 2007), esp. chapter two, "Cosmopolitan Hospitality and Secular Ethics: Kant Today" (46–86). Equally important are the discussions I had with colleague Irina Aristarkhova as she wrote her recent book, *Hospitality of the Matrix: Philosophy, Biomedicine, and Culture* (New York: Columbia University Press, 2012).

28 Siebers, *Heterotopia*, 8.

29 Toni Morrison, quoted in Channette Romero, "Creating the Beloved Community: Religion, Race, and Nation in Toni Morrison's *Paradise*," *African American Review* 39 (2005): 425. Romero's is just one of the critical pieces looking into Morrison's use of "a multiplicity of religious beliefs" (415), including the Afro-Brazilian religious practice called *candomblé*. In addition to its hybrid origins, this religion privileges the spiritual power of the female. As Maha Marouan explains, "by introducing an ancient female deity and an ancient religion that views the world in terms of multiplicity and ambiguity, the novel ruptures the dualistic oppositions associated with the perception of deity in Christianity. Consolata [in Morrison's novel] ... celebrates the complexity of the feminine element and expresses her opposition to Christian dualities [and] insists on the merging of the two opposite images of the sinning flesh and the immaculate soul associated with Christian tradition" (*The African Diaspora and the Study of Religion*, ed. Theodore Louis Trost [New York: Palgrave Macmillan, 2007], 114). This aspect of Morrison's writing is also discussed in: *Toni Morrison and the Bible: Contested Intertextualities*, ed. Shirley A. Stave (New York: Peter Lang, 2006); Majda R. Atieh, "The Revelation of the Veiled in Toni Morrison's *Paradise*," MELUS 36.2 (Summer 2011): 89–107.

30 See Susan Bowers on African-American apocalyptic writing, and Morrison's insistence on spiritual renewal springing from "an invasion of the world beyond the veil" (211).

31 See Timothy Aubrey, "Beware the Furrow of the Middlebrow: Searching for Paradise on *The Oprah Winfrey Show*," *Modern Fiction Studies* 52:2 (Summer 2006), 364.

32 Morrison, from *The Salon Interview – Toni Morrison*, with Zia Jaffrey. Retrieved from http://www.salon.com/books/int/1998/02/cov_sI_02int.

33 Sontag, *At the Same Time*, 205. See Holly Flint, 585–612.

34 Flint's discussion of the "coevality" of black and white histories in this novel (see esp. 592–599) is relevant to this point. Romero concurs, proposing that the setting of the novel's opening crisis on July 4, 1976, "urges readers to consider how closely tied these characters are to the values and exclusions used to create this nation" ("Creating the Beloved Community," 420).

35 Toni Morrison interview with Farnsworth. Retrieved from http://www.pbs.org/newshour/bb/entertainment/jan-june98/morrison_3–9.html

36 Aubrey, "Beware the Furrow," 364. Philip Page's conclusion is as elegantly put as any: Morrison's novels are "postmodern, not in the sense of extreme self-referentiality or in the mockery of narration, but in their privileging of polyvocalism, stretched boundaries, open-endedness, and unraveled binary oppositions" ("Home Matters: Longing and Belonging, Nostalgia and Mourning in Women's Fiction" [review], *Modern Fiction Studies* 48.2 [2002], 534–35).

37 On this effacement, see Aubrey, "Beware the Furrow," 360–364; and Keren Omry, "Literary Free Jazz? Mumbo Jumbo and Paradise: Language and Meaning," *African American Review* 41.1 (Spring 2007): 137–138.

38 Rob Davidson, "Racial Stock and 8-Rocks: Communal Historiography in Toni Morrison's Paradise," *Twentieth-Century Literature* 47.3 (Fall 2001): 372 n.4.

39 Morrison, *Salon Interview* with Zia Jaffrey. Retrieved from http://www.salon.com/books/int/1998/02/cov_sI_02int.

40 Romero, "Creating the Beloved Community," 7.

41 Gerard Delanty, "Two Conceptions of Cultural Citizenship: A Review of Recent Literature on Culture and Citizenship," *The Global Review of Ethnopolitics* 1.3 (March 2002): 64.

42 Aubrey, "Beware the Furrow," 359. See Romero on the novel's method of "bring[ing] about material change by encouraging its readers to view themselves as part of a collective history of oppression and resistance," extending the reader's imagination and interpretation "beyond the boundaries of the novel, the ethnic community, and the nation-state" to "new imaginings of community" ("Creating the Beloved Community," 425).

43 Morrison, in an interview with Carolyn C. Denard, in *Toni Morrison: Conversations*, ed. Carolyn C. Denard. (Jackson: University Press of Mississippi, 1998), 191.

44 Delanty, "Cultural Citizenship," 64.

CHAPTER 5

1 Fatima Mernissi, *Women in Moslem Paradise* (New Delhi: Kali for Women, 1986), n.p.
2 See Nawal El Saadawi, "She Has No Place in Paradise," in *The Anchor Book of Modern Arabic Fiction*, ed. Denys Johnson-Davis (New York: Anchor Books, 2006), 364–371. Subsequent references are given in the text.
3 Abdelwahab Bouhdiba, *Sexuality in Islam*, trans. Alan Sheridan (London: Routledge & Kegan Paul, 1985), 86.
4 Henri Lefebvre, *The Production of Space*, trans. Donald Nicholson-Smith (Oxford: Blackwell Publishing, 2004), 391.
5 Barbara Harlow, "'All That Is Inside Is Not Center': Responses to the Discourses of Domination," in *Coming to Terms: Feminism, Theory, Politics*, ed. Elizabeth Weed (New York: Routledge, 1989), 165.
6 Nevertheless, notes Persis M. Karim, her work has "continued to influence an emerging generation of young writers who are confronting not only the expectations and edicts of the Islamic Republic, but also an excessive and unpredictable censorial establishment that regularly closes down publications dedicated to women's issues and writing," review of *Women Without Men*, in *MESA Bulletin*, 35.1 (Summer 2001).
7 Shahrnush Parsipur, with Golbarg Bashi, "The proper etiquette of meeting Shahrnush Parsipur in the United States" (interview, July 9, 2006). Retrieved from www.shahrnushparsipur.com/wp/the-proper-etiquette-of-meeting-shahrnush-parsipur-in-the-united-states/Also see Farzaneh Milani (esp. 201–207) in *Veils and Words: The Emerging Voices of Iranian Women* (Syracuse: Syracuse University Press, 1992), 236–237, on the "perils of writing" – in particular, the taboo against the disclosure of private aspects of women's lives; a text representing women as visible and vocal is thus doubly illicit.
8 Shahrnush Parsipur, "A Prelude to Touba and the Meaning of Night" (lecture, Seattle Asian Art Museum, October 7, 2006, trans. James M. Gustafson). Retrieved from http://www.shahrnushparsipur.com/wp/a-prelude-to-touba-and-the-meaning-of-night/
9 Shahrnush Parsipur with Mohammed Al-Urdun, "Iran's literary giantess is defiant in exile ... but missing home" (interview published in *Camden New Journal*, June 19, 2007). Retrieved fromhttp://www.shahrnushparsipur.com/wp/irans-literary-giantess-is-defiant-in-exile-but-missing-home/
10 Sepideh Saremi, "Interview with Shahrnush Parsipur, Author," January 2008, retrieved from http://www.shahrnushparsipur.com/wp/interview-with-shahrnush-parsipur-author/Also see Asghar Massombagi on the "male dominated" field of modern Iranian prose, "From Utopia to Reality: *Women Without Men*.'" Retrieved from http://www.iranian.com/AsgharMassombagi/2001/August/Utopia/. On Parsipur's stated "mission" as an intellectual vanguard for Iranian women, see Isabel Stümpel, "Zeugin, Chronistin, Aufklärerin? Zum Selbstverständnis einer zeitgenössen persischen Autorin," in *Conscious Voices: Concepts of Writing in the Middle East* (Stuttgart: Orient-Institut der Deutschen Morgenländischen Gesellschaft, 1999), 197–220.

11 Parsipur, with Golbarg Bashi, "The proper etiquette," n.p.

12 Parsipur, with Golbarg Bashi, "The proper etiquette," n.p.

13 Parsipur, with Sepideh Saremi, "Interview," n.p.

14 See Asma Barlas, *"Believing Women" in Islam: Unreading Patriarchal Interpretations of the Qur'an* (Austin: University of Texas Press, 2002) and Leila Ahmed, "Feminism and Cross-Cultural Inquiry: The Terms of the Discourse in Islam," in *Coming to Terms: Feminism, Theory, Politics,* ed. Elizabeth Weed (New York: Routledge, 1989), 143–151.

15 See Magda M. Al-Nowaihi, "Re-envisioning National Community in Salwa Bakr's *Golden Chariot.*" In *Intersections: Gender, Nation, and Community in Arab Women's Novels,* ed. Lisa Suhair, Majaj, Paula W. Sunderman, and Terese Saliba. (Syracuse, NY: Syracuse University Press, 2002), 86.

16 "Shirin Neshat with Carol Becker and Phong Bui," interview, September 2009. Retrieved from http://www.brooklynrail.org/2009/09/art/shirin-neshat-with-carol-becker-phong-bui

17 Also see William L. Hanaway's review: "Parsipur navigates skillfully between the extremes of mainstream discourse and overt opposition … keeping [the text] in the disputed territory between tract and trance" (*World Literature Today* [1999]). Retrieved from http://www.complete-review.com/reviews/iran/parsips2.htm

18 Annemarie Schimmel, *My Soul Is a Woman: The Feminine in Islam,* trans. Susan H. Ray (New York: Continuum, 1997), 25.

19 S. Gulzar Haider, "On What Makes Architecture Islamic," in *Understanding Islamic Architecture,* ed. Attilo Petruccioli and Khalil K. Pirani (London: RoutledgeCurzon, 2002), 20.

20 Gerard Grandval, "Preface," in M. R. Moghtader and Mehdi Khansari, *The Persian Garden: Echoes of Paradise* (Washington, DC: Mage Publishers, 1998), n.p. Retrieved from http://www.iranian.com/History/Oct98/Garden/index.html

21 Nader Ardalan, "'Simultaneous perplexity': The Paradise Garden as the Quintessential Visual Paradigm of Islamic Architecture and Beyond," in *Understanding Islamic Architecture,* 10.

22 For an account of nature and interpretation of the story of Sassi, and her relevance to Islamic mysticism, see Annemarie Schimmel, *My Soul Is a Woman,* 139–155.

23 Milani, *Veils and Words,* 236–237.

24 Massombagi, "From Utopia to Reality," n.p.

25 Schimmel, *My Soul Is a Woman,* 154.

26 Schimmel, *My Soul Is a Woman,* 154.

27 Massombagi, "From Utopia to Reality," n.p.

28 Milani, *Veils and Words,* 238.

29 María Martínez González, "Feminist Praxis Challenges the Identity Question: Toward New Collective Identity Metaphors," *Hypatia* 23.3 (Summer 2008), 24–25. Emphasis in the original.

30 Lucy Sargisson, *Contemporary Feminist Utopianism* (London: Routledge, 1996), 9.

31 González, "Feminist Praxis," 24–25. Emphasis in the original.

32 González, "Feminist Praxis," 29.

33 Sargisson, *Contemporary Feminist Utopianism*, 14.

34 See Amin Malak, *Muslim Narratives and the Discourse of English* (Albany: SUNY Press, 2005) notes that "[t]he confinement of women [in this memoir] evokes Foucauldian notions of borders and boundaries, erected in prisons or mental institutions, as symptoms of power relationships.... The prohibition on women to leave their quarters, except on special occasions and only when accompanied by a male relative or guardian, represent not only a limitation on freedom but also an asphyxiation of creative potential" (113); see full discussion of the memoir on 114–122.

35 Mernissi has written elsewhere and often on this topic, including in her *Shahrazad n'est pas marocaine* (Casablanca: Editions Le Fennec, 1988) and more recently in *Scheherazade Goes West* (New York: Pocket Books/ Washington Square Press, 2001; see esp. 33–60). Many critics remark on Mernissi's rich use of the figure of Scheherazade: see Suzanne Gauch's reading of *Dreams of Trespass*'s "speaking in between" in *Liberating Shahrazad: Feminism, Postcolonialism, and Islam* (Minneapolis: University of Minnesota Press, 2007), 35–54; Malak, *Muslim Narratives*, 116–117; Melissa Matthes, "Shahrazad's Sisters: Storytelling and Politics in the Memoirs of Mernissi, El Saadawi and Ashrawi," *Alif* 19 (1999): 68–96; Fedwa Malti-Douglas's wonderful *Woman's Body, Woman's Word*, esp. 11–28 and 91–117); Chikwenye Okonjo Ogunyemi, *Juju Fission: Women's Alternative Fictions from the Sahara, the Kalahari, and the Oases In-Between* (New York: Peter Lang, 2007), 67; and Huff-Rousselle's review of Mernissi's work, "A Contemporary Scheherazade's Tales of a Borderless World," in *Cairo Times*, May 2003. Retrieved from http://www.mernissi.net/civil_society/portraits/ fatimamernissi.html

36 Western misrepresentation of the Qur'anic Paradise is an ongoing topic of exploration. See: Rana Kabbani, *Europe's Myths of Orient* (1986). But also see Fatwa Malti-Douglas on Arab culture's own version of "island utopia" (*Woman's Body*, 85–110), al-Waqwâq. These medieval portraits of Paradise, by Ibn Tufayl and others, are a consistent touchstone for figurations of medieval sex and gender ideologies in the Islamic world (see esp. 93–110).

37 Amin Malak, *Muslim Narratives*, 120.

38 My reading challenges Amin Malak's characterization of Mernissi's text as one in which the "limitation on freedom" is also "an asphyxiation of creative potential" (*Muslim Narratives*, 113).

39 Malak also remarks on the "[deliberate] drawing [of] a parallel between the division of the national homeland and the domestic household" and "the suggestion here ... that the women were doubly colonized: as citizens of a foreign-occupied country and as secluded inhabitants of a male-controlled household" (*Muslim Narratives*, 114).

40 This is of course a trope common to many female speculative visions; see Marleen Barr, "A Dream of Flying," ch. 3 in *Feminist Fabulations: Space/ Postmodern Fiction* (Des Moines: University of Iowa Press, 1992), 51–94.

41	On the *hammam* as a type of paradise, see Moris Farhi's "Lentils in Paradise" in *Imagined Masculinities: Male Identity and Culture in the Modern Middle East*, ed. Emma Sinclair-Webb and Mai Ghoussoub (London: Saqi Books, 1996), a humorous coming-of-age account involving his childhood experience of gendered spatiality of the *hammam*; like Mernissi's boy-cousin, he is expelled once "the innocence of his gaze is questioned" (15).

42	On body politics in Mernissi and Assia Djebar, see Brinda Mehta, *Rituals of Memory in Contemporary Arab Women's Writing* (Syracuse: Syracuse University Press, 2007), 121–151.

43	See Amin Malak, who explores these symbolic acts of resistance (*Muslim Narratives*, 115–116).

44	Mernissi can be added to Rosi Braidotti's list of feminist writers who have identified "female identity with a sort of planetary exile," which, Braidotti notes, "has since become a topos of feminist studies" (see *Nomadic Subjects* [New York: Columbia University Press], 21).

45	On a book tour in the West for *Dreams of Trespass*, Mernissi is routinely "shocked by [the] grins" of male journalists at the mention of the word "harem." But following her grandmother's Sufi-inspired philosophy, "I needed to transform my feelings of shock … into an openness to learn from them" (2). As the tour continues, she finds "the secret to gaining enlightenment … was to increase one's listening capacity. Where to start? Well, by shedding your arrogance, or at least trying to, and by respecting the other" (25).

46	Henri Lefebvre, *The Production of Space*, trans. Donald Nicholson-Smith (Oxford: Blackwell Publishing, 2004), 393.

47	The argument about "investment of time" comes from Lefebvre. See Joseph T. Zeidan, *Arab Women Novelists: The Formative Years and Beyond* (Albany, NY: State University of New York Press, 1995), detailing writers' fierce push for education for women, without which women could not articulate demands or fight for them.

48	Rajaa Alsanea's *Girls of Riyadh* (2005). Translated by Rajaa Alsanea and Marilyn Booth (New York: Penguin Books, 2007). Subsequent references are given in the text.

49	See M. Hakan Yavuz, "Media Identities for Alevis and Kurds in Turkey," in *New Media in the Muslim World*, ed. Dale F. Eickelman and Jon W. Anderson (Bloomington: Indiana University Press, 1999), 180–199. Yavus explains why "new communications networks promote such shifts in the production and control of knowledge" by introducing "more abstract and flexible frames of reference to cope with the evolving socio-political landscape" (181).

50	See Eikelman and Anderson, in *New Media*, 2. Eickelman and Anderson outline the association of new media with an "interstitial space between the super-literacy of traditional religious specialists and mass sub-literacy or illiteracy." This space, obviously dangerous to traditionalists, producing a "creolized discourse that is not authorized anywhere but instead links others in an intermediate discourse" (9). This is the space that "urban" media users – such as *seerehwenfadha7et*'s friends – are building, inhabiting, and finding themselves most comfortable in.

51 Eickelman and Anderson, *New Media*, 15.
52 Eickelman and Anderson, *New Media*, 2.
53 Eickelman and Anderson, *New Media*, 38 and 6.
54 Eickelman and Anderson, *New Media*, 4.
55 Mernissi, "The Meaning of Spatial Boundaries," in *Feminist Postcolonial Theory: A Reader*, ed. Reina Lewis and Sara Mills (New York: Routledge, 2003), 489.
56 Fereshteh Nouraie-Simone, *On Shifting Ground: Middle Eastern Women in the Global Era* (New York: The Feminist Press at CUNY, 2005), 72.
57 Nouraie-Simone, *On Shifting Ground*, 72.
58 Eickelman and Anderson, *New Media*, 8.
59 Eickelman and Anderson, *New Media*, 15.
60 The term is Asma Barlas's, *"Believing Women,"* 9.

CONCLUSION

1 Epigraphs: G. K. Chesterton, "In Defense of China Shepherdesses," in *The Defendant*, ed. Dale Ahlquist (New York: Dover Publications, 2012), 36; Sonallah Ibrahim, in an interview with Elliott Colla, "The Imagination as Transitive Act: An Interview with Sonallah Ibrahim," *Jadaliyya* (June 12, 2011). Retrieved at:www.jadaliyya.com/pages/index/1811/the-imagination-as-transitive-act_an-interview-wit.
2 Louis Marin, "Frontiers of Utopia: Past and Present," *Critical Inquiry* 19 (1993), 413.
3 This formulation is, of course, Fredric Jameson's, from his 2005 *Archaeologies of the Future: The Desire Called Utopia and Other Science Fictions* (New York: Verso, 2007).
4 Hélène Cixous's essay, "Castration or Decapitation" (*Signs* 7.1, 1981) also explores the fundamental opposition of the couple: "A couple posed in opposition, in tension, in conflict … a couple engaged in a kind of war in which death is always at work." Cixous also wonders "what a completely different couple relationship would be like, what a love that was more than merely a cover for, a veil of, war would be like" (44).
5 Rosi Braidotti, *Nomadic Subjects: Embodiment and Sexual Difference in Contemporary Feminist Theory* (New York: Columbia University Press, 1994), 32.
6 Susan Buck-Morss, *Thinking Past Terror: Islamism and Critical Theory on the Left* (2003. New York: Verso, 2006).
7 See the Online Etymological Dictionary, retrieved at www.etymonline.com: O. E. gamen "game, joy, fun, amusement," common Germanic (cf. O. Fris. game "joy, glee," O. N. gaman, O. S., O. H. G. gaman "sport, merriment," Dan. *gamen*, Swed. *gamman* "merriment"), regarded as identical with Goth. *gaman* "participation, communion," from P.Gmc. *ga- collective prefix+*mann*, "person," giving a sense of "people together."

8 Jennie Molz and Sarah Gibson, "Introduction," in *Mobilizing Hospitality*, 1.

9 Jeanette Winterson, *The Stone Gods* (New York: Mariner Books 2009), 195, 203. Hélène Cixous also wonders "what a completely different couple relationship would be like, what a love that was more than merely a cover for, a veil of, war would be like" ("Castration and Decapitation," 44).

10 Fatima Mernissi, *Women in Moslem Paradise* (New Delhi: Kali for Women, 1986), n.p.

11 Karima Laachir, "Hospitality and the Limitations of the National," in *Mobilizing Hospitality: The Ethics of Social Relations in a Mobile World*, ed. Jennie Germann Molz and Sarah Gibson (Burlington, VT: Ashgate Publishing),182.

12 Tobin Siebers, *Heterotopia: Postmodern Utopia and the Body Politic* (Ann Arbor: University of Michigan Press, 1995), 19–20.

13 Seyla Benhabib, *Situating the Self: Gender, Community, Postmodernism in Contemporary Ethics* (Oxford: Polity Press, 1992). Her support of Carol Gilligan's position regarding feminist contributions to moral philosophy suggests a role for speculative standpoint: "The contextuality, narrativity and specificity of women's moral judgement is not a sign of weakness or deficiency, but a manifestation of a vision of moral maturity that views the self as a being immersed in a network of relationships with others" (78).

14 In addition to Siebers, see Kathleen M. Wheeler's "Modernist" Women Writers and Narrative Art (New York: NYU Press, 1994) on the renewed attention to "the self as a rhetorical position" (16) toward a revision of "what present processes of socialization do to our potentialities, our self-regard and the regard of others" (17, emphasis added). Patricia Waugh also anticipates an alternate form of communality as "a collectivism that preserves the individual self," in *Feminine Fictions: Revisiting the Post Modern* (New York: Routledge, Kegan and Paul, 1989), 169.

15 Margaret Atwood, *The Year of the Flood* (New York: Nan A. Talese/Doubleday, 2009), 165.

16 Martin Halliwell, "Awaiting the Perfect Storm,'" in *Waltzing Again: New and Selected Conversations with Margaret Atwood*, ed. Ingersoll (Princeton, NJ: Ontario Review, 2006), 261–262.

17 Margaret Atwood, *Curious Pursuits: Occasional Writing 1970–2005* (London: Virago Press, 2005), 323. Emphasis in the original.

18 On the "self-disempowerment" of the public in politics see Beck, *Risk Society*, 187–200 and 225–228.

19 See Beck, *Risk Society*: reflexive modernity required science's essential skepticism to be "turned on itself" (232), and in which the "circle of self-disempowerment and loss of credibility" (227) that creates victims of the rest of us "neuronormals" is broken.

20 Barbara Adam and Joost Van Loon, "Introduction," *The Risk Society and Beyond: Critical Issues for Social Theory*, ed. Barbara Adam, Ulrich Beck, and Joost Van Loon (London: Sage Publications, 2000), 7 (emphasis added).

21 Barbara Adam and Joost Van Loon, "Introduction," *Risk Society and Beyond*, 2.

22 Atwood, in *Waltzing Again*, Ingersoll (ed.), 183. I am reminded here of Nadine Gordimer's statement, quoted by John Su, that "[t]he Writer himself knows that the only revolution is the permanent one – not in the Trotskyite sense, but in the sense of the imagination, in which no understanding is ever completed, but must keep breaking up and reforming in different combinations if it is to spread and meet the terrible questions of human existence" (Su, 33). And see Egyptian novelist Sonallah Ibrahim, who, following the logic of a Marxian "negation of the negation," asserts that "any situation is composed of contradictory elements, and that the struggle between them sets in motion a transition to a new, different situation which is itself the result of one of the opposing sides beating out the other. And this victory of one side over the other is, naturally, then subject to its own conditions and so on. The transition to a new situation is not the end of the cycle, because the process continues. The new situation creates new contradictions that set in motion a struggle between them." Real literature, he concludes, "gives expression to people's lives and the natural aspirations of [an] individual people. And this means that it necessarily runs against power. To be a real writer entails having a total image of society, history and the future. And this vision must certainly have a kind of oppositional, resistant stance toward lived reality and its limitations" (from "The Imagination as Transitive Act" interview with Elliott Colla. Retrieved at:www.jadaliyya.com/pages/index/1811/the-imagination-as-transitive-act_an-interview-wit).

23 Atwood, in *Waltzing Again*, ed. Ingersoll, 220.

24 Tobin Siebers, *The Subject and Other Subjects: On Ethical, Aesthetic, and Political Identity* (Ann Arbor: The University of Michigan Press, 1998). His notion of the "nausea" of ethics stems from the recognition of "the same old story" of human violence, in all its forms, and immoralities: "Ethics is nauseating because it involves repetition … in the sense of the inescapable familiarity, intimacy, and redundancy of our dilemmas" (2). Aesthetics and politics begin, he observes, "when self-reflection discovers an object other than itself or reaches a conclusion. For both aesthetics and politics obey the need to bring an end to the nausea of ethics" (7–8). Such reflections – or speculations – create narratives that "[plot] against ethical conflicts and humiliations. They are utopian in their desire to solve these problems; they are dystopian in the recognition that resolving a conflict once will not prevent that conflict from reappearing.... Increasingly, because of these repetitions, postmodern ethics defines itself as dystopian, which is to say that it is an ethics skeptical about the possibility of ethics" (4–5). This would also explain this artist's own interest in the role of art itself in resisting repetition – a particularly strong structural theme in *Paradise*, in both Winterson novels, in all three Atwood novels and in Mernissi's *Dreams of Trespass*. Also see Earl G. Ingersoll, "Survival in Margaret Atwood's Novel *Oryx and Crake*," *Extrapolation* 45 (2004): 174–175. As Atwood "becomes more intensely concerned with the survival of the civilization that generates and celebrates art," the more interested she becomes in "what-if" scenarios.

25 See my "'Doomed by Hope': Environmental Catastrophe and the Structured Ignorance of Risk in Margaret Atwood's Oryx and Crake," in *Changing the Climate: Utopia, Dystopia and Catastrophe*, ed. Andrew Milner and Simon Sellars (Melbourne: Arena, 2011), 173–195.

26 This etymological information is retrieved at: www.etymonline.com/index.php?term=regard

27 See Niamh Moore's "Imagining Feminist Futures" (125–141 in Gillis, Howie, and Munford) for an outline of possible directions for third-wave, eco-feminist approaches to the urgencies of climate change and other environmental challenges.

28 See Sarah Nuttall, *Entanglement: Literary and Cultural Reflections on Post-Apartheid* (Johannesburg: Wits University Press, 2009). Nuttall's theory of entanglement teases out connections between feminism and environmental politics. A focus on entanglement "speaks to the need for a utopian horizon" – particularly as it "returns us to a concept of the human where we do not necessarily expect to find it" (12).

29 Margaret Atwood, "*The Handmaid's Tale* and *Oryx and Crake* in Context," *PMLA* 119 (2004): 517.

Index